Supplier Diversity

by Kathey K. Porter, MBA, MSE, CPSD

P9-CBT-140

for
dummies®
A Wiley Brand

Supplier Diversity For Dummies®

Published by: **John Wiley & Sons, Inc.**, 111 River Street, Hoboken, NJ 07030-5774, www.wiley.com

Copyright © 2022 by John Wiley & Sons, Inc., Hoboken, New Jersey

Published simultaneously in Canada

For general information on our other products and services, please contact our Customer Care Department within the U.S. at 877-762-2974, outside the U.S. at 317-572-3993, or fax 317-572-4002. For technical support, please visit https://hub.wiley.com/community/support/dummies.

Wiley publishes in a variety of print and electronic formats and by print-on-demand. Some material included with standard print versions of this book may not be included in e-books or in print-on-demand. If this book refers to media such as a CD or DVD that is not included in the version you purchased, you may download this material at http://booksupport.wiley.com. For more information about Wiley products, visit www.wiley.com.

Library of Congress Control Number: 2022936112

ISBN 978-1-119-84301-6 (pbk); ISBN 978-1-119-84302-3 (ebk); ISBN 978-1-119-84303-0 (ebk)

SKY10034269_042622

Supplier Diversity

by Kathey K. Porter, MBA, MSE, CPSD

A Wiley Brand

Supplier Diversity For Dummies®

Published by: **John Wiley & Sons, Inc.,** 111 River Street, Hoboken, NJ 07030-5774, www.wiley.com

Copyright © 2022 by John Wiley & Sons, Inc., Hoboken, New Jersey

Published simultaneously in Canada

For general information on our other products and services, please contact our Customer Care Department within the U.S. at 877-762-2974, outside the U.S. at 317-572-3993, or fax 317-572-4002. For technical support, please visit https://hub.wiley.com/community/support/dummies.

Wiley publishes in a variety of print and electronic formats and by print-on-demand. Some material included with standard print versions of this book may not be included in e-books or in print-on-demand. If this book refers to media such as a CD or DVD that is not included in the version you purchased, you may download this material at http://booksupport.wiley.com. For more information about Wiley products, visit www.wiley.com.

Library of Congress Control Number: 2022936112

ISBN 978-1-119-84301-6 (pbk); ISBN 978-1-119-84302-3 (ebk); ISBN 978-1-119-84303-0 (ebk)

SKY10034269_042622

Contents at a Glance

Table of Contents

Introduction

Welcome to *Supplier Diversity For Dummies*. As I embarked on this project, the timing for this book couldn't have been more perfect given the predictions about entrepreneurship, demographic growth, and the workplace of the future. It has been an honor to write the first-ever book of this type in this series. I'm Kathey K. Porter, MBA, MSE, CPSD, and I've held a variety of leadership roles in supplier diversity and now as a supplier diversity consultant with a minority-, woman-, and veteran-owned business. My experiences (both professional and personal) have prepared me to create this work, and I'm excited to be able to share with you what I've learned along the way.

About This Book

Supplier Diversity For Dummies is your one-stop resource guide to get a comprehensive understanding of what supplier diversity is all about, how it contributes to an organization's success, what your role is as a leader, and how to implement supplier diversity in every area of your organization. In this book, I explain everything from the common terminology to the continued evolution of supplier diversity to how outside factors influence your organizational policies. I also cover strategies for tasks like these:

>> Assessing your organization's current culture and cultivating and sustaining inclusion and equity programs

>> Making the business case for supplier diversity and addressing the obstacles to supplier diversity

>> Aligning supplier diversity with your organization's strategic priorities and creating a supplier diversity strategic plan

>> Measuring the success of your supplier diversity efforts

>> Fostering partnerships with the community to drive supplier diversity efforts

Throughout this book, I share from my experience, proven strategies, and results achieved as a supplier diversity leader across a number of industries, including government and higher education, an advocate with leading agencies, and a consultant to several global organizations. I also bring a personal perspective as an entrepreneur who frequently utilizes these programs. I'm also happy to share insights from other leading professionals and historians in this space.

This book answers questions, explains misnomers, and addresses concerns that I receive from supplier diversity and procurement leaders across the country. True to the *For Dummies* form, it demystifies supplier diversity to make it practical, understandable, accessible, and implementable. My hope is that it speaks to everyone with an interest in supplier diversity, from seasoned professionals to new practitioners to stakeholders responsible for leading this effort to senior leaders at the top. In other words, leaders at all levels can benefit from this book.

I want to quickly point out a few things to help you better navigate and use this book:

>> Important terms and key words are in *italics* and are followed with a quick definition or explanation.

>> Keywords and action steps in lists appear in **bold.**

>> Sidebars (look for the shaded boxes) feature content that's interesting and informative but not essential to your understanding of a topic. If you're wanting to get in and out quickly, you can safely skip them.

Foolish Assumptions

Generally, I know it's not a good idea to make assumptions. But for this book, I've made a few to better serve your needs:

>> You're working at an organization in a manager or leader role.

>> You recognize that the world of work is changing, and you want to better understand it.

>> You have little or no knowledge and experience in leading supplier diversity initiatives and want to pick up the fundamentals.

>> You may be uneasy about supplier diversity and curious about how it can help your organization.

>> You want to develop into a more effective and impactful supplier diversity leader.

Icons Used in This Book

Throughout this book, you find icons that help you navigate the information. Here's a rundown of what they mean:

TIP

This icon alerts you to helpful hints. Tips can help you save time and avoid frustration.

REMEMBER

This icon reminds you of important information you should read carefully.

WARNING

This icon flags actions and ideas that may cause you problems. Often, warnings accompany common mistakes or misconceptions people have about supplier diversity.

TECHNICAL STUFF

This icon highlights information that goes a bit beyond need-to-know but is still helpful and interesting. You can skip this stuff if you're pressed for time and just want the absolute basics.

Beyond the Book

This book contains lots of ideas, strategies, checklists, tools, resources, references, best practices, and other sources that give you more than enough to work with. But there's more! It includes an online Cheat Sheet that provides guidance and tips for spotting and dealing with common supplier diversity barriers, a list of questions to determine your organizational readiness, and ways to gain internal and external stakeholder support. To access this handy Cheat Sheet, go to www.dummies.com and type **Supplier Diversity For Dummies Cheat Sheet** in the search box.

Additionally, if you, your team, or members of your organization need supplier diversity training, coaching, a keynote speaker, or consulting on any of the processes I share in this book, or want to obtain a certificate in supplier diversity, you can access information and a number of free resources at www.sdti.co.

Where to Go from Here

Like supplier diversity, this book isn't linear. Feel free to use the table of contents as a guide to move around to get exactly what you need. Part 1 gets you off to a great start and sets the foundation for really understanding supplier diversity. Part 2 looks at your internal environment. Part 3 discusses your suppliers and developing a program that's supplier-centric. Part 4 examines the external environment and your community. Part 5 talks about technology and analytics and the role they play in today's supplier diversity programs. Part 6 looks at how to build or expand a career in supplier diversity.

This book isn't designed to be an exhaustive or definitive work on supplier diversity. And I don't expect you to become an expert on all things supplier diversity in order to become an effective practitioner. Supplier diversity is a process and a journey, and you won't get to the Billion Dollar Roundtable overnight. Hopefully, though, you'll be able to sharpen your skills and apply what you read here so that you can help your organization and the diverse businesses you work with. Focus on being that champion that everyone wants to support because they believe in the mission behind supplier diversity and the value it brings to the organization and the community.

1

Getting Started with Supplier Diversity

Chapter **1**

Understanding the Growing Demand for Supplier Diversity

upplier diversity is a proactive business strategy that encourages buying from businesses that identify as belonging to a specific socioeconomic, historically disadvantaged, or underutilized demographic as suppliers, vendors, and contractors. The Small Business Administration, commonly called the SBA, classifies businesses in a number of categories. The most common are minority-owned or disadvantaged, women-owned, veteran-owned, and service-disabled-veteran owned. Corporations have expanded their definitions to also include LGBTQ to be more reflective of their local communities.

Supplier diversity has continued to progress from legislation to stabilize social unrest during the late 1960s to an economic imperative and a bona-fide management strategy. Supplier diversity programs recognize that when an organization buys products and services from suppliers that have been historically underutilized, it helps nurture and transform its own supply chain. Supplier diversity also gives organizations access to agile businesses with timely business solutions that allow them to gain a competitive advantage in the marketplace.

In this chapter, I cover what supplier diversity is (and isn't) and why it's still needed. I also identify some of the factors redefining supplier diversity and why organizations are recommitting to it.

Breaking Down What Supplier Diversity Is and Isn't

Throughout my career as a supplier diversity professional, I've worked in a number of industries and have been housed in a variety of departments: economic development, procurement, business operations, and community relations. I've had a range of supervisors, including those who knew nothing about supplier diversity, which gave me the freedom and flexibility to do a number of things. I've had supervisors who *thought* they knew supplier diversity, which created an epic battle to execute anything. Then I had those who understood and embraced the mission, which led to a real group effort.

Organizations have any number of reasons why departments end up where they do on the org chart. Sometimes they make perfect sense, and sometimes — well, I'll just say they don't ask me for my input. Inevitably, where supplier diversity ends up says a lot about the value the organization places on it and determines how you're able to behave in the role. Ultimately, this positioning affects what you're doing and the results you're able to deliver. For example, I've found myself involved in things that were really outside my scope, some that expanded my view of supplier diversity and how it touches the community.

REMEMBER

Through my experience and my conversations with supplier diversity colleagues, I know that where supplier diversity sits in the organization must be intentional. It sets the tone for how the program operates; how it interfaces with others throughout the organization; how it establishes influence; how it carries out tasks; and how it interacts with the community, stakeholders, and senior leaders. Additionally, it unconsciously sways how others view the role, which can lead to confusion about what supplier diversity actually is. The following sections dive into the true functions of supplier diversity as well as those it doesn't actually cover.

What it is

So, what exactly is supplier diversity? It's

>> **A procurement function:** Supplier diversity ensures that any business has an opportunity to do business with the organization regardless of race, gender, sexual orientation, and so on. It does so by developing policies, processes, and procedures that make the procurement process inclusive, fair, and equitable.

>> **A business and management strategy:** Supplier diversity is a strategy that supports the economic development of diverse communities who are customers and consumers by giving them opportunities to sell to the organization. It's a management strategy that allows organizations to progressively transform a company's supply chain and gain a competitive advantage by doing business with diverse businesses.

>> **An economic driver and entrepreneurial resource:** Supplier diversity provides support, education, and mentorship to small and diverse businesses. When an economic gap exists, whether through lack of work prospects or access to business opportunities, the entire community suffers. This scenario creates a drag on social services and leads to the overuse of other community resources. Organizations, especially those that are large economic engines in the community, have a duty to look at their resources, step in, and create solutions. The access to resources supplier diversity gives entrepreneurs helps drive business growth and create economic stability for the entire community.

What it's not

Here's what supplier diversity isn't:

>> **A diversity and inclusion/HR function:** Supplier diversity doesn't focus on hiring and retaining a diverse workforce, creating employee resource groups, or cultivating an inclusive work culture (I discuss this difference in greater detail in Chapter 4).

>> **A philanthropic function:** As a procurement and business function, supplier diversity doesn't award contracts or enter into contractual agreements with businesses based on need or hardship. It involves a competitive process that businesses must be qualified for and able to perform.

>> **An external community relations or PR function:** Yes, supplier diversity is community-facing thanks to its close relationship with the small and diverse business community, but it's not a "voice" of the entire organization, nor does it act as a general spokesperson for all things happening.

>> **A set-aside or affirmative action program:** Supplier diversity creates a pathway for small and diverse businesses to get a foot in the door. It encourages the utilization of small and diverse vendors but doesn't "set aside" contracts for one particular group or advocate that contracts be awarded based solely on how businesses may identify. *Remember:* This distinction is especially relevant in the public sector, where public dollars are being spent. In fact, the federal government is the only entity that can legally set aside contracts for vendors based on their identification as part of a specific socioeconomic demographic.

>> **A catchall for other functions:** Supplier diversity isn't a job description that captures multiple, traditionally stand-alone functions into one position, and it's not an add-on "get to it when you have time" job.

REMEMBER

Although supplier diversity is a frequent collaborator with many departments and relies on internal relationships to advance its mission, keeping these points in mind helps programs avoid spending time on tasks that aren't productive or don't always contribute to the set goals. For example, although production and marketing often work together, having someone from production make marketing decisions for the organization may not be a good idea.

Investigating Whether Supplier Diversity Is Still Necessary

Every few years, this question pops up for debate as society (and a few detractors) try to move beyond the conversation of race- and gender-based initiatives and quotas and focus solely on qualifications, merit, and so on. The assumption is that the legislation, hours of training, and countless programs people have endured over the years have done their jobs. Now, everyone has equal access to anything they choose: jobs, housing, healthcare, business, you name it. This argument implies that the playing field is now equal and fair and assumes that humans no longer harbor implicit biases, prejudices, or favoritisms. If this description sounds like your organization, congratulations — you did it! If not, keep reading.

As Chapter 2 explains, the motives behind supplier diversity have shifted from complying with federal law (we *have* to) to doing the right thing (we *want* to) to creating a business case (we *need* to). Arguably, these shifts likely came because someone brought up the question of whether it was still necessary.

The United States has definitely come a long way since the affirmative action legislation of the 1960s, but any progress that's been made validates that these types of initiatives work and that there's really no such thing as "we've made it." If anyone working in diversity will tell you one thing, it's that supplier diversity isn't a destination but rather a continual process that requires a long-term commitment to change.

One argument in favor of the ongoing need for supplier diversity is the continued economic disparity that exists between diverse business owners and non-diverse business owners, whether it's lack of access to capital or networks, lack of resources, or any other number of issues that derail business growth.

Take, for example, the impact the COVID-19 pandemic has had on diverse businesses. Of course, entrepreneurs across the board took a tremendous beating, but COVID-19's effect on minority-owned small businesses in the United States was much more dire and extreme, according to an article by McKinsey & Company. It noted that of all vulnerable small businesses, minority-owned businesses were the most at risk and that many were in financially precarious positions even before COVID-19 lockdowns began. The pandemic disproportionately impacted minority-owned small businesses for two critical reasons:

>> These outfits tend to face underlying and systemic issues that make running and scaling successfully more difficult.

>> They're more likely to be concentrated in industries most immediately affected by the pandemic, making them more susceptible to disruption.

Their vulnerability was compounded because many minority-owned businesses lacked emergency funding. A large percentage of minority businesses weren't able to take advantage of relief funds from the government because they didn't have the commercial banking relationships that larger companies had. (Many banks focused on their larger, long-term clients with established credit relationships.) The Center for Responsible Lending, a nonprofit group that combats abusive lending practices, estimates that nearly 90 percent of minority-owned businesses had little chance of receiving a Paycheck Protection Program (PPP) loan through a mainstream bank or credit union.

The Center for Responsible lending further broke down its estimates by demographic; here are the rough numbers:

>> 95 percent of Black-owned businesses

>> 91 percent of Latino-owned businesses

>> 91 percent of Native Hawaiian or Pacific Islander-owned businesses

>> 75 percent of Asian-owned businesses

Looking at reasons supplier diversity is still necessary

Obviously, as a supplier diversity consultant and author, I have definite opinions around this subject. However, this section isn't a declaration on how I feel. My leanings are based on factual and anecdotal observations that support the need for supplier diversity.

>> **When goals are attached to projects, utilization improves.** *Goals* in this context are percentages established on projects administered by public agencies — that is, local/state governments, higher education institutions, K-12 schools, and the federal government. Conducting disparity studies can help justify the utilization of goals. A *disparity study* is an analysis that examines whether differences exist between the percentage of dollars that minority- and women-owned businesses received in contracts during a specific period and the percentage of dollars that those businesses would be expected to receive based on their availability to perform those contracts. It may also look at other factors, such as legal considerations around creating programs for these businesses, conditions in the local marketplace for these businesses, contracting practices, and business assistance programs currently in place.

Based on the results of such a study, organizations can establish goals, usually on their subcontracting opportunities, with the hopes of improving the utilization of diverse businesses. For example, a project can have a goal of 30 percent, which means that a prime contractor (a contractor who has a direct contract with an organization) must ensure that at least 30 percent of the total contract value will be spent with small or diverse businesses. If it can't do so, it must provide a valid reason. In my experience, prime vendors often *overindex* on the utilization of small and diverse business spend when a goal is attached — that is, they spend more than 30 percent (or whatever the goal is) because they want to maintain a good relationship with a client and to report this number for future project pursuits. With a robust program, a prime vendor may be penalized for not meeting goals and risk winning future contract opportunities with a client.

>> **When tracking, compliance, and reporting measures are in place, utilization improves.** Accountability measures such as project tracking, contract compliance, and reporting let project teams and supplier diversity monitor the progress of a project in somewhat real time and take action if the prime contractor looks like it's not going to be able to fulfill a goal. This approach is a more collaborative one where supplier diversity can provide support to help connect the prime contractor to small and diverse businesses.

>> **When organizations or individuals think their livelihood may be in jeopardy, they change their behavior.** This concept is a relatively new one that many organizations are embracing. According to supplier.io, many of the Top 50 Companies for Diversity (as recognized by *DiversityInc* magazine) are placing more emphasis on achieving diversity/supplier diversity goals and tying executive compensation to the effort. This move not only provides additional incentive to hit supplier diversity goals but also reinforces the importance of diversity as a core value in the company.

Considering what supplier diversity needs to do to stay relevant

If supplier diversity is to continue to evolve, maintain its relevancy, and usher in a new era of supplier diversity, some pointed actions need to occur:

>> **Continued investment in current and pipeline professionals:** As supplier diversity evolves, so must the professional profile of its leaders. Organizations have to have a clear understanding of the function when drafting job descriptions and hiring (as I note earlier in the chapter, this position isn't a catchall). Today, certification and training programs offer professionals an opportunity to build their skills in this area to ensure that they're prepared to hit the ground running and not necessarily learning on the job. I discuss building a career in supplier diversity in Part 6.

>> **Development of industry standards:** People have long complained that the industry can be fragmented because of different standards and requirements across industries. For a long time, supplier diversity took its cues from the federal government. But as corporate supplier diversity grew, those programs began establishing their own standards, which sometimes creates confusion for the small and diverse businesses (and even industry professionals). It has also created a bit of a chasm between professionals that work in public supplier diversity and private (corporate) supplier diversity. The industry has to work together to create standards that help uplift the entire industry, an act that would likely go a long way in crafting a message that makes gaining buy-in at the organizational level easier.

>> **Proactive mindset shifts from senior leadership:** Like anything, priorities shift. New leaders have different ideas for where the organization should focus its energies. As much as you may want everyone to be proactive and progressive, they just aren't. This area is one of the reasons supplier diversity is a continual process that requires constant work on culture and change management. So much so that everyone, even a leader, will have to get with the program, or they may find themselves a poor culture fit.

- >> **A strategic focus with key performance indicators (KPIs) that align with big-picture goals:** Supplier diversity has to shift its narrative to one focused on strategy. Some organizations still likely treat this initiative as a charity or philanthropic effort rather than a true strategic management function. Supplier diversity has to develop those KPIs that align with the organizational goals to demonstrate the value that it brings in achieving them.

- >> **Reputation management:** Supplier diversity can sometimes be a mixed bag of results in a mixed bag of perceptions. I've seen programs that are wildly successful and those that are just treading water. Unfortunately, the latter programs/leaders are the ones that give the impression that all supplier diversity does is "help landscaping and janitorial companies." Supplier diversity has always done a good job of building positive relationships and converting them into advocates and allies. It has to continue to influence this decision making to earn its seat at the table and level up how people perceive supplier diversity.

TIP

- >> **An emphasis on conviction, compliance, and courage:** I saw this three C's idea for another industry but thought it was very applicable. Supplier diversity must lead with conviction to communicate why it's doing what it is and why that's important for the organization. It has to educate on compliance — the processes that are there to protect the organization and not expose it or the program to risk. Finally, supplier diversity has to have courage to continue to push for change so that it can add value and create impact that shapes the community.

- >> **Measurement of economic impact:** Externally, supplier diversity has to be able to tell its story of the economic impact it adds to the small and diverse businesses, the organization, and the community at large.

Examining External Drivers Redefining Supplier Diversity

As I discuss in Chapter 2, the groundwork for supplier diversity as it exists today began in the 1960s. In its early days, corporations' motives for taking on supplier diversity may have been a little self-serving, in that they were likely more concerned about preserving their standing in the eyes of the government and maintaining their own contracts than with helping small and diverse businesses succeed. It wasn't until the 1990s (the Right Thing to Do Era) that organizations really began to dissect their efforts and view supplier diversity as a strategic component to their overall operations. In fact, using Google Ngram, Figure 1-1 illustrates how frequently the term *supplier diversity* has been used in book titles, which directly coincides with key periods in its existence.

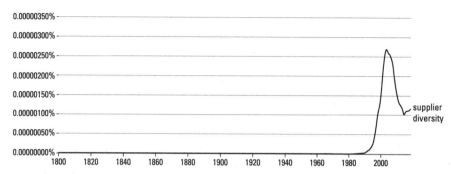

FIGURE 1-1:
Supplier diversity
title frequency.

Supplier diversity is once again experiencing a resurgence in organizations. In the following sections, I take a look at some of the societal factors driving this resurgence.

Growth of minority entrepreneurship

The desire to achieve the American Dream allows entrepreneurship to experience explosive growth with minority populations. Supplier diversity as a strategy makes business-to-business (B2B) and business to government (B2G) contracting a viable and achievable path for many entrepreneurs. The federal government alone is required to set aside at least 23 percent of its total spending specifically for small and diverse businesses.

TECHNICAL
STUFF

According to research released by the U.S. Department of Commerce's Minority Business Development Agency (MBDA), in collaboration with the U.S. Census Bureau (Census), the following list highlights recent growth trends for minority business:

» In 2017, the nation's minority nonemployer firms (firms with no employees; using primarily 1099 contractors) generated over $279.3 billion in receipts.

» The number of minority nonemployer firms grew by 16.7 percent to 8.169 million between 2014 and 2017, nearly four times the 4.2 percent growth in the number of non-minority nonemployer firms.

» Of the 8.169 million minority nonemployer firms in 2017,

  • 3.635 million (44.5 percent) were Hispanic-owned (By official definition, the owner of a Hispanic-owned firm may be of any race.)

  • 2.951 million (36.1 percent) were Black or African American-owned

  • 1.960 million (24.0 percent) were Asian-owned

  • 84,500 (1.0 percent) were American Indian or Alaska Native-owned

  • 38,500 (0.5 percent) were Native Hawaiian and Other Pacific Islander-owned

- » Minority women-owned nonemployer firms totaled 3.779 million (46.3 percent of total minority nonemployer firms), with receipts totaling over $83.7 billion.

- » Minority veteran-owned nonemployer firms were 312,000 (3.8 percent of total minority nonemployer firms), with receipts totaling over $9.3 billion.

Demographic shifts: The changing face of the majority

According to census figures, by 2042, *racial minorities* (those that identify as part of a race other than non-Hispanic, single-race whites) are poised to become the new majority, making up more than half the U.S. population. By 2050, 54 percent of the population will be minorities. In a country whose history has been shaped by the boundaries among racial groups, this projected demographic shift is undoubtedly important. Additionally, U.S. society is increasingly represented by a cross-section of generations, including seniors and *millennials* (typically defined as those born between 1981 and 1997).

But what does it mean for the supply chain? As diverse populations increase, so does their spending power and influence. Gone are the days when companies told you what to think, do, and buy with no questions asked. Today's buyers are very savvy. They're looking for connections to the brands they buy from, whether that connection is in the organization's principles and beliefs or its leadership. These buyers want to know that organizations stand for something that makes society better. And if that's something that they value and believe in, that's even better.

Forrester, a leading consumer research and consulting firm, refers to them as the *values-based consumer*. Customers are becoming more aware of — and sensitive to — social issues and using this to make purchasing decisions.

Social activism/economic inclusion

Activism has always played a part in the causes agencies and corporations take on. Though internal stakeholders can champion a cause, true activism starts from the outside, usually in an area that people feel the organization isn't supporting or being responsive enough to.

Supplier diversity got its start based on calls for economic inclusion within the Black community. It has expanded over the years to include women-, LGBTQ, and veteran-owned businesses. Because of their positions in the community — often as large employers and major economic engines — organizations are realizing they have the power (and a responsibility) to address economic disparities through their supply chains and how they purchase the goods and services needed to run their organizations. In addition to being responsive to the needs of the community, they're finding that it also makes business sense.

Accountability to secondary stakeholders

Stakeholders are individuals or groups that have an interest in the organization and, whether directly or indirectly, are impacted by its actions. Stakeholders can be broken into two different groups: primary and secondary. Organizations have a different responsibility to each group.

Primary stakeholders are employees, suppliers, boards of directors, owners, shareholders, and customers. *Secondary stakeholders* are external groups such as government and regulatory agencies, trade and labor unions, political and social groups, the media, and so on. They drive supplier diversity in the external environment. In this age of cancel culture, they can wield tremendous influence, both positively and negatively, on the actions that the organization takes. They indirectly affect the organization by taking actions that either support the organization's efforts or make success difficult.

In some communities, supplier diversity can be an emotional and highly charged subject. When I was a practitioner, usually once or twice a year, I'd get a call from a reporter wanting to know for an article how much we were spending with small and diverse businesses. It usually came after a politician announced "increasing opportunities for small and diverse businesses" as part of their platform.

This usually created a frenzy about who would respond and what exactly should be shared (going on the record can be tricky). If the results were good, it would be nothing more than an informative article. If the results weren't so good, it usually created a firestorm in the community resulting in meetings with community leaders pushing for reforms for increased opportunities, an overhaul of the program, or even the removal of the supplier diversity leader. These stakeholders hold organizations accountable to their commitment to create opportunities for small and diverse businesses and push them when they feel their actions aren't enough or results aren't being achieved.

That's how external stakeholders can drive change. Sometimes public outcry is needed before the organization takes action. Also, this interaction forms the basis for a long-term collaborative relationship. External stakeholders know what businesses in the community need. Internal stakeholders know what resources are available and how to navigate internally to get it done.

Recognizing Why Organizations Are Recommitting to Supplier Diversity

As the new law of the land, the diversity-related executive orders of the late 1960s and early 1970s were based on the government's desire to do something to address systemic economic disparities within the Black community. (See Chapter 2 for more on these orders.) Arguably, supplier diversity didn't always live up to its expectations for any number of reasons, whether it was lack of total commitment by the organization; little or no compliance, oversight, and enforcement; or just the vagueness regarding exactly what to do. Today, society is still facing calls for change to address the same economic disparities.

But companies have a chance to get it right. Many organizations are doubling down on supplier diversity efforts and strengthening the commitment to developing impactful programs that focus on the whole system of supplier diversity management (SDM) and deliver on the promise of economic inclusion. The following sections explore a few of the internal reasons organizations are recommitting to supplier diversity.

Complex business challenges/ strategic advantage

If there was a mantra for running a business, it would be "stay prepared for the unexpected." So many elements are involved, and things can change at the drop of a hat. As markets move faster and grow increasingly complex, organizations are looking for efficiency and innovation in every aspect of the business, including their supply chain.

TIP

Organizations are realizing that having a diverse supplier pool makes good business sense. The gains they can receive — whether through price competitiveness or access to industry expertise and know-how, not to mention the intrinsic value in community goodwill — are all things that provide organizations with the strategic advantage needed in order to remain competitive in the 21st century. Supplier diversity isn't just the right thing to do but an economic imperative.

Increased focus on collaboration in the supply chain

As interest increases in the supply chain, so does the interest in supplier diversity. Expanding market reach, greater customer focus, and increasing market and cost pressures are forcing many organizations to reevaluate the effectiveness of their supply chains. The disruption caused by the COVID-19 pandemic has also required supply chains to become more flexible and responsive than ever before. As many industries experience challenging transitions, supply chain partners are increasingly important to improve supply chain capabilities, efficiencies, and impact to the bottom line. As organizations become more dependent on their suppliers, collaborative planning becomes more central.

Compliance with the law

Although simply staying out of trouble was the prevailing reason for diversity measures in the beginning, it's still a relevant goal today. The government remains the only entity that can mandate the utilization of a business based on its socioeconomic status. Though many supplier diversity practitioners' focus is on small businesses, corporations and other public entities (local governments, higher education institutions, hospitals, and so on) have relationships with the federal government. Corporations make up a large portion of government contractors, and many smaller public institutions receive federal funding in the form of grants. Thus, each of them is required to comply with the mandate that a portion of their project be set aside for small and diverse businesses.

Accountability to primary stakeholders

Primary stakeholders have a vested interest in how the organization performs and the activities it engages in to achieve results. In short, they drive supplier diversity inside the organization. Primary stakeholders benefit when organizations are doing well, but their actions can also directly impact the organization's success and failure.

REMEMBER

Even with a push or outcry from secondary (external) stakeholders, nothing gets done internally without the efforts of the primary stakeholders, whether it's the supplier diversity leader, senior leadership, or employees advocating for change. I've even seen organizations where supplier diversity was a personal purpose for members of the board, and they felt the organization could do more to support small and diverse businesses. Many organizations create supplier diversity councils consisting of a cross-section of internal and external stakeholders and use public input to help them shape and conceive their supplier diversity efforts. I know this may sound a bit reactive, but that's okay.

Corporate social responsibility/stewardship

Corporate social responsibility is a self-regulating business model that helps a company be socially accountable to itself, its stakeholders, and the public. By practicing corporate social responsibility, also called *corporate citizenship,* companies can be conscious of the kind of impact they're having on all aspects of society, including economic, social, and environmental.

As more and more organizations evaluate the impact they have on their communities and the world, businesses are taking this responsibility one step further by seeking out ways to address challenges, ultimately making the communities they're part of better.

Chapter **2**

Understanding the Foundation of Supplier Diversity

When compared to other areas within your organization, supplier diversity is relatively young as a department or even a strategic initiative. Despite its auspicious start during the 1960s, it languished for many years and wasn't always embraced or welcomed. Not until the 1970s did organizations and communities across the country begin to get intentional about their commitment and create programs that can have a lasting impact on their communities.

In this chapter, I look at the foundation of supplier diversity — where it began, its evolution, and some trends shaping its future. I haven't designed this chapter to be a big history lesson. It's here to provide more context to why supplier diversity programs were started, how they've evolved, and how certain elements became part of the structure you know today. This background can inform your thinking as a practitioner so you can move beyond a cookie-cutter approach to create or build your program to be responsive to the businesses within your community.

Looking at Where It All Began

The 1950s ushered in a new era of prosperity in the United States. It marked the end of WWII, which positioned the United States as the world's strongest military power. One of the benefits awaiting soldiers returning home was the opportunity for entrepreneurship. The Small Business Act of 1953 established the Small Business Administration, commonly called the SBA. The SBA, now recognized as the leading federal agency focused on small-business growth and development, was required to guarantee a fair percentage of public or government-structured contracts to various small-business owners throughout the country.

The Small Business Investment Act of 1958 expanded services provided to small businesses. Its purpose was to counsel, assist, and protect the interests of small-business concerns in order to preserve and encourage free competitive enterprise. It also ensured that a fair proportion of the government's total purchases and contracts/subcontracts for property and services were placed with small-business enterprises.

During this time, the economy was booming, and the bounties of this success were available to more people than ever before. The American economy experienced a shift that created more income for more Americans than in previous decades. This prosperity helped establish a solid middle class and provided the foundation for generational wealth. However, only a portion of society was benefitting from this newfound wealth and financial security. As the economic disparity gap widened, the 1960s were marked with uprisings, protests, and civil rights/Black Power movements within the Black community. This unrest brought new calls for equality and access to economic opportunities for the Black community.

Over the next few years, several presidents issued key executive orders to address economic issues impacting the Black community — employment, contracting, and entrepreneurship issues. For a while, these orders did quiet the calls for justice and access to economic opportunity. However, subsequent orders continued to be issued, highlighting the fact that this complex issue couldn't be solved with a one-and-done order.

The following sections highlight the executive orders that had a direct impact on supplier diversity. They're the foundation for how it has evolved today.

REMEMBER

Understanding the context of supplier diversity allows organizations to create a program that fits their culture while addressing the issues of their small business community.

Executive Order 10925 (1961): Established Committee on Equal Opportunity Employment

Issued by President John F. Kennedy, this order established the President's Committee on Equal Employment Opportunity (EEO) and included a condition that government contractors "take affirmative action to ensure that applicants are employed, and employees are treated during employment, without regard to their race, creed, color, or national origin." It also gave federal contracting agencies authority to institute procedures against federal contractors who violated their EEO obligations, including contract cancellation, debarment from future contracts, and other sanctions. This order is significant in that it was the first use of the term *affirmative action,* and it set the stage for future orders that address socioeconomic disparities.

Executive Order 11246 (1965): Established Requirements for Non-discriminatory Practices

Issued by President Lyndon B. Johnson, this order prohibited organizations that received federal contracts and subcontracts from discriminating based on race, color, religion, and national origin in employment. In 1967, after outcry from women's groups, the order was amended (Order 11375) to include sex on the list of attributes. Executive Order 11246 also requires federal contractors to take affirmative action to promote the full achievement of equal opportunity for women and minorities. The Office of Federal Contract Compliance Programs (OFCCP), part of the Department of Labor, is in charge of overseeing this requirement for all federal contractors and has developed regulations for these contractors.

Executive Orders 11458 (1969) and 11625 (1971): Economic Entrepreneurial b Equality

There is a scene in the Lee Daniels movie, *The Butler,* that shows Washington, D.C., burning after the assassination of Martin Luther King in 1968. In that scene Nixon asks his aides what do "they" want? One of the few African American advisers to Nixon told him that Blacks wanted to do business like every other American but were discriminated against in government contracts. That was the supposed seed of supplier diversity.

Issued by President Richard Nixon, this order specifically addressed economic entrepreneurial equality. It provided a framework for developing a national program for minority business enterprises and establishing the Office of Minority Business Enterprise (OMBE) and the Advisory Council for Minority Business Enterprise. *Note:* In 1977, Executive Order 12007 terminated the Advisory Council for Minority Business Enterprise. OMBE became the Minority Business Development Agency (MBDA). In 2021, the U.S. Department of Commerce announced that the MBDA would be a permanent agency and expanded, and it was elevated with the passage of the Minority Business Development Act of 2021.

Initially, Executive Order 11458 was viewed as a step in the right direction. Unfortunately, the goodwill was short lived because the order didn't provide language clarifying who can be considered a minority-owned business. This gap left the interpretation of who'd be eligible up to agencies and organizations, so the order had little to no impact on fostering economic inclusion.

Nixon replaced Executive Order 11458 with Executive Order 11625, which attempted to solve the problem of defining who was eligible for these business programs. The order introduced vague language such as "socially and economically disadvantaged persons" and defined *minorities* as not just Black people but also Puerto Ricans, Spanish-speaking Americans, American Indians, Eskimos, and Aleuts. Many felt this language diluted the initial intention of the executive orders, which was to address the need for social justice for Black Americans. Because of an outcry from women's rights groups, women were also included in this category and would go on to be classified as minority or disadvantaged, a designation that continues to this day.

Public Law 95-507 (1978)

On October 24, 1978, President Jimmy Carter signed Public Law 95-507 to amend the Small Business Act and the Small Business Investment Act of 1958. This change made federal procurement contracting more readily accessible to all small businesses. The law PL 95-507 specifies that the government's policy is to provide viable opportunities to small businesses, small disadvantaged businesses, and women-owned businesses in both its acquisitions and its awarding of subcontracts.

Examining the Evolution of Supplier Diversity

The executive orders I cover in the earlier section "Looking at Where It All Began" were based on the government's desire to do something to address systemic economic disparities within the Black community. The orders stated what needed to be done with regard to inclusive hiring and business practices, but they didn't provide a framework for how it should be done. This vacuum left the field wide open to interpretation, resulting in abuse, fraud, and neglect. Organizations and agencies were left with their own understanding and created programs that they felt worked for them and were reflective of their cultures at the time. For better or worse, the organizations of yesteryear aren't the culture-centric organizations of today. Not every organization was successful with its efforts. But despite these mixed results, supplier diversity programs forged ahead and began to really take shape during the 1970s.

According to Dr. Fred McKinney, one of the country's foremost supplier diversity historians (not to mention technical editor and contributor for this book), supplier diversity includes three distinct periods: compliance, right thing to do, and making the case. Figure 2-1 looks at each period of supplier diversity and the shift in organizational priorities during each phase.

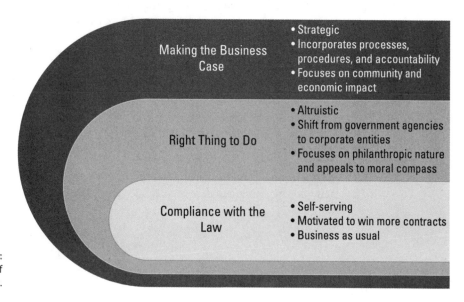

FIGURE 2-1:
Evolution of supplier diversity.

Making the Business Case
- Strategic
- Incorporates processes, procedures, and accountability
- Focuses on community and economic impact

Right Thing to Do
- Altruistic
- Shift from government agencies to corporate entities
- Focuses on philanthropic nature and appeals to moral compass

Compliance with the Law
- Self-serving
- Motivated to win more contracts
- Business as usual

MAYOR MAYNARD JACKSON AND SUPPLIER DIVERSITY IN ATLANTA, GEORGIA

A legendary example that resulted in the creation of some of the most substantial Black businesses that still exist today is the one created in Atlanta by the Honorable Mayor Maynard Jackson. This demonstrated the potential of supplier diversity.

Maynard Jackson, Atlanta's first Black mayor, is one of the most revered mayors in Atlanta's history; many regard him as the father of modern-day supplier diversity. He won the election partly on his promise of economic prosperity for all Atlantans. His approach made him a legend and made Atlanta a model for economic inclusion.

At the time of Jackson's election in 1974, Atlanta was embarking on one of its most ambitious projects ever — expanding the Hartsfield Airport (now commonly known as the Hartsfield-Jackson International Airport) into an international hub. Upon assuming office, Mayor Jackson met with business leaders and told them he would move forward with the expansion of Hartsfield Airport on one condition: 25 percent of all contracts were to be set aside for minority firms. Jackson reportedly told those in opposition that the city wouldn't build the airport if they didn't agree to this stipulation, and he held fast to his offer of 75 percent of the project or 100 percent of nothing. As expected, the business elite recoiled, and Jackson's administration prepared for a long fight.

Over the next two years, Mayor Jackson fought some of the most powerful men in the South who were using their clout to call in political chips to get the governor and state legislature to take control of the airport expansion project. For Mayor Jackson, the stakes were high. This was not only a campaign promise but also an opportunity to provide Black business owners something previously denied them: access to a share of contracts on a major public works project initially valued at $450 million. The mayor used the delay to sell corporations on creative ways to work with Black firms. One novel concept at the time was creating a joint venture with minority firms. This model is now widely used across the world and is often a requirement on public construction-related projects.

By 1976, the parties finally came to an agreement. All parties would eventually agree to Jackson's modified version of his plan: a goal (not a mandate) of 20 to 25 percent participation of minority-owned firms.

Five years later, Jackson increased the percentage of contracts awarded to minorities from less than 1 percent in 1973 to roughly 39 percent. This surge strengthened the Black middle class and created an affluent business community that still exists today.

Compliance with federal law (1969–1990)

Supplier diversity got its start with the federal government, but by 1968, several leading companies, such as General Motors and IBM (who were also federal contractors), were compelled to launch their own supplier diversity programs. Large corporations and the government have always had a close relationship. In the early days of the United States, it was nothing for the government to borrow money from private bankers when it ran a little short.

To this day, many corporations are vendors that provide the government with a variety of goods and services. With the establishment of the executive orders I cover earlier in the chapter, these vendors were under regulatory pressure to provide contracts to minority-owned businesses. Although some were inspired to create their own programs, many were motivated to simply remain compliant in order to continue to win contracts. This period came to a close because of legal challenges and backlash against laws designed to promote minority business development.

The right thing to do (1990s–early 2000s)

Up until this time, the government or the public sector was the main force creating opportunities for minority businesses. But as legal challenges abounded, businesses began to shift their focus to look at opportunities in the private sector with corporations. The leading organization that certified minority firms and advocated for minority businesses interested in doing business with corporations was (and still is) the National Minority Supplier Development Council, or NMSDC.

During this time, NMSDC strategically shifted its focus from a publicly funded organization to an organization funded by and focused on corporations. Corporations began to publicize their efforts in their communications, often touting supplier diversity as the right thing to do, and to formalize their programs by hiring personnel, developing processes, and investing in systems that allowed them to track utilization, which then can be reported.

This era was the first time a true business ecosystem was created, and minority businesses benefitted greatly. It also created a model for advocacy and certifying organizations that represent other socioeconomically disadvantaged groups such as women, the LGBTQ community, and veterans.

Making the business case (2000s–present)

The 2000s were marked by several shifts in the marketplace — the tech industry, changes in demographics, the growing influence of consumers, and the increased globalization of business — that had a tremendous impact on corporations, the likes of which they hadn't experienced before. Each of these factors presented new challenges and raised the stakes for supplier diversity to not simply comply with government regulations or push its feel-good message as the right thing to do. Supplier diversity needed to help the organization maintain a competitive advantage by making the business case to support its reason for being.

As I describe in Chapter 7, a strong business case for supplier diversity focuses on the tangible impact or metrics you can monitor through measured performance results. It's sustainable in ways that the phases in the two preceding sections weren't. Compliance allows programs to be challenged or risk being shut down based on court rulings. Programs based on an emotional appeal like "the right thing to do" can shift depending on leadership's priorities or be difficult to justify when decisions are based solely on numbers.

Pondering the Future of Supplier Diversity

Earlier in the chapter, I discuss the different phases of supplier diversity and how the industry has grown and evolved to become a strategic pillar within organizations and in communities. Just like the civil unrest of the 1960s led to the start of these programs, the civil unrest of 2020 has created a reawakening and refocus on supplier diversity as a driver of entrepreneurship and economic inclusion.

As markets continue to get more complex and competitive and external factors influence business like never before, organizations have to look at every nook and cranny to gain or maintain a competitive advantage. For instance, market factors such as the supply chain shortages of the 2021 holiday season impacted everything from food to clothing to toys to electronics. This promoted organizations to take a closer look at supplier diversity and diverse businesses as a potential solution. It's clear we've moved to a hybrid phase that combines all the previous eras and also includes social equity.

As the industry continues to advance, you have to wonder what will drive the next phase of supplier diversity. Will it be a subtle shift or a major disruption? Whatever it is, you should be aware of the issues that are poised to have an impact on supplier diversity in the future.

TIP

Today's business challenges have created a reawakening and refocus on supplier diversity as a driver of entrepreneurship and economic inclusion.

Business and program globalization

If you're part of a global organization, I'm sure international business is an important aspect of your organization's overall business. Whether looking to gain efficiencies or appeal to the local market, you may be tasked with extending your efforts, not just domestically but also internationally. A number of countries have aligned with leading U.S. groups to form their own programs focused on creating access to opportunities, including the following:

>> The Canadian Aboriginal and Minority Supplier Council

>> Minority Supplier Development in China

>> Minority Supplier Development UK (MSDUK)

>> Supply Nation (Australia)

>> The South African Supplier Diversity Council

Many international markets are at the early stages of business inclusion for diverse populations. Global supplier diversity not only helps local businesses where you may be operating but also provides another capacity-building opportunity by connecting domestic businesses to international opportunities.

Strategic advantage

Just as the demographics of the consumer markets are changing, so too is the makeup of the labor markets. Today's employees are looking for more than just a job. They're motivated by a higher cause and want to believe that the things they and their organizations do make society better.

Just a few short years ago, departments like sustainability; diversity, equity, and inclusion (DEI); and supplier diversity weren't part of the traditional structure and weren't always embraced. Now they're an integral part of business operations and are prominently on display in communications, websites, annual reports, articles, and so on. Being able to make the business case and communicate program impact can be helpful for functions like recruiting, grant funding, or marketing, to name a few.

Economic imperative

The makeup of the U.S. population continues to become increasingly diverse. The U.S. Census Bureau indicates more than half of all Americans will identify as a part of a minority group by 2040. This shift is already impacting areas such as consumer markets. These groups are demanding access to employment and entrepreneurial opportunities and are using their voting power, or sometimes protesting, to influence change.

As this group continues to grow, improving minority access to business opportunities will be more than a social issue; it'll be an economic imperative.

REMEMBER

Chapter **3**

Supplier Diversity Management: A New Way of Thinking

From organizations to entrepreneurs, supplier diversity is on everyone's minds. For entrepreneurs, it's knowing how to leverage supplier diversity to create business relationships, win contracts, and grow a sustainable business. For organizations, it's developing an impactful program that brings value to the organization and the community. As each group tries to gain that understanding, supplier diversity has grown from a cursory academic construct to a viable management and entrepreneurship strategy and worthwhile organizational pursuit.

Whenever I begin working with a new client, I always like to get a sense of their current supplier diversity operation. Often, they explain their desire for a program. They have available opportunities and are performing the requisite activities, but they're still not getting the results they want. After I hear about their challenges, I can always tell they're still looking at supplier diversity as an initiative rather than as a process. They usually have one, maybe two aspects, but they're missing another phase of the model that's necessary to make their efforts work. When I begin to explain this component, I love it when the "a–ha" moment occurs. It's like you can see the light bulb come on as their eyes light up.

In this chapter, I define and explain supplier diversity management, discuss supplier diversity management as a process, and introduce the supplier diversity management (SDM) model.

Defining Supplier Diversity Management

People often think of supplier diversity as an endless number of luncheons, breakfasts, and dinners (the chicken dinner circuit) with a few workshops thrown in. It's easy to disparage these "chicken dinners," but historically, prior to organizations like the National Minority Supplier Development Council, diverse business owners never had the opportunity to socialize with nondiverse business leaders. In the South, it was not only illegal — it could be deadly.

Yes, as part of the entrepreneurial ecosystem, supplier diversity professionals are very visible at community events such as these, and informational workshops make up a large part of supplier diversity programming, but those are just snapshots of everything involved in supplier diversity. Looking at the field collectively rather than the individual events provides a fuller picture of what it really entails.

Depending on the leadership, some view supplier diversity as an optional initiative and not a true management function. When you actually think about the myriad of activities involved in supplier diversity, it really is a system or process, one I call *supplier diversity management* (SDM).

REMEMBER

Supplier diversity management is a new way of thinking about supplier diversity. It comprises the planning and coordination of all the people, policies, processes, procedures, and stakeholders working together to connect small and diverse businesses to opportunities while creating value for the organization. It requires aligning your internal efforts and external resources to focus on value creation and on driving results for the small and diverse business community.

Supplier diversity management involves many interconnected functions that are difficult to manage separately and expect worthwhile outcomes, such as the following:

>> Supplier development

>> Contract compliance

» Creation of the 4 P's (people, policies, processes, and procedures; see Chapter 6)

» Project management

» Stakeholder engagement and collaboration

» Community relations

As organizations shift to build programs that are impactful and focus on adding value, they have to ensure that these functions are aligned and working together.

TIP

Think of SDM like a car. A car needs all its internal parts (battery, engine, electrical systems, and so on) and its external parts (wheels, doors, windows) in order for it to work properly. Some of the items are required for it to work at all. It may still technically function without some of the others, but if it doesn't work the way you'd hoped, it's nothing more than a useless heap of scrap metal which has no value to you. The same goes for a supplier diversity program; sure, you can technically run it without all the pieces, but it isn't as effective.

Perusing Supplier Diversity Management as a Process

In the chapter introduction, I mention clients' a-ha moments when they first hear about supplier diversity management as a process. Well, here's what happens after the light bulb comes on: We usually have a conversation about the gaps in their programs and whether the gaps are intentional or unintentional. If they're unintentional, it may be because the organizations weren't aware that this process was something they needed. If the gaps are intentional, it's usually because the supplier diversity people haven't been able to get buy-in from the top to incorporate all the phases into their program. Either way, whether it's increasing knowledge or developing tactics to secure buy-in, there's a solution.

As supplier diversity has evolved over the years, the outcomes organizations have required to justify their programs have also shifted. During each phase, they adopted new tactics or measures in response to what was important to the organization at that time. (You can read more about the phases of supplier diversity history in Chapter 2.) Today, supplier diversity is a management strategy, and the outcome is delivering value to the organization.

Organizations that evolved successfully became synonymous with best practices. They're often comprehensive programs, incorporating activities (whether that's internal policies and in-reach or external outreach, accountability, and supplier development) in each step of the process. As I discuss in the preceding section, that comprehensiveness is a hallmark of SDM.

Conversely, programs that aren't so successful usually include only one aspect of the process. For example, they may have an internal policy but no external outreach, communication, or supplier development plan. This setup may limit the number of small and diverse businesses that engage in their program or their contract readiness for contract opportunities with the organization. Another company may have a heavy focus on supplier development and conducting workshops but not have policies strong enough to be impactful or inclusive or a clear process to connect businesses to opportunities.

A *process* is a series of actions or steps taken to achieve a particular end. Consider the process involved in running a bakery. It's made up of a group of functions represented in a tiered plan, starting at the top. These tiers include all the functions needed to operate a bakery, such as production, marketing, HR, supply chain, and so on. You can break down the high-level processes that make up each function into more granular tasks.

For example, you can divide the production process into smaller sub-processes, such as preparing the batter, making the icing, adding toppings or designs, baking the cakes, and packing and shipping. Each of these sub-processes has its own sub-processes (all the ingredients needed, ideal storage conditions). You keep repeating these steps until you reach the lowest level of the process, or activities, to get a finalized and detailed plan of all the company's processes.

The same principles make up the supplier diversity management model. When you're working on one aspect, or something that you're more comfortable with, focusing on just that one element and neglecting others is easy. But if you don't realize the interconnectivity between each part, the process can be ineffective, inefficient, or both.

Figure 3-1 illustrates the supplier diversity management process.

Each of these functions is interconnected, and they work together to create a push and pull effect to reach the goal of creating value for the organization and the community. External community stakeholders have an interest in creating a strong small and diverse business community and can drive action. To do so, they may push organizations to ensure that small, diverse, and local business are able to compete and have opportunities to be considered for contract awards. They then pull information from these organizations to stay abreast of what's happening and hold them accountable to comply.

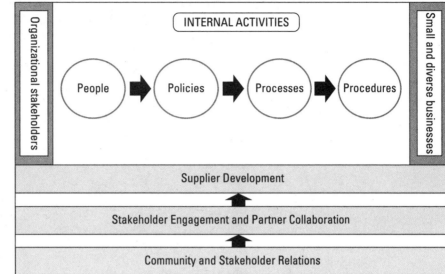

Value Creation

INTERNAL ACTIVITIES

Organizational stakeholders

People ➡ Policies ➡ Processes ➡ Procedures

Small and diverse businesses

Supplier Development

Stakeholder Engagement and Partner Collaboration

Community and Stakeholder Relations

FIGURE 3-1: The supplier diversity management process.

Organizations may create programs or adjust their program activities in response to this movement. They push information about their programs, upcoming opportunities, and results out to stakeholders, the small and diverse business community, and internal departments and senior leaders. After the program is in place, organizations work to develop small and diverse businesses so that departments are able to engage businesses that are ready and able to successfully perform on projects. The success of these businesses allows them to build sustainable businesses and remain viable contributors to the business community.

Introducing the Supplier Diversity Management (SDM) Model

Supplier diversity management focuses on building a full, holistic program that includes all the areas necessary — not just one or two aspects — to maximize benefits. The supplier diversity management (SDM) model is a guide that helps map out the key functions for any type of organization or agency looking to implement a full-scale supplier diversity program that achieves results and delivers value to the organization.

When you build a program that is in alignment with your organization's goals and focuses — not just conducting activities or going through the motions but also adding value to the organization — guiding your actions toward meaningful activities becomes easier. The SDM model ensures that your internal and external activities and supplier development converge (see Figure 3-2), allowing you to deliver on this promise.

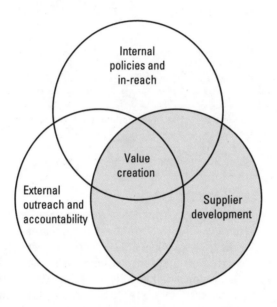

FIGURE 3-2:
Supplier diversity
interconnectivity.

Figure 3-3 illustrates how the SDM model works and how each aspect works together and complements the other.

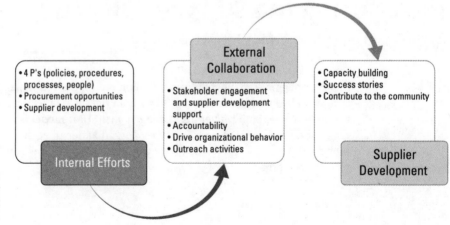

FIGURE 3-3:
Supplier diversity
management
model.

The internal process

Everything starts here. This part focuses on all your internal activities, your 4 P's, your in-reach efforts, and your programs and determines the robustness of your program. It's the heart of your supplier diversity efforts, but, like a human, your program needs more than a heart to function healthy and strong.

Many organizations have an "if we build it, they will come" approach, in that they think businesses will line up to do business with them if they create a program. In reality, the most qualified and capable firms are in high demand, especially in industries that don't have many small or diverse businesses. These companies have the luxury of being very selective about who their partners are. They aren't interested in processes that are cumbersome and unwelcoming, no matter who you are or how big your organization is. But entrepreneurship is alive and well. Every day, more people are deciding to pursue their dreams of owning a business. This boom creates many opportunities to show would-be entrepreneurs why you're a good partner and that their next client is you.

The external process

This part may be two-fold:

>> **External stakeholders:** Whether they're consumers, community leaders, business partners, or the small and diverse businesses themselves, external stakeholders can provide the motivation and push that organizations sometimes need in order to take action. As I discuss in Chapter 2, supplier diversity started in response to the social and economic inequality of the 1960s. Over the years, as it entered different phases, the shift was usually in response to some kind of external force. In fact, even the resurgence supplier diversity experienced in 2021 was a result of the racial and social unrest of 2020.

    External stakeholders are also resource partners in that they team up with an organization to deliver programs to small and diverse businesses, especially if the organization doesn't have enough resources to fully devote to this function. Further, they're prime partners (suppliers with a direct contract with the organization) that may provide subcontracting or other businesses partnering opportunities to small and diverse businesses.

>> **Community outreach:** *Community outreach* involves actively engaging in the community to scout and recruit companies to do business with your organization. The supplier diversity industry has done a great job of creating opportunities to connect small and diverse businesses to decision makers. Before the COVID-19 pandemic, on any given day in any city, there was no shortage of events in which small and diverse businesses participated.

The supplier development process

Through external collaborations (see the preceding section), organizations realized that they could provide additional support in a way that was cost effective yet still impactful. It also engaged their prime partners and encouraged them to adopt their own supplier diversity efforts providing additional opportunities for small and diverse businesses. This relationship gave rise to the importance of supplier development.

As the name indicates, the focus is on development — proactively creating a pipeline of small and diverse businesses ready to work with your organization. As organizations become more intentional about supplier diversity and allocate more time and professional resources to their programs, they have to look beyond just spend analytics. Supplier development allows you to do that and has become one of the most important facets of the model. Investing in small and diverse businesses not only prepares them for the rigors of doing business with your organization, but it also primes them for contract opportunities with other institutions. This boost helps build their capacity, which is vital for long-term growth and entrepreneurial sustainability.

Supplier development is probably the process that's missing from most supplier development programs. Supplier development comes in many forms, from informal efforts such as workshops and networking events to more structured programs including mentoring programs, accelerators, and matchmaking. What you decide to do depends on the stage of your program, your budget and resources, your organization's goals, and what makes sense for your organization.

REMEMBER

Supplier development doesn't mean you're investing in or managing the businesses. It's about giving them the necessary tools to help understand their capability or competency and allow them to increase their competitive advantage (and, hopefully, match them to opportunities within your organization).

Supplier development is also an important step in the strategic sourcing and the supplier relationship management (SRM) processes. With *strategic sourcing,* supplier discovery and engagement allow the organization to identify and work with the best suppliers to create win-win situations. Strategic sourcing looks beyond just price as the basis for making decisions to award.

Supplier relationship management is an intentional and system-wide assessment of suppliers' strengths and capabilities and how they match to opportunities within your organization. It's the planning and execution of all interactions with suppliers, in a coordinated fashion throughout the relationship life cycle, to maximize the value of the relationships.

Because of the strategic focus of both strategic sourcing and SRM, they're great complements to supplier development activities and provide the perfect springboard to transition small and diverse businesses into actual suppliers. Supplier development doesn't focus solely on developing the professional capacity of these businesses. It focuses on building relationships, which is the foundation for every successful procurement transaction, to deliver greater levels of innovation and competitive advantage than can be achieved otherwise. Further, it moves the relationship beyond just a traditional, transactional purchasing arrangement. It's like that old proverb: If you give someone a fish, you feed them for a day; if you teach someone to fish, you feed them for a lifetime.

WARNING

Programs with a heavy focus on supplier development and not enough on their internal processes run the risk of being viewed as one-dimensional — offering training (which, honestly, businesses can get anywhere) but no real access to opportunities. Many argue that small and diverse businesses don't need more training; they need access to contracts. This belief is due to the overgrowth of training programs that offer nothing more than a certificate and words of encouragement at the end.

REMEMBER

The benefit of creating your own supplier development program, and the incentive for these businesses to commit their time and energy to participate, is that they can build relationships and learn your processes, which will, hopefully, lead to a business opportunity. Successful supplier development programs not only train but also have an end goal in mind — to leverage the training to create a pathway to opportunity within the organization.

Getting Started with SDM

Many supplier diversity programs start with the end goal in mind, approaching it as a destination rather than a long-term organizational process. This method isn't necessarily the wrong way to think about supplier diversity, but it may not allow you to identify the gaps because you aren't deconstructing the process and considering every step needed to achieve your goal of adding value. Having properly designed business processes in place is the key to efficiency, scalability, and competitiveness and ensures that the program will be a vital part of the organization for years to come. This area is where the SDM model is an effective tool. You can read more about the model in the earlier section "Introducing the Supplier Diversity Management (SDM) Model."

The SDM model is a guide that helps you identify the key functions at every phase of the process and map out the activities you should incorporate based on your organizational culture. It's not a cookie-cutter approach. Rather, it allows you to consider those details that are unique to your organization and adapt your program activities to those that allow you to achieve your outcomes. In this model (refer to Figure 3-3), you see how each phase impacts the next phase. Starting at the left, organizational stakeholders (external process) drive internal activities (internal process) which then impacts diverse businesses (supplier development process). These activities work collectively to create value.

The following sections offer a few tips to consider as you begin using the SDM model in your organization.

Phase 1: Internal efforts

Internal efforts include a focus on the 4 P's — policies, procedures, processes, and people — your in-reach efforts, and your programs. The following are some key questions to consider:

>> Can we create a map for our supplier diversity process?

>> How comprehensive do we want our efforts to be?

>> Are we willing to devote necessary resources to develop this process?

>> How do we view/value supplier diversity?

>> What are our expected outcomes? What value do we want to add?

Phase 2: External efforts

External efforts focus on collaboration. Here are a few questions to ask yourself:

>> What resources do we need for support?

>> What community resources are available — that is, large businesses, industry experts, other business development agencies, and so on?

>> How will they add value to our program?

SDM — BRINGING THE RESULTS TO STRUGGLING ORGANIZATIONS

When organizations come to me about their programs, it's usually because they're not getting the results they'd hoped for. They have the willingness and the elements of what can be a strong program, but it's still not coming together. By deconstructing their program using the SDM model, they can readily see the gaps. For example, they might be experiencing challenges in finding small and diverse businesses. They may have the requisite internal elements, but they haven't incorporated the supplier engagement and development program to get firms into their pipeline. Or they may be having issues increasing departmental utilization with small and diverse businesses. This usually indicates that their internal programs, specifically the 4 P's, may need to be reviewed to ensure that each area has been addressed.

Phase 3: Supplier development

This last phase is about (wait for it) development. Keep the following in mind:

- » How much can we devote to supplier development?
- » How will we incorporate supplier development into our program?
- » How will supplier development fit into our program?
- » What happens after?
- » How do we keep businesses engaged?

IN THIS CHAPTER

» Knowing the differences between supplier diversity and DEI

» Understanding how the two programs can work with each other

» Discovering some common dangers in lumping both initiatives together

Chapter **4**

Distinguishing between Supplier Diversity and DEI

The global COVID-19 pandemic, polarizing politics, and social justice movements have made *diversity, equity, and inclusion* (DEI) a high-trending theme and one of the hottest topics in organizations today. You hear about it everywhere: on the news, in company press releases, and in everyday conversations. According to research by management consultancy Russell Reynolds Associates, the hiring of chief diversity officers for companies listed on the S&P 500 nearly tripled from December 2020 to March 2021.

That organizations have recommitted themselves to ensuring that their environments are diverse and inclusive is certainly great news. However, organizations must also remember that they can't have a fully actualized diversity strategy if it doesn't include all facets of diversity: the workforce *and* its suppliers — a side that is sometimes overlooked.

This chapter discusses the differences between supplier diversity and DEI, why they're collaborative partners, and the pitfalls of combining the two.

Surveying the Programs' Similar Names and Mission

Since the 20th century, groups have long advocated for equal and fair treatment in the workplace. If you do any research on when diversity became part of the conversation, you find that, like suppler diversity, it has had many iterations over the years to arrive where it is today.

Starting with diversity

As I explain in Chapter 2, calls to address diversity began in the 1960s, when the postwar prosperity still hadn't reached all segments of society. This disparity inspired unrest and new demands for equality and economic access within the Black community.

President Kennedy first introduced affirmative action legislation in 1961, a method of rectifying discrimination that had persisted despite civil rights laws and constitutional guarantees. It focused on education and jobs and required companies to take active measures to ensure that Blacks and people from other marginalized groups enjoyed the same opportunities for promotions, salary increases, career advancement, school admissions, scholarships, and financial aid that had been nearly exclusively reserved for whites. It was designed as a temporary remedy that would end after a level playing field for all Americans had been attained.

The Civil Rights Act of 1964 signed by President Lyndon Johnson prohibited employment discrimination based on race, sex, color, religion, and national origin and gave rise to the creation of the Equal Employment Opportunity Commission (EEOC) to enforce Title VII and eliminate unlawful employment discrimination. As discrimination in the workplace persisted, the Equal Opportunity Commission (EEOC) set guidelines focused on the culture-at-large and made it a lawful offense. Their goal was to make sweeping changes in the U.S. workplace culture and address how to expand the workforce to include "historically underrepresented populations."

Most historians agree diversity initiatives began in earnest because of a report during the late 1980s. The report indicated that "only 15 percent of the new entrants to the labor force over the next 13 years will be native white males, compared to 47 percent in that category today," and that for the United States to keep thriving, lawmakers needed to address three things:

>> "Maintain the dynamism of an aging workforce" (In other words, ensure that the workforce is able to stay active and engaged.)

>> Address the "conflicting needs of women, work, and families"

>> "Integrate Black and Hispanic workers fully into the economy"

This realization really hit home, especially within the business community. The 1980s were a formative decade in history. The United States was trying to reestablish itself as a global power, especially compared to other up-and-coming economies such as China. Diversity initiatives became an important piece to advance the U.S. workforce, expand industry, and maintain America's global dominance.

During this time, an increasing number of corporations launched diversity initiatives. They focused largely on recruitment and getting workers of different backgrounds in the door. However, they soon found that they had no guarantee those workers would stay.

Introducing inclusion

Constant employee turnover created a revolving door that not only became costly but also created some questions about the organizations' commitment to diversity. Some companies realized they needed to focus on the working environment just as much — that inclusion needed to be another prong of the strategy. The field became diversity and inclusion.

Inclusion isn't just superficial recruitment diversity or celebrating differences. It examines how employees can feel accepted for being themselves while having access to the decision making table. Some inclusion strategies include the following:

>> Business and employee resource groups (ERGs)

>> Formal mentoring programs

>> New methods of engaging and leveraging all employees' knowledge and skills

>> More transparent paths for employees to succeed within a company and the leadership structure

Expanding for equity

In recent years, diversity and inclusion initiatives have expanded to include equity. *Equity* focuses on ensuring that everyone has just and fair access to the same information, opportunities, and environment regardless of their experience or specific social position. Each person has unique needs, advantages, and barriers; everyone starts from a different place, so everyone needs different resources to level the playing field. To be successful, inclusive environments require equal access and fairness. Equity enhances inclusion and looks at systemic issues that allow inequality to continue.

REMEMBER

If this sounds a lot like supplier diversity, you're right. Whether you're talking about employees or vendors, diversity on its own isn't enough. To leverage both strategies to drive bottom-line results, the goal is to *recruit* desired groups to the organization, to create and foster an *inclusive* environment where they feel welcomed and like a valued part of the culture or process, and to ensure they have *equitable* access to the same opportunities as everyone else.

A NEW SENSE OF URGENCY: PUTTING THE FOCUS ON SUPPLIER DIVERSITY AFTER THE GLOBAL PANDEMIC

I started this project when the world was facing some of the most unparalleled and disruptive events in history — the COVID-19 pandemic and the social unrest sparked by the murder of George Floyd. The world as we knew it came to a halt, with businesses and schools closing and operations shifting to a virtual environment. Groups used this time not only to protest for social reforms but also to demand access to increased economic opportunities.

The death toll from the global pandemic was devastating with the effects still being felt. From an economic perspective, some businesses were able to adapt to this shift to virtual, work-from-home orders, or limited staff. Many, particularly small and diverse businesses, were not and were among the hardest hit. According to CBS News: "There were more than 1 million black-owned businesses in the U.S. at the beginning of February 2020, according to research from the University of California at Santa Cruz, which drew from census survey estimates. By mid-April, 440,000 black business owners had shuttered their company for good — a 41 percent plunge. By comparison, 17 percent of white-owned businesses closed during the same period, the UC Santa Cruz research shows."

This was a tipping point, where organizations began looking internally at how they could step up and support, putting supplier diversity squarely in the middle. With supplier diversity professionals, there was a renewed sense of urgency to create creative solutions that would have a lasting impact. Global organizations announced financial commitments, pledged resources, and opened their doors to diverse businesses like never before. The year 2021 was definitely a defining moment in supplier diversity work to get small and diverse businesses back to work.

Diving into Their Different Audiences, Tactics, and Results

As a department or even a strategic initiative, diversity programs are still relatively green when compared to other functions within an organization. Despite diversity's auspicious start during the 1960s, for many years it languished and wasn't always embraced, welcomed, or even understood. But during the 1970s and 1980s, it became clear that the focus on diversity wasn't going away. Organizations had to quickly get intentional about their commitment, develop strategies that worked, and create programs that could have a lasting impact on their communities.

Understanding the key differences in supplier diversity and DEI programs helps you balance and use them collaboratively and complementarily to avoid hyperfocusing on one area and neglecting the other. The following sections break down a few of these major differences.

Customers/target audience

DEI focuses on recruiting and fostering a culture of inclusion for current and future employees regardless of ethnicity, gender, age, disability, sexual orientation, religion, nationality, or educational level. DEI may also focus on niche groups within the organization that may have historically been overlooked, such as parents that are adopting or fathers that want to take paternal leave. These groups have a tremendous voice in shaping the benefits that an organization offers its employees.

Supplier diversity focuses on developing and nurturing the contracting relationship with suppliers, vendors, and consultants that have been historically marginalized and excluded from business opportunities because of ethnicity, gender, sexual orientation, and veteran status.

Tactics used

Supplier diversity and DEI deploy different methods to appeal to their target audiences. Because internal feedback is so important to the culture-building process, DEI directs its efforts primarily in the internal environment. It may deploy a combination of methods including recruitment fairs, ERGs, and climate surveys to direct its program efforts.

Supplier diversity uses a combination of external and internal efforts to achieve its results. Because it's targeting small and diverse businesses from the community, it participates in outreach events and conducts workshops and training, all directed at the external community. It may even use councils of external small and diverse businesses and other community stakeholders. Internally, it works with employees, senior leaders, and allies to help them understand supplier diversity and encourage them to buy from small and diverse vendors.

TIP

Understanding the context of supplier diversity allows organizations to create a program that fits their cultures while addressing the issues of their small business communities.

Measuring results

DEI and supplier diversity use varying metrics to demonstrate their value and measure success. The types of instruments they use definitely overlap, but ultimately, it's a bit like comparing apples to oranges. They're both fruit, but they taste totally different.

REMEMBER

Understanding the differences in the types of metrics tracked by each program and the context of the information gathered is important. Combining metrics may not consider outliers or one-off scenarios that exist in supplier diversity. Focusing on the wrong metrics may make you overlook gaps in your program.

DEI may focus on the number of hires, efforts taken to accommodate specific groups, the number of new initiatives that recognize and celebrate different nationalities, the creation of programs that create a pipeline to senior leadership positions, and so on.

With supplier diversity, spend and utilization with small and diverse vendors are the most common metrics. And, for a long time, they were the standard metrics. With the heavy investment in supplier development, supplier diversity today may look at the number of small and diverse businesses responding to solicitations, the award and project completion rates for small and diverse business, the conversion rate for workshop attendees becoming actual vendors, the number of repeat awardees, whether contract awards are increasing or decreasing, and so on.

REMEMBER

In addition to their core metrics, both programs are looking for additional ways to capture and demonstrate their value by looking at the quality of life and economic impact investments in these programs are having on the community. Measuring diversity results is all about assessing success, identifying gaps to drive necessary behaviors, and determining corrective action to make the organization and these programs better.

Figure 4-1 provides examples of metrics used by each and shows how they compare to each other.

	Supplier Diversity	DEI
Climate-based. Measures feelings and sentiments; can be used to understand how target audience feels about the organization	• I feel like I can win contracts. • I feel like I have access to business opportunities. • I feel like they care about my success. • I feel respected. • I feel like a valued partner.	• I feel like I belong. • I can express my opinions. • I can engage with co-workers regardless of status, seniority, or level of authority. • I feel respected. • I feel like I have access to opportunities. • I feel like a valued member of the team.
Program-based. Measures your responsiveness to the targeted audience; initiative focused — metrics are things that you can track easily and are tied to progress made	• # of businesses engaged in your program • % of businesses that respond and win/lose bid solicitations	• # of entrances/exits that are accessible. • # of bathrooms that are neutral. • % of physical accommodation requests accommodated. • % demographic data (for example, % of workforce that identifies as a certain gender or other demographic identity) • Attrition rates. • Promotion rates.
Demographic/socioeconomic-based. Most commonly tracked for both; however, shouldn't be used as the primary indicator of progress; may be illegal in DEI	• Ethnicity • Gender • LGBTQ identities • Nationality • Disability status • Veteran status	• # of hires by ethnicity • # of hires by gender • # of hires by age • # of hires by LGBTQ identities • # of hires by religion • Nationality • Disability status
Organizational-based. Looks at the impact efforts have on the organization		• Overall sales growth correlated to increases in diversity or changes in ranked metrics • Sales per revenue-generating department (including any relevant support departments) • Revenue per employee (segmented by department or correlated with demographics to understand diversity impact) • Brand sentiment (done through social listening and correlated to any public conversation the company has about diversity, equity, and inclusion)

FIGURE 4-1:
Differences in measuring results.

Becoming Collaborative Partners

Supplier diversity and DEI definitely have aspects that make them great collaborative partners. Based on their timelines and history, in many ways DEI and supplier diversity have grown together. Each started by government executive order, with little guidance other than the intended outcome. Unfortunately, the path to get there was never completely laid out. Through trial and error, both programs have had to figure out their respective roles and how best to deliver value to the organizations.

Based on the differences I describe in the earlier section "Diving into Their Different Audiences, Tactics, and Results," each has forged a distinct path and role — DEI in HR and supplier diversity in procurement — and both have managed to grow and become strategic staples by working together as natural collaborative partners.

REMEMBER

In Chapter 8, I discuss the relationship between supplier diversity and DEI; for the purposes of this chapter, you should understand the three ways in which supplier diversity and DEI collaborate:

>> Help gain active stakeholder involvement

>> Help increase visibility and engagement across the organization

>> Help keep the diversity conversation top of mind

Perusing the Pitfalls of Combining Supplier Diversity and DEI

In recent years, two trends have appeared to sometimes blur the line between supplier diversity and DEI. Understandably, how your diversity efforts are structured depends on budget, personnel, or exactly how your organization views diversity. Whatever the reason, it should align with what your organization wants to accomplish and how you want the public and your stakeholders to perceive your diversity efforts. But in this setting, for the two programs to exist without one cannibalizing the other is a challenge. The following sections cover some of the current trends and the problems they present.

WARNING

Few things are more disruptive to any program than poor execution. Building a poor structure can run counter to what you're trying to accomplish. Further, it can negatively impact program results, which can lead to internal resentment and dysfunction. When that sets in with an organization, it's hard to overcome.

Best practice is for these functions to work alongside each other, not one under the other. You're creating supplier diversity *and* DEI rather than supplier diversity *or* DEI. As important as both of these are and will continue to be in the future, setting up a choice would be a hard, and maybe costly, decision to make.

Combining diversity efforts under one umbrella

This structure presents challenges for a few reasons:

>> **Leadership woes, part one:** For starters, determining who leads this effort — a supplier diversity professional or a DEI professional — is tricky. Just as HR and procurement are two distinct functions, each with different sensibilities and competencies, so are supplier diversity and DEI. You wouldn't hire a procurement professional to run HR and vice versa.

>> **Leadership woes, part two:** Because the professional competencies are different, managing them under one umbrella usually ends with one person woefully unprepared to lead or manage the other program. They end up directing much of their time where they're most comfortable while not paying enough, if any, attention to the other program.

>> **Perceived prioritization:** Having someone from one program lead the combined effort may give the impression that that program is more of a priority than the other.

The changing role of the Chief Diversity Officer

Using an umbrella approach also impacts the leader tasked with managing it — the Chief Diversity Officer, or CDO. There have been quite a few hires and announcements of newly appointed CDOs. With some organizations, it's the same as it's always been, focused on DEI. In others, it's an all-encompassing position covering all things diversity, including supplier diversity.

The emphasis on diversity is definitely a positive one. However, does the CDO title truly reflect what's happening with diversity? For example, the CDO title has primarily been associated with DEI. However, if a comprehensive diversity strategy includes creating equitable opportunities for employees *and* suppliers, are diversity professionals, who are usually trained to support one portion of a program, equipped to handle the rigors of another aspect of diversity that includes different audiences and has its own set of challenges, objectives, and KPIs? Will this merging of the two require CDOs to be well versed in both areas, or is it setting diversity efforts up to fail by overreaching the capacity of the professional in charge?

WARNING

I've heard many colleagues express feelings of burnout and being overwhelmed managing the demands of both and still being able to be effective. As stated earlier, the umbrella approach is problematic to diversity for several reasons. The title and what it entails adds to this challenge.

Changing the name of supplier diversity to "supplier diversity and inclusion"

This change has been subtle and is still relatively new, but it's showing up more in job descriptions or job titles across the board. The premise is that, like DEI, diversity gets businesses in the door, and inclusion ensures that they feel welcomed after they're there. This point may be semantics, but it gives the impression that it's a blended function. But as I discuss in the preceding section, that blending is difficult to execute and still devote the same level of priority to each one.

Chapter **5**

Digging into Supplier Diversity within the Organization

Before you can effectively manage an initiative, you have to understand the role it'll play within the organization. Many organizations have or plan to start supplier diversity programs, but often they fail to consider how these initiatives will work within the organization. This lack of planning makes fully integrating the program into the organization and getting buy-in difficult. This chapter takes a deeper dive into supplier diversity within the organization: the many roles required of the supplier diversity professional, how supplier diversity works within the organization and specifically the procurement process, and what the potential conflicts and resolutions are.

Understanding the Role of the Supplier Diversity Professional

In today's complex organizations, culture is as important as ever. In fact, it's one of the most pressing issues executives face. A recent study by Boston Consulting Group found that companies that focused on culture were five times more likely to achieve breakthrough results in their transformation initiatives than those that didn't. Supplier diversity is one of those transformation initiatives in which having the right culture and understanding where supplier diversity fits within your organization is extremely important.

It's in this transformation culture that the supplier diversity professional is a layered, multifaceted role, often wearing what I like to call the Seven Hats of the Supplier Diversity Professional. Take a look in your supplier diversity closet; on any given day (maybe even several times a day), you've probably reached for at least one of these hats shown in Figure 5-1 and described in the following list:

>> **Leader:** As the supplier diversity leader, you direct and champion the efforts within the organization.

>> **Influencer:** Part salesperson, part evangelist, your role as an influencer focuses on shaping and persuading external actions and stakeholder activities to support supplier diversity policies and strategies.

>> **Change agent:** This part of your role is similar to that of influencer but focuses on changing internal entrenched behaviors to make long-lasting, transformative shifts in the organization's culture.

>> **Recruiter:** You're the primary bridge between opportunities within the organization and small and diverse businesses. You're always on the lookout for vendors that may be a good fit for the procurement pipeline and ensure that they're prepared for contract opportunities.

>> **Advocate:** You're a champion for small and diverse businesses for opportunities across the organization while looking for new ways to increase engagement and utilization.

>> **Collaborator:** Whether you're conducting internal activation or external outreach, collaboration is the foundation for most supplier diversity activities.

>> **Employee:** With all these functions, you're still an employee, which means carefully balancing all your other hats while still keeping the best interests of the organization top of mind and minimizing exposure to risk (such as disputes, legal action, or even having the program shut down). I hope your workspace has high ceilings.

TIP

I like to think of the supplier diversity professional as a chameleon of sorts. Depending on the audience and what you're trying to achieve, you have to change your messaging and adapt to your surroundings.

REMEMBER

Culture doesn't change overnight or by accident. The supplier diversity professional should incorporate a tactical plan to lead the transformation and culture shift that needs to occur.

Surveying How Supplier Diversity Fits into the Organization

I am a big supporter of understanding how your entire organization — not just your section of it — works. My first job out of college was with a small personal care company as an assistant marketing brand manager. Although the company sold products all over the world, it was still a family-owned company where everyone knew each other's names.

One of the benefits of working in a small company was the ability to learn the inner workings. In consumer products, marketing is one of the functions that everything emanates from. When we'd launch a new product, we had to coordinate with research to see whether it could make it, with purchasing to see whether it could buy the materials at the price I needed, with production to ensure that it could produce it, and with sales to ensure that it could sell it. If I made a unilateral decision on the formula (or packaging, production, or sales strategy) without consulting any of these departments, the move could spell disaster for the launch and success of my product and cost the company hundreds of thousands of dollars, not to mention my job. Not only did I need these departments, but I also needed to understand how they worked and how every decision or request I made impacted them. I needed to understand their roles within the organization, not just mine. This experience definitely framed my ability to build relationships and collaborate with departments across the organization.

Supplier diversity is similar in that success comes from working with departments across the organization. Some departments are more integral than others, so you have to cultivate the relationship more. Understanding how supplier diversity works with each department requires knowing which of the seven hats is required to achieve desired results. (Head to the preceding section for more on the Seven Hats of the Supplier Diversity Professional.)

With supply chain/procurement

Although procurement is the primary relationship for supplier diversity, the best way to describe it is as *yin and yang* — the ancient Chinese concept of dualism, where contrary forces may actually be complementary, interconnected, and interdependent. In short, they may not always see eye to eye, but they're interrelated and rely on each other.

At first glance, procurement and supplier diversity appear to have opposing interests for a couple of reasons:

>> The role of procurement is to buy what the organization needs at the best price possible, so price is often its deciding factor. Procurement's ability to save the organization money is one of its departmental key performance indicators (KPIs).

>> Most people like the status quo, or keeping things the way they are. Developing relationships with vendors and settling into a routine when making purchases without giving it any additional thought is easy.

Supplier diversity is a bit of a disruption to this departmental model. Supplier diversity requires departments to be more intentional with their actions. It asks departments to build relationships with small and diverse businesses who may be new to their organization and to consider factors other than low price when making buying decisions. Understandably, this shift can be a challenge depending on the purchase. Considering a new or small vendor is much easier for routine, everyday items than it is for more complex and specialized items.

I talk about how supplier diversity is involved in the procurement process later in this chapter, but here are few ways supplier diversity works with procurement:

>> Ensure that small and diverse businesses are aware of buying opportunities throughout the organization

>> Facilitate the relationship-building process

>> Create policies that encourage small and diverse business use in all opportunities

>> Support an inclusive process that levels the procurement playing field

>> Partner on outreach and events targeting small and diverse businesses

With facilities/construction

The relationship between supplier diversity and the facilities/construction department is much like the one with procurement in the preceding section, just on a larger scale. Depending on the structure, organizations may have a facilities or construction department that manages all their construction projects. Whereas procurement typically awards contracts directly to small and diverse businesses, facilities/construction usually has a relationship with a larger firm, or *prime* (this may also be a diverse business). The relationship between supplier diversity and the facilities/construction department is important because it comprises the majority of *tier* 2 or subcontracting spend.

Tier 2 spend requires prime contractors to report to the organization how much they've spent or will spend with small and diverse businesses to complete a project. Some organizations implement a goal, which is a minimum percentage of the total contract to be spent with small and diverse businesses. For example, if a project valued at $2 million has a small and diverse business goal of 20 percent, that means that at least $200,000 of the total contract must be spent with small and diverse businesses. (I discuss goal-setting in detail in Chapter 18.) Depending on the market, this goal may be a strongly suggested condition or a mandated requirement.

For supplier diversity programs, managing a tier 2/subcontracting effort is an important part of a comprehensive program and, increasingly, an important capture point for reporting overall utilization. But it's also essential for the entire ecosystem:

>> It encourages prime companies to develop a program and create opportunities for small and diverse firms within their own organizations. It also allows them to create positive goodwill as a partner to their respective clients that value these programs.

>> It gives small and diverse businesses access to high-value contracts. This access lets diverse businesses scale and increase their capacity at a much faster rate.

Supplier diversity works with facilities/construction to

>> Ensure that small and diverse businesses are aware of opportunities in order to build strategic partnerships

>> Create opportunities for small and diverse businesses to meet and build relationships with prime contractors and departmental personnel

>> Develop policies, such as goal-setting, preferential points on request for proposal (RFP) evaluations, compliance, and an accountability process, that encourage prime contractors to utilize small and diverse businesses

With diversity and inclusion

Although the two departments' priorities are different, diversity and inclusion (also known as diversity, equity, and inclusion [DEI]) is a natural collaborator for supplier diversity. DEI focuses on creating an inclusive culture for employees and internal stakeholders. Because culture is the foundation for successful supplier diversity efforts, the fact that these groups frequently work together to leverage each other's networks and partner on activities and programs makes sense.

Supplier diversity works with DEI to

>> Connect with internal stakeholders to understand diversity efforts

>> Establish diversity as an organizational strategy rather than just a short-term initiative

>> Leverage resources to expand the diversity message/platform throughout the organization and community

With senior leadership

Senior leadership may be VPs or any senior-level stakeholder with an interest in the program. It isn't a formal department, per se, but it carries lots of weight with supplier diversity. Supplier diversity usually relies on senior leadership to set the tone for implementing the strategy within the organization and to create the right culture for it to be successful.

Supplier diversity is also accountable to this group to report program activities and results. Translation: Senior leadership is responsible for deciding the level of influence supplier diversity has within the organization — whether it's an actual program with teeth or a lame-duck program with no real authority or impact. The relationship with senior leadership can determine the life or death of the supplier diversity program.

REMEMBER

Supplier diversity works with senior leadership to

>> Set meaningful and impactful objectives for the program and the community

>> Ensure that these objectives are communicated and integrated throughout the organization

>> Establish an internal culture that embraces diversity

With community relations

Supplier diversity is often viewed as a community function because many of your programs and activities, such as outreach and business development, are community-facing. In large organizations, community relations often buys tables at community events and asks you to attend on the organization's behalf. This situation is a great opportunity to network and interface with community leaders and stakeholders that may have interests similar to yours. It helps bring awareness to your program while solidifying your position as a leader for small and diverse businesses and puts you in a position to meet your next collaborative partner or sponsor.

REMEMBER

Supplier diversity works with community relations to

>> Demonstrate the organization's commitment to diversity to external stakeholders — community, businesses, customers, and others

>> Leverage community relationships to bring awareness to the supplier diversity program

With other departments and organizational initiatives

For supplier diversity to work, you need other departments with buying responsibilities to carry out the mission of procuring from small and diverse firms. Depending on what is needed, the level of interaction is different. It may mean giving department reps program information, collaborating on a project, introducing them to suitable vendors, or sponsoring supplier diversity events.

REMEMBER

Supplier diversity works with departments and organizational initiatives to

>> Ensure that they understand supplier diversity and how to integrate these principles into their departmental procurement routines

>> Find opportunities to align missions to create partnership opportunities

>> Facilitate the relationship-building process

Getting Involved in the Procurement Process — From Beginning to End

Earlier in the chapter, I describe the yin and yang relationship that can exist between supplier diversity and procurement/facilities and construction. Their interests sometimes appear conflicting, but they actually need each other in order to be successful.

Supplier diversity has to build and maintain strong relationships with these departments and have a seat at the table. Figure 5-2 shows the steps that may be used in procurement and what supplier diversity does at each step. The following sections provide more detail on each of these steps.

Forecasting upcoming opportunities

Getting involved as early as possible in the process is key. You do so by staying in communication with procurement. Forecasts are more widely available in public procurement than with private institutions (corporations may not want to let competitors know what they're planning to buy). Supplier diversity should be involved to ensure that small and diverse businesses are aware of opportunities and have enough time to get the resources needed to prepare a response.

Procurement function	Supplier Diversity function
Forecasting	• Advise small and diverse businesses of opportunities • Determine support businesses need to respond
Reviewing	• Review bid documents for inclusive language • Ensure policies are inclusive and within legal guidelines
Evaluation	• Serve on evaluation committee for appropriate projects • Advocate for small and diverse businesses on non-evaluation projects
Onboarding	• Ensure small and diverse businesses are registered in the portal • Ensure portal/process is searchable to internal departments
Informing	• Let vendors know about upcoming opportunities • Ensure small and diverse businesses understand bid requirements
Tracking	• Monitor projects for compliance to organization goals • Monitor projects for small and diverse business utilization
Sourcing	• Find capable vendors for internal opportunities • Evalute capacity to match small and diverse businesses to the right opportunities
Contract Resolution	• Assist vendors with issues • Mediate, if necessary, when there are issues with partners

FIGURE 5-2:
Supplier Diversity
Procurement
Relationship
Model.

Reviewing and ensuring bid documents/RFPs are inclusive

Bid documents can be very complex and confusing. Because they're legal documents, they have to outline everything required for the advertised opportunity. Supplier diversity should be involved to ensure that the documents:

>> Include the organization's stance of using small and diverse businesses

>> Communicate established policies on small and diverse business utilization

>> Indicate how submissions will be evaluated if responding businesses (primes) plan to include small and diverse business in their proposal. This can include detailing how many points a responder's submission receives for their small/diverse business utilization plan.

Participating on selection/evaluation committees

Companies usually use *selection or evaluation committees* to evaluate solicitations using RFPs for construction projects. This two-step process goes something like this:

1. The company receives responses from interested firms, and the evaluation committee selects a smaller list, or *shortlist,* of firms.

2. The shortlisted firms make a final presentation to the evaluation committee.

The vendors receive points based on their responses to established criteria such as team expertise, prior experience, supplier diversity, safety, project approach, and so on. The final award is based on the scores received during the final presentation.

TIP

Supplier diversity should advocate for participating as a voting member of this evaluation committee because the organization has the opportunity to hear the vendor's approach to getting small and diverse businesses on the project. It's also a chance for internal departments to see one aspect of the supplier diversity function and reinforces with its vendors the importance the organization places on supplier diversity.

Establishing the vendor onboarding process

The onboarding process is one of the first steps small and diverse businesses take to establish themselves as potential vendors. Also called the *vendor portal*, it's usually found on the procurement page and managed by procurement. Many of the functions that supplier diversity relies on originate from the vendor portal, including identifying which vendors are diverse, sending notifications of upcoming opportunities to vendors, and tracking how much has been spent with small and diverse businesses. Supplier diversity is involved to establish the functionality and capabilities of the vendor portal so that each department can get what it needs. For more on the vendor portal and how it can help (or hinder) small and diverse businesses' ability to get in the door, check out Chapter 6.

Informing and preparing prospective diverse vendors

Having a relationship with procurement ensures that you stay in the loop of upcoming opportunities. The earlier you know about them, the earlier you can then pass the information on to small and diverse vendors that may be interested.

REMEMBER

Because of the time-sensitivity usually associated with responding to bids, time to prepare and access to information are two of the most valuable resources for small and diverse businesses looking for consideration for opportunities.

Tracking performance and utilization

This task is largely a supplier diversity function, but it relies heavily on procurement systems to get the necessary data to report. Several solutions provide support for tracking small and diverse business utilization. Some organizations may opt to get a third-party solution to maintain this function, but any solution still needs to interface with the vendor portal (see the preceding section) to be effective.

Sourcing and advocating for small and diverse businesses

Having a strong relationship with procurement means it'll share information on upcoming opportunities and turn to you as a resource when sourcing diverse vendors that may be a good fit for opportunities. (This is one place the recruiter hat I discuss earlier in the chapter comes in.) Because you aren't responsible for making an award, this step is where you not only can provide names of firms you're aware of but also can strongly advocate for their utilization.

Mediation and conflict resolution

Providing support to vendors throughout the supplier diversity life cycle is a crucial component to their success. This aspect may include answering questions when vendors have pay issues, challenges on the contract, or even problems with the prime contractor. *Note:* Some programs may help with internal issues but limit their involvement in resolving issues with prime contractors because the contract is technically between the vendor and the prime contractor. This is often a source of conflict between finance, procurement, and supplier diversity. The great supplier diversity professional is a consummate diplomat who knows what battles to fight and how to fight them. (Does this sound like another hat?)

Anticipating Potential Conflicts and Identifying Resolutions

Conflict is a thorny but natural dynamic between functions. Although supplier diversity is an integral part of the procurement process, the two departments sometimes have a "friendly" back and forth where the mood feels more like procurement versus supplier diversity than procurement *and* supplier diversity. Anecdotally, this tension usually occurs because their priorities are occasionally on the opposite ends of the spectrum and the KPIs they measure success with are completely different.

But when I speak to colleagues about their supplier diversity efforts, whether they're starting a new program or trying to create a more robust program, their biggest challenge to success is internal conflicts.

REMEMBER

Internal conflicts may indicate that issues go beyond personality or ideological differences. The challenge is in creating the synergistic relationship necessary for the two to work together. In order to create that, you have to understand why the friction occurs.

No organization is immune to experiencing conflict. A number of factors can contribute to organizational conflict. In his book *Macro Organizational Behavior* (Scott, Foresman, and Company), Robert Miles indicates several examples that are relevant to the relationship between supplier diversity and procurement:

- » **Task interdependencies:** The more departments that have to work together or collaborate to accomplish a goal, the greater the likelihood of conflict if different expectations or goals exist. The interdependence makes avoiding the conflict more difficult because high task interdependency makes relationships more intense. A small disagreement can get heated very quickly and stall program efforts.

- » **Status inconsistencies:** Depending on how the organization is structured, procurement may feel that supplier diversity falls lower within the organization hierarchy and therefore works for procurement rather than with it.

- » **Jurisdictional ambiguities:** *Jurisdictional ambiguities* occur when who's responsible for what isn't always clear. For example, although supplier diversity may give input on key processes such as the vendor portal, onboarding processes, and bid language, these are procurement functions and reside in procurement. Who has the final say may be a point of contention.

- » **Communication problems:** Communication problems or ambiguities in the communication process are arguably one of the most common causes of conflict. When one person misunderstands a message, information is withheld, or a breakdown occurs in the method of delivery (email, text, or whatever), people can easily respond in frustration and even anger.

- » **Lack of common performance standards:** Differences in performance criteria and reward systems provide more potential for organizational conflict. Procurement teams are evaluated and rewarded for their ability to save the organization money (which sometimes conflicts with using a small or diverse vendor). Supplier diversity is evaluated on the utilization of small and diverse businesses the organization contracts with. Even though buying from small and diverse suppliers is an organizational goal, nobody but the actual supplier diversity department is specifically evaluated on this. This means other departments have no incentive to shoot for it and make it a priority. Conflict arises when each department focuses squarely on meeting its own performance criteria without regard for the other.

- » **Individual differences:** A variety of individual differences, such as personal abilities, traits, and skills, can influence interpersonal relations. Individual dominance, aggressiveness, authoritarianism, and tolerance for ambiguity all affect how a person deals with potential conflict. Often, these characteristics may influence whether conflict even exists.

Some additional conflicts specific to supplier diversity and procurement include the following:

>> Procurement focusing on price and not considering other factors

>> Procurement unwilling to work with new and unproven vendors

>> Supplier diversity advocating for firms that may sometimes be at the expense of using local businesses

>> Procurement not always embracing supplier diversity as a strategic advantage

REMEMBER

The type of conflict determines how quickly it can be resolved. But conflict *has* to be resolved for your organization to go about its business and achieve its mission. This necessity may mean making trade-offs to achieve objectives.

Unfortunately, many organizations aren't the most adept at managing or resolving conflicts.

TIP

The following are a few simple solutions for resolving conflicts between supplier diversity and procurement:

>> Supplier diversity and procurement teams coordinate and agree on goals and targets. This task may sound simple, but many organizations struggle to make it work.

>> Supplier diversity and procurement teams work together to establish policies and processes that are heavily dependent on the other, such as the onboarding process, vendor notification of opportunities, vendor evaluation, and developing inclusive contract policies and language.

>> Supplier diversity and procurement teams meet frequently to stay connected and discuss opportunities for collaboration. (Communication is important, especially if supplier diversity isn't housed in procurement.)

FIVE MODES OF RESOLVING CONFLICT FOR SUPPLIER DIVERSITY

One model that I particularly like for assessing situations and managing conflict is the Five Modes of Resolving Conflict developed by Kenneth Thomas and Ralph Kilmann. This model specifically focuses on organizational conflict in a business setting and includes five modes for handling any situation.

I've adapted this model and made it applicable to supplier diversity. Understanding that there's always some resistance to change, you have to know when to be persistent and when to fall back and regroup. As you dig into your organization and begin the process of making lasting change, you can't expect to resolve every situation on the first try. But following these modes can help you make the necessary adjustments so that you can get people to see things your way in no time.

Conflict Handling Mode	Situation
Competing	1. Quick, decisive action is necessary.
	2. Important issues where unpopular actions need implementing (cost-cutting, enforcing unpopular rules, discipline, and so on)
	3. Solutions vital to achieving the organization mission.
	4. Against people who take advantage of noncompetitive behavior.
Collaborating	1. Trying to find a win-win solution when both sets of concerns are too important to be compromised.
	2. Your objective is to learn or get more information.
	3. Trying to get insights from people with different perspectives.
	4. Gaining commitment by incorporating concerns into a consensus.
Compromising	1. Goals are important but not worth the effort or potential disruption they'd cause.
	2. Opponents with equal power are committed to different agendas.
	3. Attempting to achieve temporary settlements to complex issues.
	4. Arriving at expedient solutions under time pressure.
	5. A backup when collaboration or competition is unsuccessful.

(continued)

(continued)

Conflict Handling Mode	Situation
Avoiding	1. An issue is trivial, or more important issues are pressing.
	2. Potential disruption outweighs the benefits of resolution.
	3. More information is required before making a decision.
	4. Others can resolve the conflict more effectively.
	5. Issues seem tangential or symptomatic of other issues, and there's no chance of a successful outcome.
Accommodating	1. You need to allow a better idea to be heard, to learn, and to show your reasonableness.
	2. Issues are more important to others than yourself — to satisfy others and maintain cooperation.
	3. Building social credits for later issues.
	4. Minimizing loss when facing a no-win situation.
	5. Harmony and stability are especially important.

2

Developing Internal (Organizational) Supplier Diversity Efforts

Chapter **6**

Gauging Your Organization's Diversity Climate

D etermining organization climate, or readiness, is a measure of how the organization is now and how it wants to be as a result of implementing a change — in this case, a supplier diversity program.

Having a strong desire to do something is just the start. You have to take active steps to make diversity a reality for the organization. This process may involve having frank discussions on how the organization views diversity and whether it recognizes diversity as a core value. Organizations often publicly tout diversity as their core value and strength only to have emails and private conversations that say otherwise.

In this chapter, I discuss how to understand your organization's diversity climate and how far it's ready to go to implement organizational change.

Surveying Supplier Diversity and Organizational Change Management

Assessing readiness involves understanding the components of change — people and process. With people, supporting the people and identifying the overall culture are two important factors. But even within the organizational culture, departments often create their own cultures. Depending on the function, these department cultures can be hierarchical, entrepreneurial, or collaborative. If the cultures or priorities of the departments clash, making supplier diversity successful can be difficult.

With process, you need to understand the organizational processes impacted by change. Doing so ensures that you're prepared to shift from current state to future state processes. Because of the collaborative nature of supplier diversity, everyone should be on board, which can be easier said than done.

Think about it: If a CEO mandates that the organization must now allocate a portion of its total spend with diverse vendors, without an active plan the target may not become a reality until the departments actively work to make it one.

To begin the evaluation process, organizations may consider some initial questions like these:

>> How has the organization historically handled change?

>> What do you need to alter in order for change to occur and stick?

>> How well does your organization function during change efforts?

>> How disruptive will the implementation process be to the organization? Are you committed for the long haul?

>> What resources do you need? Is your team ready at all levels to implement?

>> Does senior leadership back and support change?

>> What are your motivations for the change? What's your resistance to it?

Organizational change management, also called OCM, is a collective term for approaches to prepare, support, and help individuals, teams, and organizations in making organizational change. It includes methods that redirect or redefine the use of resources, business process, budget allocations, or other modes of operation that significantly impact an organization.

Looking at supplier diversity through the lens of OCM (see Figure 6-1) helps an organization ensure that its culture, processes, strategy, and (the most important part) its people are aligned. To some, OCM can be very complex and feel cumbersome or even like a burden. However, if the organization is committed to making the change, it can start by investing in what's needed for lasting change to occur.

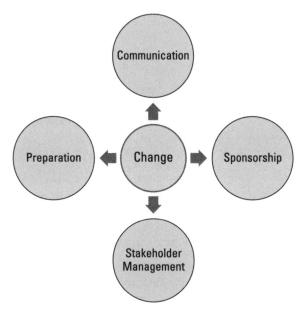

To start the OCM process, four mainstays are necessary to allow the process of change to occur:

>> **Communication:** Communication is fundamental for change. People need and want to know what's happening, when it's happening, why/how they're doing it, and how it impacts them. Communication provides the awareness and understanding needed for them to commit, engage, and execute the necessary change successfully. By setting expectations, employing tools to improve communication, and proactively seeking ways to reduce misinformation, you're more likely to get stakeholders to buy into making change. They'll also stay more engaged and committed, which is how long-term organizational transformation occurs. Good communication should be intentional, consistent, and a two-way street.

To build on your communication planning for change, ensure that your organization establishes an adequate communication plan and overall strategy for the change effort and confirm that communication is flowing at all levels in the organization.

>> **Sponsorship:** A successful change needs active sponsorship and engagement at the executive level. When change occurs, people turn to leaders for direction and support. A sponsor helps build commitment and authenticity across the organization. Sponsors have ultimate responsibility for projects. You can directly link the success of a project to an active sponsor who champions the change, mitigates resistance, and builds organizational alliances.

To build on your sponsorship of change, determine whether the change has the right level of sponsorship — that the level of your primary sponsor matches up with the size and type of the change — before moving ahead.

>> **Stakeholder management:** Stakeholder management involves identifying all stakeholders and getting buy-in. This task involves making them aware of the change and its benefits throughout the process. Actively engaging stakeholders early during the change process directly correlates to the success of the change.

To build on stakeholder management, conduct a stakeholder analysis with your leadership team, and make sure that this analysis is continually revisited and refreshed. Too often, stakeholders are replaced with others that may have a different agenda. Effective stakeholder management provides you the tools to look ahead and anticipate problems before they happen.

>> **Preparation:** The primary goal of preparation is to understand need gaps in stakeholders' skills and provide them opportunities to expand their knowledge and understanding before the change happens. Preparation, in whatever form, should nurture understanding, acceptance, and commitment and build confidence for all involved in the change.

To build on your preparation, design training to educate teams on the specifics of the change and what they need in order to understand and support it.

Examining Your Organizational 4 P's

A great way to think about supplier diversity is as a system — a group of interacting or interrelated elements that act according to a set of rules to form a unified whole. The components that make up a supplier diversity program are its people, policies, processes, and procedures — the 4 P's. You have to assess and manage each of these parts to determine your organization's readiness and to make sure that the supplier diversity system functions as desired. In this section, I examine each component and its importance in the supplier diversity system.

Establishing your process

By definition, a *process* provides a high-level perspective of the various tasks required to complete the work and is driven by the organization's goals and the accomplishment of its intended results. Simply put, your processes are the required tasks that, when combined, turn your inputs (activities) into desired outputs (increased use of diverse vendors) and answer the question "How can my business do business with your organization?"

You should be able to articulate what a vendor will experience when doing business with your organization so that it feels supported throughout the process. Often, these are new or small vendors that may not be familiar with the complexities or layers involved in doing business with your organization. Many supplier diversity systems focus on one facet of their programs, such as outreach or planning workshops, because it's easier and more fun. Unfortunately, they don't spend enough time on establishing processes that lay out what happens after businesses are in their pipelines. This area is one of the biggest points of frustration for small businesses.

Several processes can occur across the supplier diversity life cycle. Because organizations use a variety of vehicles to buy the goods and services they need, a one-size-fits-all process strategy isn't practical or realistic. Telling vendors to "just register in the vendor portal" and wait for opportunities that fit their business to come around won't work with today's procurement systems.

REMEMBER

In today's procurement environment, the process begins long before a solicitation is out or the organization needs to make a purchase. It starts with understanding the small or diverse business — their history, their capacity and capabilities, and so on — and building the relationship. That way, when an opportunity becomes available, they're better able to make a strong match, leading to successful completion.

TIP

In public procurement, many organizations may create a forecast of what opportunities are coming up, which allows businesses to prepare to respond beforehand. With private corporations, this information may be a little harder to find as many of them don't publish their current or future solicitations on their website because they don't always want their competitors to know what they're sourcing at the time. In this environment, the relationship building is even more important. As it relates to your organization's readiness, here are a few questions to ask:

» Do departments readily engage and support your events?

» Do other colleagues advocate for you and supplier diversity when you're not around?

» Are departments open to meeting with small and diverse firms?

» Do departments consider firms for procurement opportunities that they manage?

» Do departments have you come talk to their teams about supplier diversity and what you do?

» Are you the lone voice in trying to make this work?

Your processes may also depend on the types of contracts you're awarding, your budget threshold, the contract length, and so on. For example, you may have processes for each of the following procurement scenarios:

For contracts $10,000 and under

For contracts between $10,000 and $100,000

For contracts between $100,001 and $250,000

For contracts $250,001 and over

REMEMBER

Generally, the higher the project amount, the more complex the procurement process is to ensure that the selected vendor has the right experience and capability to successfully perform. Additionally, contracts over a certain dollar amount may be required by law to have certain safeguards in place to protect the organization in case the project takes a negative turn. For example, on construction projects over $100,000, many states require the contractor to provide a bond or have a certain level of insurance. Conversely, projects under $100,000 may not.

This variation gives you greater latitude in establishing the vendor criteria and process for procuring these projects, which also creates greater opportunity for small and diverse vendors.

The more time you spend understanding your opportunities, the more time you can devote to developing, establishing, and creating a clearly defined process. Doing so makes engaging the right vendors for available opportunities easier.

Identifying your procedures

Your *procedures* concentrate more on the fulfillment of particular activities identified inside the business process. Many confuse processes and procedures or use them interchangeably.

WHEN POLICIES AND PROCEDURES COLLIDE

I am reminded of a time when I witnessed policies and procedures collide, and the organization was open to change. There was a situation with a response to a solicitation. Usually, when a firm submits a proposal, the policy outlines the documents required and specifies that if even one of the items is missing the submitting firm is immediately disqualified (or DQ'd), and the submission is rendered nonresponsive. (This is not uncommon and is usually done to thin the herd.) I was usually notified when firms were DQ'd, especially if they were small or diverse, to understand why they were considered nonresponsive. One of the firms, a minority firm, was DQ'd because they'd forgotten to include their proof of insurance. It was devastating for the business, but it was even more disheartening because they were already doing work with the organization at the time on another project. Also, their disqualification meant that there were no diverse firms submitting a proposal.

That evening, I drafted a change to the procedures. Rather than render a firm nonresponsive when only one or two documents were missing in their submission, we would contact them and allow them time (24 hours) to get the document(s) submitted in order to complete their package.

In the bustle of trying to submit a proposal on time, it's easy for oversights to occur. With this change, they can at least have their proposal reviewed and still have a fighting chance to be considered for an award. And the process remained fair because this new procedure became the standard for everyone.

I know you're wondering what happened. Well, they lost this bid, but they learned from it and went on to win several other projects. They became a very successful prime partner for the organization.

Though the process provides the high-level look (as I describe in the preceding section), your procedures add details to the components for each activity. They look at specifics: What does your onboarding/vendor registration system look like? What certifications are required? How do businesses engage user departments? How can they be considered for tier 2/subcontracting? How do businesses get paid after they perform the work?

I like to think of processes and procedures like peanut butter and jelly. They're great by themselves, but together, they're one of the greatest duos of all time.

Understanding your procedures as part of your diversity climate assessment helps you see where the boulders are that may block your progress. Procedures that are unnecessarily burdensome and taxing give the impression that you want businesses to get frustrated and give up. This sends the message that you're not really committed to making your supplier diversity program work.

Understanding the "Who-What-How" of Your Organizational Spend

I'm a big proponent for understanding how your organization works. As with any structured program, processes and procedures define the who, what, and how for your program.

The "who-what-how" are kinda like the guts of your organization. They all work together to make your program go and provide a blueprint for a clearly defined process. As part of your organizational readiness, understanding how they work together sends the message that you've invested in establishing a process and that you're serious about your supplier diversity program.

The more you're able to communicate your process — who makes buying decisions, what you buy, and how you buy — the easier it becomes to demonstrate that you're ready for small and diverse firms to engage with your organization.

Who makes buying decisions?

Who makes the buying decision can depend on the type of contract, type of solicitation vehicle used, or whether procurement is centralized or decentralized. Many organizations use a combination of a centralized and decentralized structure. This hybrid setup means departments have delegated authority to make purchases under a certain amount (decentralized), but procurement is involved in purchases over a certain amount or maybe with items that are complex, hard to find, or sole-sourced (centralized).

Understanding who makes the buying decision also determines what type of policy (for example, requiring at least one quote from a diverse vendor) or training may be required to ensure that departments are applying inclusive practices even when you (supplier diversity) aren't directly involved.

TIP

One of the ways I've helped businesses navigate the organization and learn who makes buying decisions is by creating an organizational user guide. This guide lists, each department, the point of contact, and the items it routinely purchases. It is updated every two years and distributed free.

What does your organization buy?

Understanding what your organization buys helps you become more effective at sourcing the right vendors for opportunities and helps your outreach become more targeted and efficient while assessing whether your opportunities are enough to help you meet utilization goals.

Additionally, it may help you find procurement gaps highlighting the need to create opportunities (that is, increased focused on tier 2/subcontracting spend, professional services, and so on). I discuss how strategic sourcing helps you understand your procurement opportunities and supplier segments in the later section "Understanding Strategic Sourcing as Part of Your Readiness Assessment."

How does your organization buy what it needs?

The same factors that define who makes the buying decisions can also impact how your organization buys what it needs. (I cover those elements in the earlier section "Who makes the buying decisions?".) For example, in a decentralized setting, departments may have the authority to purchase small items (under a specific amount) by using a p-card, or purchasing card. This leeway allows them to forgo the process of putting it out to bid, which can be long, especially for simple purchases. For diverse vendors, it creates another entry point into the organization and gives them the flexibility to meet directly with user departments to build relationships — benefits this structure relies on.

Assessing Your Organization's Vendor Relationship Management (VRM)

Another part of gauging organizational readiness is the emphasis placed on developing processes involved throughout the vendor life cycle, or *vendor relationship management* (VRM). In order for any program or initiative to work, understanding how you're perceived in the market is probably a good idea. Unfortunately, most organizations never take the time to ask themselves, "What do small and diverse businesses actually think of us?" From onboarding to navigating your organization to getting paid, you may have a hard time recruiting diverse vendors if they find your processes cumbersome, challenging, and hard to navigate or if you provide little interaction or communication.

REMEMBER

Vendors' willingness to do business with you is just as important as your desire to utilize them. Details matter, and the first impression is everything.

Not long ago, the interaction between supplier diversity professionals and small and diverse businesses was very different from today. Organizations paid little attention to vendor engagement or development; the main focus was on having an up-to-date database or getting as many businesses signed up in the vendor registration portal as possible. In some ways, it was an "if we build a program, the businesses will come" approach. As procurement departments have shifted their focus to not only saving money but also increasing efficiency, they've started looking at the entire supply chain, retrieving and analyzing purchasing data, and segmenting the supply chain, or strategic sourcing.

Now, the way organizations purchase the items they need has changed drastically. It has become a complex system that makes VRM increasingly important. VRM focuses on the relationship and requires more interaction between the organization and the vendor. It deepens the buyer-supplier relationships to achieve the desired outcome.

The following sections cover some of the steps in the VRM process and common mistakes organizations make when understanding how to use their process to interact with small and diverse vendors.

REMEMBER

Organizations that are ready to adopt inclusive practices need to commit to creating clearly defined processes and investing resources behind VRM. Doing so allows you to move beyond the transactional phase and get to know vendors better, directing them to opportunities they're suited for, informing them of the procurement process, and making them a collaborative partner in your organization.

Vendor onboarding

One of the first steps in VRM is *vendor onboarding* or *vendor registration*. Onboarding is usually the initial point of contact and the start of a future business relationship with a vendor. It indicates that a vendor is ready to do business, and it's required in order to have purchase orders issued and to get paid. But organizations miss some important points with this part of the process:

» The vendor portal is sometimes perceived as a black hole that leads nowhere. Vendors are shuffled to register in the vendor portal, and then it's a "don't call us, we'll call you" mentality where vendors wait to get notified of opportunities via email (before that it was via fax) inviting them to respond if they're suited for it.

» Depending on what's being purchased, opportunities may not come through procurement, so they aren't always announced via email notification, and small and diverse businesses that may have been able to respond may miss them (this is still the process for many organizations).

» Organizations sometimes create a separate database solely to capture diverse businesses. Vendors may register in the main vendor portal and then register again in a "diverse vendor portal." Sometimes this practice exists to provide a list of available diverse vendors for internal departments to select from. Though that intention is good, this double list usually indicates that the databases aren't integrated into the main system. Also, perception is everything. Grouped on a different list, diverse vendors appear separate and probably not equal. This discrepancy is a conflicting dynamic when the goal is to expand equity and access, not perpetuate exclusion.

For supplier diversity, vendor onboarding is the first connection point to gather vendor data important for tracking diverse business spend, contract compliance, and so on. Many organizations don't pay enough attention to this crucial part of the process. The initial interaction (or lack thereof) may be an indication of what businesses can expect in support from the organization in the future.

Years ago, I recall having initial conversations with a large multinational company to provide some training. After several conversations, the company told me to keep the ball rolling, I should register in its vendor portal. I got a link to register in the portal, but for the life of me I didn't see anywhere to register. I searched for the company's procurement page and was taken to a different page that said the company was migrating to a new portal and the old page was no longer valid. The new page contained lots of information but still didn't have anywhere to register.

During our next meeting, I didn't want to make waves and look like I didn't follow directions, but I had to mention that I was unable to register and that the process was confusing. My contact casually replied, "Oh yeah, that's something we're working on." I was a little shocked because this was a large organization. They followed up by saying that they had my information and would share it with colleagues. After that, our interactions became fewer and fewer until I finally gave up. It was clear the company didn't have a process for engagement and, despite touting its commitment to doing business with small and diverse businesses, wasn't ready to engage in a meaningful way.

Today's ERP systems and diversity management software allow greater connectivity and management of the entire supplier diversity life cycle process. You want to determine what type of systems (and level of investment) you put in place to support your program. I discuss technology systems in Part 5.

The first impression is everything. Investing in the onboarding phase of VRM allows you to move beyond the transactional phase and get to know vendors better, making them a collaborative partner in your organization.

Connecting vendors to internal stakeholders

Depending on the size of your organization, navigating it can be a monster. This navigation is another process that organizations don't pay enough attention to, and vendors are often left to fend for themselves. One of the biggest questions that I used to get from potential vendors was "How do I market my business to your organization?" Yes, entrepreneurs need to do their research and know their customer, but you can't expect someone new to the organization to fluidly navigate its inner workings and know exactly what's required, how the company likes things done, and whom to speak with. (I worked in an organization with nearly 30,000 employees and was always meeting someone new.)

When considering this aspect of your process, you want to establish processes for engagement and create opportunities that allow the initial dialogue to occur or introductions to happen. Programs may include meetings with appropriate departments and decision makers, industry days, matchmaking/strategic sourcing sessions, vendor conferences/fairs, one-on-one meetings — anything that allows the conversation to begin and keeps the lines of communication flowing.

Examining the vendor payment process

Another part of VRM to consider (and if you ask a vendor, perhaps one of the most important parts) is the payment process. Small businesses live and die by their cash flows. Studies show that one of the top reasons small businesses fail is that they don't have enough cash on hand. Doing business with organizations can be a great boon for a small business but can also cause significant damage or worse if the business isn't fully prepared. After it wins a contract, a small business may be bound by the same terms and conditions as a large firm. Unfortunately, small businesses don't always have as strong a financial foundation to withstand delayed payment terms that can reach anywhere from 30 to 120 days, depending on the organization. And no one wants to see a small business go out of business after working with them.

REMEMBER

Organizations committed to diversity need to consider what policies or training may be necessary to make getting paid a more navigable process for suppliers. Through policies, you can institute prompt payment clauses that allow vendors to be paid within seven to ten days of submitting an approved invoice. Some organizations offer payments within the same week if an invoice is received by their processing department's cutoff time (usually a Wednesday). Smaller organizations certainly have greater flexibility than larger ones in approving policies such as these.

Some organizations may have policies or secret payment clauses that, while designed to help businesses, aren't necessarily published. Vendors have to ask about them before a contract is signed. Committing to training suppliers on payment policies is another area in which organizations can address issues. Creating training programs that help suppliers understand your standard terms and conditions, how to complete a request for payment, what special processes may allow them to get paid faster, and what happens between when they submit an invoice and when they actually get cash in hand helps businesses feel supported throughout the entire process.

Understanding Strategic Sourcing as Part of Your Readiness Assessment

As procurement has evolved from buying based just on low bid to implementing a more strategic approach, supplier diversity has also had to evolve to ensure that small and diverse businesses aren't left out of the equation. One way organizations have accomplished this is through *strategic sourcing,* which basically just means being intentional about identifying the ideal supplier for what you're buying. Strategic sourcing got its start with large Fortune 500 companies and became popular in the late 1980s and early 1990s. It's now standard in most procurement departments across the world.

Strategic sourcing happens at the start of the procurement process. After all, before you issue any solicitation, award any project, or sign any contract, you have to source suppliers. Doing it strategically helps you optimize the performance of your entire supply chain.

TIP

For more information on strategic sourcing, a good resource to check out is the latest edition of *Supply Chain Management For Dummies,* by Daniel Stanton (Wiley).

Strategic sourcing is part of the diversity climate gauging process for several reasons. If you're establishing a new program, you need to understand the investment required to create opportunities for potential suppliers. If you're managing an existing program, you're likely looking for ways your program can become more impactful, not just focus on increasing spend (which should be the result of your efforts).

For strategic sourcing to be successful, you have to understand your procurement opportunities and supplier segments. Figure 6-2 shows some common procurement category segments. However, your procurement opportunities, or spend categories, may vary depending on the organization.

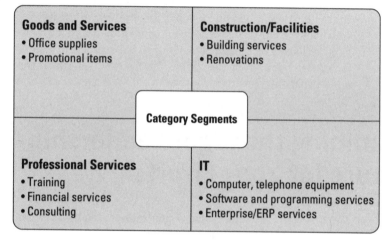

FIGURE 6-2: Common procurement category segments.

Of these categories, you can then look at which opportunities are direct and which are indirect. *Direct opportunities* are for items you use, well, directly in the making of your products or services and are usually purchased straight from the supplier. These suppliers are considered *tier 1* or *prime* suppliers. For example, suppose you make candles. The companies that sell you jars, labels, wax, and wicks are your tier 1 suppliers.

Indirect opportunities are those that aren't directly involved in the manufacture of your products but are still an important part of what keeps your organization going. These opportunities include purchases such as office supplies, promotional items, cleaning supplies, and so on.

TIP

Breaking down your procurement opportunities by direct and indirect categories also allows you to segment your suppliers. Based on your future spend, you can look at the tier 1 suppliers you have in each spend category to see whether you have opportunities to increase their spend. You can also suggest that your tier 1 partners evaluate their supply chains for opportunities to increase their spends with these businesses.

Another idea is to look at chances to move tier 2 suppliers up to tier 1. *Tier 2 suppliers* are the companies that sell your tier 1 partners the supplies they need to make your items; in the candle example, that's the glass for the jars, paper for the labels, cotton or fiber for the wicks, and so on. This approach allows the tier 2 suppliers to grow and expand their capacity while establishing their own contract relationship with you. (Tier 2 is another way to increase utilization. I discuss this topic further in Chapter 17.)

Although indirect opportunities tend to be smaller purchases, you have lots of flexibility there. You can consider longer-term contracts (two or three years), which allows you to lock in pricing while providing the supplier the stability of a long-term contract. Also, depending on your structure (centralized or decentralized), you can see whether opportunities exist for them to provide products to other departments within your organization if they aren't already doing so.

Determining the Right Leadership Structure for Your Efforts

The final step in gauging your organizational readiness is determining the right leadership structure to lead this effort. In "Examining Your Organizational 4 P's" earlier in the chapter, I talk about how important determining the structure that fits your organization and your commitment to supplier diversity is.

When you consider the many roles you have to take on and the stakeholders you have to engage in implementing supplier diversity across the organization, you can clearly see that having the right leadership structure is vital to the success of the program. Working with the right leadership structure does the following:

>> Sets the tone for your program

>> Displays your commitment to this effort as a valued strategic initiative

>> Determines how much bite or impact you have

>> Defines your ability to deliver the necessary supplier development support and programming to small and diverse businesses

>> Determines the time available to devote to necessary functions

>> Defines your ability to engage stakeholders

Organizations usually fill the supplier diversity leader position in three ways: direct hire, contract with a consultant, or shift the function to someone internally as an employee add-on function. Table 6-1 takes a look at the differences with each structure.

TABLE 6-1   **Comparing Leadership Structures**

Consideration	Consultant	Direct Hire	Employee Add-on
Decision making authority	None	Full	None
Ability to get internal support	None	Full	Limited
Ability to get collaborative partners	None	Full	Limited
Ability to advocate for small/diverse businesses	None	Full	Limited
Cost implications (salary versus fees)	Full	Full	Limited
Ability to recruit new businesses	Limited	Full	None
Time commitment	Limited	Full	Limited
Ability to conduct events and business development	Limited	Full	Limited
Ability to develop policies and procedures	Limited	Full	None
Ability to provide strategic direction	Limited	Full	None

Consultant

In supplier diversity, a consultant can assist in a number of ways, from developing a framework for creating a program to running training to advising on or conducting research such as disparity studies. They can bring industry knowledge and best-in-class expertise that you may not already have in-house. Some organizations opt to keep the consultant on a short-term basis while they ramp up or decide exactly how they want to staff this role.

Some of the challenges with having a consultant include the following:

>> Limited time to carry out many of the tasks required in a robust supplier diversity program

>> Time split between other clients, responsibilities, and so on

> » Doesn't allow the internal or external relationship building to occur

> » No vested interest in organization's long-term success

Direct hire

After years of mixed results, many organizations are making the investment to hire a dedicated person to manage and implement supplier diversity throughout the organization. Do any search of jobs in supplier diversity and you'll see a number of listings from organizations large and small. This quantity is definitely a good sign for the industry. Supplier diversity was my sole responsibility as a practitioner in all the organizations I've worked in. The key to my success was having the ability to focus my efforts on advocating for small and diverse businesses, creating programming for them to increase their capacity and opportunities to connect with decision makers throughout the organization while building external collaborations and partnerships.

Through this advocacy piece, I was also able to build trust, which is a key component in the relationship-building process. The suppliers trusted me to enough to share their hopes for their businesses as well as challenges they may have experienced on a project.

REMEMBER

Organizations need to determine the level of authority and control this position carries and where it's housed within the organization.

Employee add-on function

With this structure, an organization adds the supplier diversity function to an existing employee's primary job function. It's usually someone in procurement or maybe someone within the organization that wants to champion this effort.

Having advocates throughout the organization is great and even necessary for supplier diversity to be successful, but adding this function to an employee's load isn't always ideal for a number of reasons:

> » Advocating can be hard when your department stresses low price.

> » With procurement, advocating may become a conflict when you also make awards (depending on the buying category).

> » Your schedule may leave you unable to carry out many of the tasks required in a robust supplier diversity program.

Chapter **7**

Making the Case for Supplier Diversity

Roy Disney once said, "When your values are clear to you, making decisions becomes easier." Before you can successfully start a program or initiative, you have to understand why you're doing it. Why does your program exist?

As organizations continually assess every aspect of their operations, looking for any opportunity to gain a competitive advantage, departments must be able to demonstrate their reason for being. Supplier diversity isn't exempt from that. A strong business case needs to be able to actively demonstrate how supplier diversity's efforts add value to the organization, the community, and, increasingly, the bottom line. When you're adding to the bottom line, ensuring that your program can survive is much easier.

Many organizations use morality to justify starting programs, and embracing supplier diversity certainly has a strong moral case. However, as the industry has evolved and business dynamics have changed, simply stating that your program exists because "it's the right thing to do" isn't going to cut it.

But for many professionals, letting people know your value can be tough (especially if that value isn't always delivered in a tangible way). They may focus their efforts on workshops or steady appearances on the lunch and dinner circuit that give the illusion of being busy without adding any real value to the organization. Don't get me wrong — workshops and community activation are a crucial part of a program's overall success. But they're just small pieces of the pie that's required for a program to be truly impactful.

No matter your intentions or the stage of your program, you must be able to justify the value supplier diversity brings to the entire organizational table. In this chapter, I discuss how to communicate that value and make a solid business case for supplier diversity.

Aligning Supplier Diversity to Organizational Strategic Goals

Supplier diversity professionals are in a unique position. You advocate for diverse businesses to get access to opportunity while you maintain professional obligations to your employers. You may not have direct responsibility for awarding contracts, but you're an important part of the procurement process and play a vital role in creating value for the organization. A good business case articulates how the policies and programs of supplier diversity work in a way that helps the organization achieve its goals by aligning with its mission and values.

Let me take a minute to talk about value. By its definition, *value* is anything of worth or importance. Thus, it can come in many forms. People have been trained to define "value" primarily as activities that produce revenues. But that's not always the case. For example, take banking. Many bankers, especially lenders, think loans are their biggest profit center and where they get most of their revenue. Yet the strength of a bank's deposits, not its loans, is what really drives its stock price. Loan interest is income to the bank, and deposit interest paid to depositors is an expense. In this example, the expense (deposit interest) is more valuable than what generates income (loan interest).

When you think about it from an ethical perspective, value is a belief that motivates people to act one way or another and serves as a guide for human behavior. Taking this a step further, value systems are prospective and prescriptive beliefs that can determine behaviors and are the foundation for intentional and deliberate activities. Although monetary value is critical, value created through beliefs can be just as key in this context. The secret sauce is to think of your organization as a complex system of value-creation processes.

Adding value can come in many forms, not just money. If it's something someone cares about, it has value.

Today's organizations commonly assign a set of values and value systems to describe what they believe and how they operate internally and externally. These values are what usually provide the foundation for strategic goals. *Strategic goals* are visions for the organization that can have measurable (quantifiable and/or qualitative) results. This means that achieving the goal must be something you can measure and track using real data. (I cover data analytics in Chapter 19.)

Here's an example from an organization I previously worked with. It had the following strategic goal and accompanying objectives based on documented statements regarding the organization's important strategic goals and long-term aspirations (names are removed):

Goal

Strengthen public engagement of organizational programs with local, national, and international communities.

> **Objective 1:** Increased engagement and outreach of programs leading to positive impacts in such areas as health, the economy, environment, and community

> **Objective 2:** Improved communication leading to increased public awareness of and value placed on organizational programs and their impact on society

> **Objective 3:** Increased technology translation and entrepreneurial activities

I was able to make the case for supplier diversity activities because the organization worked with small businesses on a local and national level. Further, the activities that supplier diversity engaged in supported its stated objectives, which focused on the economy (Objective 1), impact on society (Objective 2), and entrepreneurial activities (Objective 3). Aligning with organizational goals removed the need to rely solely on feel-good messaging or positioning supplier diversity as some type of philanthropic initiative.

Finding Value-Creating Opportunities

Organizations where supplier diversity aligns with the primary buying departments — procurement and facilities — are better able to find value-creating opportunities and use them to their competitive advantage. You create value when you meet or exceed expectations and impressions. Doing so allows both internal and external stakeholders to place a higher value on the organization, whether as an employer, a provider, or a business partner. *Value-creating opportunities* look at every aspect or stakeholder of the organization and find ways to further align them. Organizations succeed when they understand the source and drivers of value creation and focus their efforts on those areas. They fail when they can't find or produce value.

Figure 7-1 shows how supplier diversity lends itself to finding value-creating opportunities with each of the stakeholder groups listed.

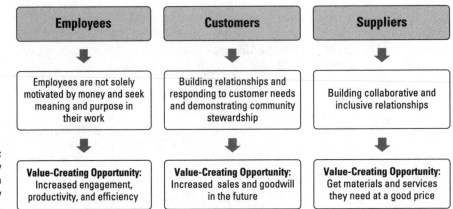

FIGURE 7-1: Supplier Diversity value creation opportunity model.

TIP

Because each group may quantify value differently, it can be hard to track and communicate value consistently. I discuss establishing metrics and KPIs in detail in Chapter 16, but some metrics to consider to calculate value include

>> The number of diverse businesses winning prime or direct contracts

>> The growth of contract opportunities versus the previous year for diverse businesses

>> The number of employment opportunities created by diverse businesses

Communicating Value

A part of making the case is also communicating that value to senior leadership (and maybe those with a vested interest in program). No matter where your supplier diversity program falls — public sector (local, state, or federal government and so on) or private industry (corporation) — you're there to carry out the wishes of your organization. You advocate for small and diverse businesses, but you

Starting with your people

People are the first part of your system and, arguably, the most important part. It starts with the person who leads this effort; they have to be able to be a champion and advocate for small business while also being an effective influencer within the organization with a knack for gaining support from internal and community stakeholders.

Another consideration is the structure in which the program will be managed, whether the organization is bringing in a consultant, making a direct hire, or delegating to an existing employee. (I discuss finding the ideal leadership in "Determining the Right Leadership Structure for Your Efforts" later in this chapter.) With each of these structures, the supplier diversity leader has a different level of authority, influence, and time, which can have varying levels of impact on the program.

Reviewing your policy

Your *policies* are what guide your activities. They're a deliberate system of guidelines to direct decisions and achieve desired outcomes. In short, they give your program its teeth. However, setting policies can be thorny because you have to consider the local, state, and federal ramifications that may limit how far you can go, especially if your program isn't necessarily based on the results of a disparity study (see the nearby sidebar).

For example, you may want to create a foot-in-the-door (FITD) policy that designates contracts under $2,500 for diverse microenterprises only to give them a point of entry with your organization. Although your intentions with this policy are good and align with your program goals, the move can be considered discriminatory. You can't exclude vendors, no matter how large, from responding to solicitations. (The only entity that can legally set aside contracts specifically for a designated socioeconomic group is the federal government.) Small contracts like these may not be of interest to larger firms, but your policy can't come across as excluding them.

A better way to execute this is to have a pre-approved list of vendors where a certain number of the slots will include diverse businesses. This way, no business was excluded and you've ensured that diverse businesses have an opportunity to participate. Usually, larger firms are not interested in lower dollar contracts, which is their prerogative. However, the objective is to ensure that everyone who's interested has a chance to respond.

work for your organization. Every initiative that an organization shoulders needs to be able to deliver some type of measurable value or return on investment (ROI). Those that can't usually find themselves tucked away somewhere (we used to call it never-never land) in a diminished capacity or even gone away altogether.

Identifying the right metrics to quantify impact should be a central focus of the communication plan. This information can be used in marketing, as a part of annual goal setting (I always included it in my annual goals), or in community meetings. I've even used it as the basis for internal training I created to inform internal departments on supplier diversity.

Determining just what metrics to report varies depending on the organization. Figure 7-2 illustrates some metrics that you can consider by sector. Further, the metrics should deliver the message that supplier diversity supports and enables existing revenue streams and can contribute incremental new revenue.

Local/state government	Federal government	Corporations
• Number of local firms utilized • Economic impact	• Response rate by demographic category/set aside • Utilization by demographic category/set aside	• Response rate by diverse firms • Win ratio based on number of submissions • Types of contracts responding • Subcontracting/tier II spend

FIGURE 7-2: Communicating value by local/state government, federal government, corporations.

Selling Your Supplier Diversity Story to Stakeholders

Putting your supplier diversity business case together to sell to stakeholders is the hard part. Because supplier diversity programs can impact so many departments — each with its own priorities, goals, and interests that may be completely opposite from another's — creating a value proposition that resonates with each of them may be challenging, to say the least.

REMEMBER

In order to effectively get buy-in, supplier diversity professionals should first understand what's important to a particular stakeholder or group and then be able to help that stakeholder view supplier diversity as a help and not a hindrance to their goals and priorities.

At one organization, I initiated a campaign to meet senior leaders in every department. Armed with reports on what each department was spending and who it was spending that with, I wanted to introduce myself and the program but also to hear more about either why they weren't using diverse vendors or how we could increase the amount they were spending. What I learned was surprising. Most were very receptive to meeting and using diverse vendors. They just needed help getting started. From then on, in addition to listening to their needs, I was able to devise a plan to assist them, whether it was seeking research funding from the government (where using small businesses is mandated) or helping them create a marketing plan for recruitment. When I knew what was important to them, creating that win-win became easier. Not all these meetings were complete wins, but over time many departments began to see some upticks in their numbers, which allowed overall utilization to increase.

In this example, I was able to sell the business case by tailoring my message to target individual departments and also be responsive to the diverse business community, which allowed me to achieve my goal. I also learned that the more stakeholders understood, the easier creating cross-functional teams/collaborations and getting the resources and budget I needed for my program to continue to grow became.

Figure 7-3 provides some examples of suggested messaging to provide in order to align with department goals.

FIGURE 7-3: Supplier diversity messaging alignment.

MAKING THE CASE BY ADDING VALUE

People will always get behind something if they see its value. The following are a few ways supplier diversity adds value to the organization, suppliers, and the community:

Organization

- Helping to achieve strategic goals
- Helping to improve image and standing
- Helping to create a procurement pipeline
- Helping to gain efficiency, better pricing, and increased innovation

Suppliers

- Helping businesses build capacity
- Helping businesses to scale and grow
- Helping businesses build legacy

Community

- Contributing to the entrepreneurial ecosystem
- Helping businesses create employment opportunities
- Building a strong small and diverse business community

IN THIS CHAPTER

» **Knowing where to look for organizational allies**

» **Conducting in-reach efforts**

» **Getting collaborators to help you help them (help you)**

Chapter **8**

Building Support for Supplier Diversity Programs

You've probably heard the old adage "It takes a village." This sentiment certainly applies to supplier diversity. Supplier diversity isn't an island or stand-alone departmental function. Achieving diversity in your supply chain requires effort from you and your colleagues in other departments, and for businesses in the community to know what opportunities are available to them. In this chapter, I discuss how to find and connect with the right resources that help build support for supplier diversity within your organization.

Seeing How Supplier Diversity Touches Many Stakeholders

Ideally, successful organizations should have a well-rounded and holistic strategy for supplier diversity. Internally, it should be an operational mindset and be applied to as many business areas as possible. Integrating it into organizational priorities to gain support from senior leadership and various departments creates the fertile environment needed to ensure that supplier diversity efforts are embraced and successful. Externally, as a community-facing function, getting support from external stakeholders is just as important to provide expertise, programming support, and access to critical networks, resources, and additional opportunities.

TIP

One great way to think about supplier diversity is as an integral part of a thriving business ecosystem. This ecosystem includes the supplier diversity practitioner/ team, operations, the internal organizational environment, the external community environment, and the business community, as Figure 8-1 shows. Through value-added functions, each plays a role in supporting the small and diverse business community, guiding them to success and long-term sustainability.

FIGURE 8-1:
Supplier diversity
ecosystem model.

Supplier diversity professionals play many roles, including influencer and collaborator. As an influencer, managing a supplier diversity program requires garnering and synchronizing support from various areas within the organization by engaging the C-suite/senior leadership to gain support and ensure connectivity across the organization. As a collaborator, you're building relationships with key stakeholders that have a vested interested in the economic success of the entire community.

Finding Allies throughout Departments in Your Organization

Supplier diversity is widely known for its work and impact on small and diverse businesses. However, the impact within the organization is just as important. As I note in Chapter 6, a key component of building support is gaining departmental allies.

Within an organization, *allies* are influential colleagues who offer backing, assistance, advice, information, advocacy, and support. Strong and mutually beneficial alliances can help supplier diversity survive and thrive by navigating the internal landscape more efficiently. This success results in getting things done more quickly and smoothly than if you were to go it alone. Additionally, strong allies can help ensure that supplier diversity's mission remains top of mind when making procurement decisions.

Building allies in your organization isn't like forming alliances on reality shows; it's a systematic process of building long-term advocates and collaborative partners. Here are seven steps for winning supplier diversity allies within your organization:

>> **Listen.** Listen to your allies, learn what they need and do within the organization, and be able to communicate what's in it for them (which I cover later in the chapter). If you're not sure what they need, ask.

>> **Be supportive.** Gaining allies is a two-way street. As you request others' support, be willing to offer your support when you can see that they need it.

>> **Nurture the relationship.** Building relationships isn't a one-off proposition. Focus on opportunities to provide support for the long term. Alliances need nurturing, so engage with potential and actual allies frequently. Demonstrate that the relationship has value and is not just transactional.

>> **Communicate effectively.** Open and timely communication is vital for any relationship to flourish. Be able to tell your potential ally what you need and how they can support that.

>> **Be mindful of your ask.** Don't ask for too much. Be realistic about the level of support you expect.

>> **Spend time with your allies.** Be available to listen, strategize, and collaborate on projects.

>> **Be patient.** Everyone you approach may not immediately be willing or able to support your cause. Be patient and professional when you hear the occasional "no."

In the following sections, I point out the various departments that can support your supplier diversity initiatives. Although they may vary in every organization, they provide a strong starting point for connecting and engaging.

Diversity, equity, and inclusion (DEI)

Diversity, equity, and inclusion (DEI) is an obvious ally and partner to build support for supplier diversity. Although its internal audiences are different (organizational culture and employee belonging), both DEI and supplier diversity are focused on creating equitable and inclusive conditions for the audiences they serve.

DEI provides the tone and tenor of how the organization views diversity internally, but I'd venture to say that no comprehensive DEI strategy is complete without a focus on supplier diversity. Now, I realize I may be biased, but supplier diversity allows the organization to externally demonstrate actions that reflect its internal views on diversity.

Most organizations embrace and adopt DEI as a mission for the entire organization. They have the support from senior level executives, often reporting directly to the president. And the DEI message is usually entrenched throughout the entire organization, which makes gaining support, influencing long-term behavior change, and achieving desired outcomes easier. This level of support is the goal for supplier diversity, so aligning with DEI allows supplier diversity to leverage this organizational support.

In some organizations, supplier diversity is part of the diversity team, with responsibility falling under the chief diversity officer (CDO). Though the CDO needs to have an understanding of the supplier diversity function, this structure is definitely ideal for collaboration.

Working with procurement

At its core, supplier diversity is a procurement function. It ensures that inclusive and equitable processes are in place that provide small and diverse businesses access to the procurement process and contract opportunities. As such, supplier diversity and procurement have an interdependent relationship. Generally, the type of procurement solicitation, whether hard bid, request for proposal (rfp), request to negotiate (rtn), request for information (rfi), or statement of work (sow), determines how the award decision is made. As an advocacy and compliance role, supplier diversity usually doesn't make the final decision but works closely to ensure that diverse businesses are aware of the opportunity and its requirements and, if interested, are prepared to respond.

Depending on whether the organization's structure is centralized or decentralized, the number of viable opportunities that flow through procurement can differ drastically.

>> With a *centralized* structure, all purchasing, regardless of the amount, flows through procurement. Supplier diversity needs to ensure close alignment so it becomes aware of opportunities a diverse business may be a good candidate for while also ensuring the buyer knows these businesses are available. You tend to find this structure in smaller organizations or organizations that don't necessarily have a defined procurement process. The downside of a centralized setup is that it tends to slow down the process and doesn't allow departments to quickly acquire the resources they need in their daily operations.

>> With a *decentralized* structure, departments have delegated authority to make purchases under a certain dollar amount. Thus, department personnel are the ones making procurement decisions. This system can create increased access to opportunities for diverse businesses, but it also requires additional learning to ensure that departments, when possible, are considering diverse suppliers for whatever they're looking to buy. This instance is one where a strong internal in-reach program, which I discuss later in this chapter, can reinforce the mission of the supplier diversity. Larger, complex organizations with established procurement protocols and procedures typically use this structure.

You can read more about these organizational setups in Chapter 6. Regardless of the structure, several tactics help ensure constant alignment with procurement. Even if supplier diversity isn't directly involved, employees in charge of making procurement decisions will keep supplier diversity top of mind and consider small and diverse suppliers as part of their vendor evaluation and award process.

>> **Reviewing policies:** Supplier diversity should review and understand the technical language used in all solicitation documents, have a role in evaluating the policies, and make recommendations to remove policies that are restrictive and don't encourage inclusive opportunities for small and diverse businesses.

>> **Buyer training:** Instinctively, buyers' objective is to buy items at the lowest price or provide the best value for the price for the organization. This model may not always allow small and diverse businesses to be competitive and may exclude them from the process, especially if competing against larger vendors.

REMEMBER

Organizations committed to utilizing small and diverse suppliers may need to look outside price and find creative ways to find opportunities. Training for buyers helps ensure that they're aware of the challenges small and diverse vendors face and work collaboratively to create policies that remove barriers.

>> **Strategic sourcing:** As organizations realize the impact that purchasing has on supply chains and operations, more have adopted an approach allowing strategic sourcing to become an important part of the overall process. *Strategic sourcing* uses data to determine what a company is buying, who it's buying the item from, and what it can do to add value to the overall procurement of the item. As I explain in Chapter 6, you can segment the supply chain in several ways. Understanding this process helps organizations become more intentional about building relationships with small and diverse vendors and creating opportunities to bring them into the procurement process.

Apprising community relations of your strategy

Organizations have a civic and moral responsibility to take an active interest in the well-being of their communities. Many do so through *community relations* — the methods companies use to establish and maintain mutually beneficial relationships within the community. Community relations confirms your organization's profile in the community while fostering goodwill and reinforcing positive sentiments with customers, other community leaders, and stakeholders. Because of their community-facing nature as a vital part of the business ecosystem, supplier diversity and community relations often have a synergistic and cooperative relationship.

TOTAL COST OF OWNERSHIP AND STRATEGIC SOURCING

Total cost of ownership (TCO) is a method for quantifying the costs for each activity along the supply chain process, including acquisition, transportation, storage, and selling of goods. It looks at the difference between the actual price paid and the long-term costs (maintenance, subscriptions, and so on). TCO allows strategic sourcing decisions to incorporate social investments (supplier relationship management, supplier diversity programs, and more), which are sometimes hard to determine. However, in strategic sourcing, these social investments are often the determining factor when making a final decision.

Those that do not fully support supplier diversity may use TCO to insinuate that it's the social investments that make the cost of using diverse businesses higher. This can't be further from the truth. In actuality, working with outside vendors, no matter the size or status, can be a complicated proposition. Conversely, investing in diverse businesses is designed to make them stronger vendors, not more expensive, and may actually help to reduce costs in the long term.

In some organizations, the community relations director may report to the top corporate communications officer with a dotted reporting line connecting to the others in the diversity office. Community relations and diversity offices often work together to create effective programs. In fact, because of this interconnectivity, some organizations may even house supplier diversity in community relations.

Informing employees and ERGs

Employees and employee resource groups (ERGs) provide another avenue for collaboration and support. ERGs are voluntary groups whose aim is to champion a selected cause (usually a diverse, inclusive workplace) aligned with specific organizational goals. Their leaders and members are usually employees who share a characteristic or have a vested interest in the success of a particular group or cause, whether it's gender equality, ethnicity inclusion, religious affiliation, lifestyle, or specific interest.

According to TopMBA, 90 percent of Fortune 500 companies have ERGs. They've accomplished many things within organizations, including improving work conditions, creating a more inclusive environment, and training, nurturing, and preparing the next generation of leaders.

ERGs can support supplier diversity by bringing employees together where conversations can flow freely and everyone can feel comfortable sharing experiences and brainstorming realistic action plans. Participants are able to discuss business opportunities within their respective departments while communicating this effort with colleagues across business units. ERGs commitment and expertise in working across the organization to tackle company-wide challenges make them a tremendous internal resource.

Looping in those responsible for sustainability initiatives

Corporations have a long history of sustainability. Although initial sustainability programs largely focused on environmental issues, during the first decade of the 2000s, many corporations began to broaden the scope of what sustainability meant within their respective organizations. It grew to encompass more issues directly related to addressing and improving quality of life and now includes interconnected areas such as environmental, economic, and social issues.

Because of this broadened definition, supplier diversity and sustainability often work together to specifically address the issue of economic sustainability, particularly when looking at business diversity from a local perspective. (In some organizations, these functions may be combined.) This collaboration makes sustainability a desirable ally to build support and champion the supplier diversity message. They may not generate revenue, but each demonstrates the organization's commitment to citizenship, responsibility, and improving economic quality of life.

REMEMBER

Sustainability and supplier diversity are both community-facing functions that address the "right thing to do" objective for the organization, so they may end up competing for the same resources, attention, and support. This potential competition makes aligning forces and taking a "two heads are better than one" approach even more critical in order to leverage each department's respective audience and stretch out resources to achieve results.

Developing an In-Reach Program

Your organizational allies must have a working knowledge of supplier diversity and be aware of the program you provide. (Read more about allies in the earlier section "Finding Allies throughout Departments in Your Organization.") Similar to traditional outreach programs, which target external businesses and stakeholders, supplier diversity programs should establish an internal strategy or in-reach program. An *in-reach* program is a comprehensive program that focuses on ensuring that your internal organization has an understanding of the supplier diversity function, its role within the organization, and how it supports departments. It also lets departments know about upcoming events, including opportunities to meet and engage with small and diverse suppliers.

The depth and breadth of your in-reach program (what you can provide, the frequency with which you can conduct engagements, and so on) depends on your available resources and your capacity to deliver services. However, successful in-reach programs consist of three key components: training, communications, and engagement.

Training

For many organizations, supplier diversity is still a new concept. You can't assume that everyone is completely aware of all the complexities of the supplier diversity function and of everything that may be going on at any given time. Thus, education is an integral part of an in-reach program.

As a supplier diversity practitioner, I designed an internal training curriculum as part of my in-reach program — Supplier Diversity Basics training. Created in partnership with human resources as part of the organization's training series, the training was conducted monthly and designed to provide participants with an introduction to the supplier diversity program and how their actions as employees would help the organization achieve its strategic supplier diversity goals.

TIP

If your organization can't implement a full-scale training program at this time, it may want to consider conducting quarterly workshops and inviting employees to participate. The more people know about supplier diversity and understand the "why," the more easily you can convert them into allies.

Communication

The communication arm of your in-reach program informs departments of your upcoming events and opportunities to meet and engage with businesses. It may even be the most reliable conduit that connects departments to the small and diverse business community.

TIP

Your communication efforts can take the form of a weekly or monthly email, newsletter, or podcast, highlighting past and future events, introducing departments to businesses, and crafting messages around the importance of utilizing small and diverse businesses. Social media has also become increasingly important for programs to communicate information. People can't become allies when they aren't aware of what you're doing.

Engagement through advisory councils/task forces

A common way to keep allies and stakeholders engaged as you build support is through an internal advisory council or task force. These groups consist of select individuals across the organization that have a vested interest in an initiative's or program's success. Usually voluntary, they help ensure the organization is on board and aware of supplier diversity efforts. They can also be effective in communicating information to their respective departments and throughout the entire organization.

TIP

If establishing a specific advisory council is a challenge, another possibility is to find and speak at other internal advisory councils or departments within the organization. The overall goal is to get in front of as many internal departments as possible to spread the word about supplier diversity. As I note earlier in the chapter, engaging allies isn't a one-time proposition. Engagement should focus on informing, collaborating, and brainstorming, not overwhelming or browbeating.

Aligning Programs to Collaborator Objectives: Solving WIIFT

A critical part of building support and gaining internal allies is the ability to communicate what's in it for them — WIIFT. (Yes, you do a bit of sales in the supplier diversity function.) You should clearly understand the objectives of the department you want to align with before approaching it with your ask. You need to talk about the benefits of collaborating instead of just talking about your job and role in the organization.

Most employees may not want to hear that you're trying to coordinate a big vendor event or that you want to conduct vendor training workshops. And why should they? These are your goals and metrics from your annual performance plan; these specific functions may not benefit other employees directly. Those people are more interested in what they can gain by working with your department and how it can help them achieve the goals for their department. By clearly articulating the benefit, you're more likely to get a positive response.

REMEMBER

Successful change, even organizational change, is personal. To motivate change, you must get people to understand how it relates to them and how they may benefit — that WIIFT. Unless you connect what you do to the individual, gaining allies will be an uphill battle. But it doesn't have to be.

TIP

Here are some suggestions for communicating WIIFT:

>> **Focus on the benefit for them.** Listen to your allies and understand their goals. Communicate how your supplier diversity program and efforts align with what they do and can help them achieve their goals.

>> **Connect with a greater cause.** Link supplier diversity to causes (such as helping small, diverse, and local businesses; uplifting the economy; and having an impact in the community) that have broad appeal. People want to know that what they do can positively impact the greater good.

>> **Tell the story.** In influencing, stories beat data every time. Instead of fixating on quantifiable metrics (which you often have to do), focus on telling stories of the impact allies' actions can have on a small business in the community.

>> **Keep communication open and frequent.** Ensure that your collaborators have as much information as they need (they may need to report on their activities as well) to talk about the work you're doing.

>> **Get them involved.** Consider adding them to an internal supplier diversity advisory group or have them as a speaker/subject matter expert at one of your events. The more entrenched they are, the more likely they are to speak on your behalf and (hopefully) sway a larger group of stakeholders within your organization.

Chapter **9**

Identifying Common Barriers to Supplier Diversity

B uilding a strong supplier diversity program doesn't happen instantaneously or overnight. Based on the number of internal and external factors involved, it's a continual and fluid process. Think of it like a diet — a *business* lifestyle change.

But just because you start a program doesn't mean it'll be a success. Despite the best of intentions, supplier diversity efforts stall or even fail for many reasons. Naturally, many people assume only external issues such as limited availability of a wide variety of firms or a lack of community resources are the leading factors that negatively impact supplier diversity. But interestingly, the most common barriers to developing a successful supplier diversity program start with the organization itself — the internal factors or inputs that you can control. The great news is that these obstacles are easy to remove, or at the very least temper, so that your efforts aren't a disappointment for the organization.

In this chapter, I discuss how to recognize common organizational and practitioner barriers, understand why supplier diversity practitioners are unsuccessful, and get over the hurdles to building a successful program.

Identifying Common Organizational Barriers

Today's organizations are complex and evolving ecosystems. Each has its own idiosyncratic characteristics, or *organizational DNA*, that make it unique and create inherent challenges that define how it adapts and executes. Execution is a key component in creating and managing a successful supplier diversity program; even the most well-planned and strategically sound initiatives can fail because of poor execution. When organizations understand their DNA, they're better equipped to make the necessary shifts to become masters at executing their supplier diversity plans.

To really understand organizational barriers, Strategy& launched an online assessment tool called the Org DNA Profiler. This assessment identifies seven types of organizational profiles. These profiles provide a baseline for an organization's ability to adopt new ideas, adapt their processes to accommodate new initiatives, and successfully execute their initiatives — in this case, a supplier diversity program:

>> **The Resilient Organization:** This organization adapts quickly to external market shifts but is focused on a clear business strategy. It anticipates changes and proactively addresses them. Motivated team players are attracted to this environment because it not only offers an inspiring work environment but also provides the resources needed to solve tough problems.

>> **The Just-in-Time Organization:** This organization can be open to new ideas, but it tends to be reactive and does just enough to appear responsive. This organization has the ability to ramp up quickly or "turn on a dime" when necessary. It does a good job with implementing changes but hasn't made the leap to being great or a leader in implementing meaningful initiatives.

>> **The Military Organization:** Usually a small but mighty force, this group is led by a hands-on senior management team and succeeds through sheer force of will. Like a military unit, it can conceive and execute brilliant strategies, but it's

heavily dependent on its senior team and can be shallow beyond that. This organization's biggest liability is preparing for growth beyond the tenure of its current leaders and having a strong succession plan in place.

>> **The Passive-Aggressive Organization:** This organization tends to want everyone to get along, so "everyone agrees but nothing changes." Building consensus to make major changes isn't the problem; implementing them is. Entrenched resistance can defeat the organization's best efforts to make change. Lacking the necessary authority, information, and incentives to undertake meaningful change, line employees may ignore mandates from senior leadership. Confronted with an apathetic organization, senior management may lack the nerve to push its agenda forward.

>> **The Fits-and-Starts Organization:** This organization has the people and resources to execute initiatives, but they aren't always working together at the same time. When they decide to do something, they may get off to a great start; unfortunately, they lack the discipline to sustain and keep it going. Because of this, they never truly reach their full potential.

>> **The Outgrown Organization:** This organization has lots of potential but has outgrown its organizational model. As it transitions to a midsize company, it's formalizing its structure and processes and can't be effectively managed by its small team. This organization tends to move slowly, even cautiously, and often finds it can't get out of its own way. Such firms routinely miss opportunities and consistently fail to execute effectively.

>> **The Overmanaged Organization:** Burdened with multiple layers of management, these organizations tend to be bureaucratic and highly political. They let analysis paralysis thwart their efforts before they even get started. When they do move, they do it slowly and reactively, never doing anything innovative or exhibiting a leadership stance. These organizations often frustrate self-starters and individuals that want to produce results.

Understanding your organizational DNA is just the first step in identifying internal challenges and barriers that may exist. Here, I discuss additional barriers that may impede your organization's supplier diversity efforts.

Implicit biases

Implicit bias most commonly comes up in discussions of recruiting and hiring practices, but it can also be prevalent in supplier diversity and procurement. According to the National Institute on Health (NIH), *implicit bias* is a bias that occurs automatically and unintentionally and impacts judgments, decisions, and behaviors. Implicit racial bias describes a psychological process in which a person's unconscious racial beliefs (stereotypes) and attitudes (prejudices) affect their behaviors, perceptions, and judgments in ways that they may not be aware of and therefore can't control.

Because implicit biases are based on past experiences and/or associations, they can also be a tremendous hindrance to advocating and recommending diverse vendors. For example, people often perceive diverse vendors as incapable or unqualified for a contract opportunity because of the vendors' smaller size, lack of experience, limited capacity, and so on when compared to non-diverse vendors. Sometimes a bad experience with one contractor sabotages a future opportunity for another diverse vendor, even if the new vendor had nothing to do with the previous situation.

The status quo

It's the organizational rallying cry that somehow manages to creep into even the most forward-thinking and progressive companies on the planet: "But this is the way we've always done it!" This comfort, known as the status quo, stifles organizations no matter how insightful or innovative they are.

Humans have a natural desire and tendency to avoid change and operate according to the status quo. This deep desire to keep things pretty much as they are becomes irrational in that even when the potential outcome may be better, people still resist change and hold onto the status quo. (I know I'm not the only one who has seen people retire rather than learn a new process.) As you can imagine, furthering the cause of supplier diversity is difficult, if not impossible, in the face of an entrenched organizational status quo mindset because the basic premise of supplier diversity is to allow diverse and often new suppliers into the procurement pipeline.

In many instances, organizations become reluctant to change when they have vendors that they've used for years. Using the same vendors becomes second nature, like letting the next episode of the show you're streaming play automatically. But contrary to popular belief, giving an opportunity to a new vendor doesn't mean removing or replacing an existing one. It does mean that the organization takes intentional action to ensure that processes are inclusive and encourages all vendors to participate in the process.

Lift and shift mentality

Lift and shift refers to the practice of *lifting* an employee from one function or department within the organization and *shifting* them into another role. Comparatively, when hiring or even recruiting for a role, organizations are very specific and targeted for the type of KSAs and experience needed for a position. Although the lift and shift strategy may work for certain functions — usually frontline or mid-level positions, or roles that don't require a high level of strategy development, specialization, or interaction with senior leadership or community stakeholders, and so on — it doesn't work for senior or executive level positions, including supplier diversity. People shifted into this role may not have a background in the field and need time to ramp up to gain the institutional knowledge they need or learn as they go. The demands that can be placed on this role can easily make this model get overwhelming to those new to the industry.

Double duty/add-on function

With double duty, supplier diversity is an add-on function. Someone hired for one job may be tasked with carrying out supplier diversity (whether voluntarily or appointed) within the organization. An organization may opt to have this as an add-on function rather than a dedicated position for many reasons: lack of budget, lack of personnel, and so on. Managing supplier diversity this way isn't impossible but it's not ideal. Advocating using a diverse firm can be a challenge when an organization decides to award solely on low price or when advocating for a diverse vendor is in conflict with your primary duties.

Legacy data systems

As a core organizational function, supplier diversity is still relatively young compared to other functions. It started in 1969 and has continued to grow and evolve, with more and more organizations adding it as part of their structure. Only around the 1990s did supplier diversity begin to move beyond empirical data and look to incorporate qualitative data and analytics not only to track participation but also to quantify results and support the growing need for communicating the business case.

Today, most organizations manage crucial business functions through an enterprise resource planning (ERP) system. This system works to automate and manage crucial business functions including finance, manufacturing, retail, supply chain, human resources, and operations. Essentially, an ERP system connects and integrates all areas, allowing processes to be streamlined and shared across the organization. For supplier diversity, an ERP system provides real-time and accurate information related to vendor onboarding, utilization, and even payments, which are basic but critical metrics for supplier diversity to track and report. But as a dedicated function, supplier diversity got left out of the ERP conversation.

Unfortunately, the increase in relevance of supplier diversity programs and the evolution of ERP systems didn't intersect in a way that allowed any consideration for incorporating the supplier diversity function into the ERP process. Thus, most ERP systems were integrated without having supplier diversity in mind or receiving input from supplier diversity or procurement.

HOW THE ERP MODEL BEGAN

The first semblance of an ERP model began in 1940 with the use of calculating machines. By the 1960s, organizations began using systems that incorporated inventory management and control. By the 1970s, these systems controlled additional functions, including manufacturing, purchasing, and delivery. The first usage of the actual term *ERP* began during the 1990s. During the 2000s, these systems evolved to include supply chain management, customer relations management (CRM), and business intelligence. Today, many systems have introduced modules that allow for tracking diverse spend by vendors.

Because of this disconnect, supplier diversity programs have had to rely on rudimentary methods for collecting and compiling data, and practitioners spend inordinate amounts of time compiling, calculating, and preparing reports. This scenario has resulted in a process that's cumbersome and inefficient while creating information that's arguably inaccurate and not a true reflection of what the organization has actually achieved. Further, it brings into question the integrity and validity of the data and potentially of the program.

Pinpointing Practitioner Barriers

Most professions have a clear process for getting the institutional knowledge needed for that career path. For example, if you want to become a doctor or lawyer, you go to medical or law school. If you want to work in procurement, you can even major in supply chain. However, professionals looking to enter the field of supplier diversity don't have a defined path or point of entry. Ask any supplier diversity professional, and I guarantee each has a different story of how they entered the industry.

In lieu of a degree in supplier diversity, people gain experience and, more importantly, competency after stepping into this role. They may get education on the job, through trial and error, or even by nontraditional learning methods such as continuing education programs and peer-to-peer learning (and, of course, books such as this one). Although most professions do involve a combination of these methods, this route is hardly the most conventional one for such an important and impactful role. Often, this lack of a concrete path creates a number of performance barriers that can prevent supplier diversity professionals from being effective even before they begin.

Just like barriers are inherent within the organization (see the earlier section "Identifying Common Organizational Barriers"), the person designated to lead this charge may have limitations coming into the role that you didn't anticipate.

REMEMBER

Recognizing these challenges doesn't indicate that they'll always hinder you, but it does help you identify and develop a mechanism to overcome them.

Despite the best preparation, motivation to do well, and mountains of enthusiasm and passion, people can still be unsuccessful in their jobs for any number of reasons. I discuss some of the most common reasons supplier diversity practitioners aren't successful in this role in the following sections.

Lack of clarity to carry out the mission

Most organizations focus first on the task at hand, their *what:* launching a supplier diversity program. They may even be clear on the customer they're serving, their *who:* diverse and small businesses. But the question they fail to define is the *why.* Understanding the why can be the single most important question that you ask. It helps you move beyond the tactical and begin to think more strategically, which is important for activating the program. Further, it provides the framework for how you'll achieve your why, which helps shape and direct your activities.

TIP

When you're clear about the what and can articulate the why, communicating and getting organizational buy-in becomes easy.

No matter the industry or the organization, I firmly believe the goal of supplier diversity is simple: ensure a diverse and inclusive procurement process that connects diverse businesses to contract opportunities.

Inability to navigate the landscape

Supplier diversity practitioners wear many hats. I liken the role to that of a TV or movie producer. They have to do the following:

>> Turn a story idea (supplier diversity program) into a profitable production (impactful and sustainable initiative)

>> Put together a creative and talented (creative and competent) cast and crew (team and professional resources)

>> Be responsible for all aspects of a production (program)

Steering this ship masterfully is as much an art as it is a skill. Although you may rely on and pull support from a variety of internal and external sources, you're the one who makes it happen. Conversely, the inability to navigate the landscape can be detrimental and cause your program to stall.

Unrealistic objectives for the organization or the community

When making the decision to start a program, most organizations have the right intentions — to help diverse businesses, build a thriving entrepreneurial ecosystem, and support economic inclusion in their communities. Unfortunately, the objectives or goals they set to measure their efforts may be flawed, unrealistic, or better suited for the long term (three to five years) than the immediate term. For example, if you're a small-to-medium-sized company located outside a major market that doesn't have a very diverse or entrepreneurial population and your program is relatively new, you're highly unlikely to make it to the *Billion Dollar Roundtable* (a unique group that recognizes corporations that have spent over $1 billion with diverse firms) in one or two years.

The problem is even more obvious when the goals the organization wants to achieve clearly haven't taken into account what's actually happening in the community. Goals should factor in organizational efforts and support; the available local, diverse entrepreneurial community; and what's realistic to achieve, and not be based on what global corporations are doing.

Lack of the resources needed to successfully achieve objectives

According to a survey by managingamericans.com, a lack of resources is one of the most common barriers that managers feel prevent them from doing their jobs effectively. Because supplier diversity isn't necessarily a revenue-generating function, this situation will likely always be the case. This positioning in the organization means that both communicating your value by aligning with organization goals and becoming more strategic to get the resources that you need is critical.

I'm not a fan of doing more with less. It's a pithy phrase that's literally impossible. Instead of committing to the impossible with limited resources, reframe your mindset to focus on what you can do with what you have. A lofty goal of joining the Billion Dollar Roundtable with limited resources isn't likely to happen (and you should say so). But an incremental increase in spending with diverse businesses over the previous year or an increase in the number of diverse businesses you're engaging or have in your pipeline is achievable, and you should look at it as progress.

No analytics/wrong metrics

You've probably heard the saying "What gets measured gets done." It means that regular measurement and reporting keeps you focused and allows you to use data to make decisions to advance your program. No matter the stage of your program — beginning, growing, or mature — you should include your most critical measurements (your *key performance indicators* or KPIs) as a part of your overall supplier diversity plan. This approach helps not to only communicate the value proposition to the organization but also to justify the business case for supplier diversity.

In recent years, organizations have been looking beyond basic spend analytics and are asking questions about impact in the community, diverse businesses, and so on. Understanding what metrics are important to which stakeholders helps you determine what analytic tools you need to facilitate this important function.

Overcoming Barriers to Build a Successful Program

Over the years, I've talked to thousands of supplier diversity professionals across the United States. Although their challenges vary and every organization has its own unique culture that can create a distinctive set of challenges, some things are consistent across the board. Understanding what the barriers are helps you create a solution. Here are some strategies to consider to overcome these obstacles and build a successful and effective program:

1. **Evaluate your organization DNA and supplier diversity readiness.**

   Determine what type of organization you have and its readiness for implementing a supplier diversity program. This helps you determine how much work is required to implement supplier diversity as an organizational initiative rather than a stand-alone function and ensures that everyone is working together.

2. **Identify your organizational *why*.**

   Determining why your organization has a supplier diversity program helps you align the program objectives to the strategic goals of the organization.

3. **Develop SMART goals — specific, measurable, achievable, realistic, and timely — for the business community and your organization.**

   Every program should establish goals by using the SMART categories, both for the diverse businesses you work with and for your organization.

4. **Understand what resources you need to achieve your SMART goals and objective identified in your *why*.**

   After you establish goals in Step 3, determining what resources they require, how you'll work, and what programmatic elements are necessary becomes easier.

5. **Ensure that stakeholders, partners, and so on understand what you do in the supplier diversity function.**

   Communication is essential for internal buy-in and support. If people don't understand, they can't advocate on your behalf.

6. **Determine the right metrics to report that accurately articulate your program activities and address your KPIs.**

   Tracking diverse spend and utilization is great, but every program should establish KPIs that articulate the full breadth of its program activities.

7. **Benchmark your program against other supplier diversity programs you admire.**

   Continually evaluate your efforts against other programs to ensure that your program remains relevant and is using the most up-to-date tools to become a best-in-class program.

Chapter **10**

Creating an Effective Supplier Diversity Plan

An old proverb (often attributed to Ben Franklin) says, "If you fail to plan, you are planning to fail." And it's true; creating an effective supplier diversity program is almost impossible without crafting a supplier diversity plan. Yet many conventional organizations, with their silos and territorial structures, sometimes overlook this step. However, silos don't work in today's modern and successful supplier diversity programs because the success of these initiatives depends heavily on internal and external collaboration.

Planning bridges the gap between where the program currently is and where you want it to go. A supplier diversity plan is important because it provides the foundation for how your organization will implement this important strategy. An effective supplier diversity plan should

» Align with the objectives senior leadership outlines in your organization's strategic plan

» Indicate how supplier diversity supports those objectives

» Detail the action items that you and your team will put into action to ensure that objectives are met

Unfortunately, many organizations don't spend the time needed during this phase and eventually end up frustrated when their efforts stall or fail.

In this chapter, I discuss the planning process and the components needed to craft an effective supplier diversity plan.

Starting Out with the Principles of Supplier Diversity Planning

Developing your plan starts with the planning process, using what I call the *principles of supplier diversity planning.* Figure 10-1 illustrates these principles, and the following list provides more details for each principle:

>> **Planning to guide direction:** Planning ensures that program activities align with the organization's objectives and anticipated outcomes. Clearly outlined objectives make gaining the necessary support to implement the program easier.

>> **Planning to decrease rate of failure:** Removing failure is impossible, but you can reduce the likelihood that your efforts are unsuccessful or don't reach your intended audience. Understanding the steps needed helps you complete tasks, and planning notes the way to deal with changes and unpredictable effects.

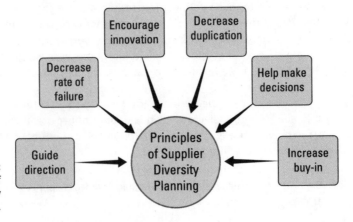

FIGURE 10-1:
The principles of supplier diversity planning.

- » **Planning to encourage innovation:** Because most supplier diversity programs have limited resources, you have to be resourceful to get stuff done. Whether you're finding creative ways to reach diverse businesses or developing inventive policies, programs, or ways to generate revenue, all facets of planning must incorporate innovation and next-generation thinking.

- » **Planning to decrease redundancy of efforts:** Planning works as the foundation to organize activities and clarify what is needed from stakeholders, partners, and collaborators. It helps you avoid wasting time on tasks that are unnecessary or don't add value to your program.

- » **Planning to help make decisions:** Planning encourages you to focus on the future and make a decision from among several alternative plans of action.

- » **Planning to increase buy-in:** Having a solid plan helps make sure that everyone is working together to achieve the same goal.

TIP

Using these planning tips helps you prioritize what's most important and organize what activities need to take place at each section of your supplier diversity plan.

Eyeing Your Vision Statement

When you look at leading brands today, most have a simple vision. Take, for instance, the Walt Disney Company. It wants to be the "world's leading producers and providers of entertainment and information." It sought to "develop the most creative, innovative, and profitable entertainment experiences and related products in the world." This vision has provided the foundation for its success, allowing it to become and remain one of the biggest brands in entertainment for many years.

A *vision statement* is a sentence or short paragraph that succinctly describes the goals of a company, nonprofit, or some other entity. It states what you're trying to build and serves as a touchstone for your future actions. A clear vision statement helps companies run more efficiently because it keeps everyone on the same page. If you can't describe what you're doing and what you want to do, your team should regroup so that you all understand what you're trying to accomplish.

Your vision statement defines how you want to be recognized, whether it's to the diverse business community, employees, collaborating partners, stakeholders, or anyone with a vested interest in your program's success. Because the statement is future-focused (it provides direction for who you want to be), it doesn't need to have a timeline or other quantifiable metrics. Some examples include the following:

Be the corporate leader in making small, woman-owned; minority-owned; HUBZone; veteran-owned; service-disabled, veteran-owned; and LGBTQ businesses

Create "real opportunities" for diverse/underrepresented (i.e., small, minority, women, veteran, LGBTQ, and persons with disabilities) businesses

Become a member of the Billion Dollar Roundtable (a designation that comes from spending at least $1 billion with diverse suppliers)

Some organizations may not have a vision statement, often because they have not taken the time to create one. However, remember that a vision statement can set the stage for everything that you do. Once an organization has defined it's vision, it should be communicated. The best way to communicate it is through action. You can how see that worked for Disney!

Clarifying Your Mission

A *mission statement* is a short statement the explains the "why" and "how" of your organization's supplier diversity program. A good mission can include the goals you hope to achieve and who you're targeting, and it aligns with the strategic goals of the organization. You want to craft a statement that clearly articulates your organization's intentions to create opportunities that encourage using diverse businesses in its procurement and contracting opportunities.

REMEMBER

Some things to keep in mind for your mission include the following:

>> **Be authentic.** People can tell when you're genuine and when it's just lip service.

>> **Be specific about your "why" and "how."** Don't just focus on "what." Stating why reminds you why it's important to your organization and why you're taking action. Expressing "how" clarifies what you're doing to make it a reality.

>> **Don't be generic.** Write a statement that tells *your* story, not one that may be for any company.

>> **Keep it simple.** Your mission statement doesn't have to be elaborate or complex.

>> **Focus on actionable items.** Again, these items don't have to be complex or lofty to be impactful. Actionable items hold you accountable to actually take action toward meeting your mission.

Locking in Your O.A.R.

After identifying the vision and mission, which I discuss in the preceding sections, you're ready for what I call your O.A.R.: objectives, actions, and results (or KPIs). On a boat, the oar helps guide your direction. Without it, you're just sitting in the water. Similarly, your O.A.R. is the heart of your plan and provides the details on how you'll execute it. The following sections focus on each component.

Communicating your objectives

Your *objectives* are outcomes that support your mission and become the priorities for the duration of your plan. They can be short- to medium-term goals and should align with your mission and vision. Like your plan, your objectives should indicate what you want to accomplish on an annual basis. (You track your KPIs more frequently, which I discuss later in the chapter). Also, indicating that objectives are ongoing and may be included in your plan for next year is perfectly okay.

TIP

I like objectives that cover each aspect of your program — external and internal. Table 10-1 shows you some examples. I have included diverse businesses on the internal and external side. In this instance, internal reflects businesses that are already doing business with your organization. External includes recruitment and building awareness with new firms that may be a good fit for contract opportunities with your organization.

TABLE 10-1 ## Sample Objectives

Internal Objectives	External Objectives
Diverse Businesses Increase spend with diverse firms by 20% Increase capacity of diverse firms by category Increase tier II/subcontracting spend by 10%	Create more partnerships with state, local, and business community and stakeholder groups
Departments Increase communication of supplier diversity efforts for internal departments	Create diverse business outreach initiative that connects, informs, increases engagement, and so on

Defining your activities

Determining the specific activities, tactics, and action items you'll deploy to help achieve your objectives can be a challenge. So many factors dictate how robust your program can be, such as existing or accessible resources, the stage of your program, your workforce, the availability of diverse businesses in your market, the needs/capacity of these businesses, and so on.

REMEMBER

Although the virtual environment has made conducting workshops and outreach events with greater frequency easier, you still have to be mindful about what you're doing. These options still require resources, and they may not always be the best use of your time. You definitely want to plan your activities before deploying an ambitious schedule and experiencing burnout.

I'm sure you have questions, like "What is a good action item?" You want to create action items that

>> **Are relevant to your market and organization:** They allow you to be collaborative and avoid duplicating efforts. You don't automatically need to do what other programs are doing.

>> **Are specific and small business centric:** They take into account the needs of your audience.

>> **Add value to the diverse businesses you're assisting:** They let you be innovative and responsive to the needs of the businesses.

>> **Have a quantifiable timeline:** This ensures that you're continuously moving forward and, hopefully, making progress. You can always reassess the timeline or objective if necessary.

Following these standards allows you to have a keen focus on activities that support your mission and address your objectives while eliminating activities that won't help you achieve your goals or benchmarks in the long run.

Activities may also cover project management functions related to supplier diversity, including implementing a new system or software or a new process. The following figure lists some internal and external goals and accompanying action items.

	Goal(s)	Action Item(s)
Internal	• Increase direct spend with diverse businesses by 10%. (This can be by demographic category, such as minority, woman-owned, veteran-owned, and so on, or by procurement category, such as Goods and Services, Professional Services, Construction, and so on.) • Increase tier 2/subcontracting opportunities for diverse businesses by 20% versus the previous year.	• Identify all active diverse suppliers and review total spend. • Increase awareness of current opportunities with diverse businesses. • Review and update relevant policies in all procurement documents. • Review processes and procedures to ensure they're inclusive and support our mission.
	• Increase awareness of the supplier diversity function within the organization. • Build stronger relationships across the organization.	• Create a communication plan that informs internal departments of our supplier diversity activities. • Launch a supplier diversity training course for departments. • Meet with one internal department per month to discuss supplier diversity and how you can help the department meet its objectives, meet diverse suppliers, and so on.
	• Increase accuracy and efficiency in reporting. • Make finding and using diverse firms easy for departments.	• Implement a new software to track vendor registration and utilization.
External	• Increase community relations and partnerships with other agencies in the community.	• Collaborate with local and state partners to host at least two events (one during the spring and one during the fall). All events will conclude before the end of the year.
	• Increase capacity of firms. • Increase outreach efforts to get new diverse businesses engaged with the organization.	• Launch a business development program for potential vendors.

Identifying your results (KPIs)

A *key performance indicator* (KPI) is a performance measurement that helps evaluate the success of an organization, activity, or initiative. For many years, programs relied on basic measures to highlight impact but were still in the dark about how they really performed.

However, in recent years, a wider group of stakeholders are questioning supplier diversity programs. Practitioners are being asked to report beyond the basics of utilization, direct spend, and so on and emphasize more complex results that support the business case, such as community economic impact, supplier development and capacity building, category management/strategic sourcing, and tier 2/subcontracting spend.

KPIs have increasingly become an important part of the supplier diversity plan. They provide you with an indication of whether you're on track to achieve your objectives by measuring performance and how you're using your resources (check out the earlier section "Communicating your objectives" for more on identifying those). For example, you can measure whether workshops on marketing to your organization have resulted in more meetings for diverse businesses with your internal departments or evaluate whether matchmaking events have resulted in an increased number of diverse subcontractors working on projects. By measuring your KPIs, you can determine the best mix of activities in which you should spend your time in order to yield the greatest results.

Here are some good practices for using KPIs:

>> Establish KPIs for each level of your program — utilization, diverse businesses, and internal departments.

>> Determine the appropriate frequency for reviewing them; you may need to make adjustments to make sure that you're in line to achieve your objectives.

>> Identify the accountability process, or who receives the results. Preferably, it's senior leadership (to demonstrate that the success of this initiative lies at the top).

Table 10-2 gives you some examples of KPIs to consider. But you can determine the right KPIs to establish based on your organization's culture, program stage, and so on. I also discuss KPIs in Chapter 16:

TABLE 10-2

Sample KPIs

Utilization	Diverse Businesses
Diverse spend versus the previous period (monthly, quarterly, annually)	Increase/decrease in number of contracts won
Number of diverse firms responding to solicitations	Number of firms in procurement pipeline
	Number of firms engaged/attending programs
	Number of new/unique visitors to your programs/events
	Increase in capacity of firms
	Percentage of firms participating in programs that win contracts
	Win/lose rate of firms that respond to solicitations
	Diverse spend by department (Internal)
	Number of departments engaged in programs/internal training (Internal)
	Number of collaborations and/or partnership events held (External)
	Number of events sponsored (External)

Putting the Plan Together

Figure 10-2 shows what a comprehensive supplier diversity plan looks like. It answers all the questions — why you're doing this, how you're doing this, and what you're doing — and provides guidance on who you want to be as a result. Now, you're ready to activate.

Supplier Diversity Plan

Mission #1: To use our organizational resources to uplift, support, and grow small and diverse businesses in our community

Mission #2: To become a trusted business partner and entrepreneurial resource of choice for small and diverse businesses in our community

Mission #3: To strengthen our connection and commitment to the community through programs that support its overall well-being, including health, the economy, and the environment

Objectives	Activities	Results (KPIs)
1) **Increase direct spend** with diverse businesses by 10%. (This can be by demographic category, such as minority, woman-owned, veteran-owned, and so on, or by procurement category, such as Goods and Services, Professional Services, Construction, and so on.)	1) Identify all active diverse suppliers and review total spend.	1) Increase in direct spend with diverse firms versus the previous period
2) **Increase tier 2/subcontracting opportunities** for diverse businesses by 20% versus the previous year.	1) Increase awareness of current prime opportunities with diverse businesses. 2) Review relevant policies in all procurement documents. 3) Review processes and procedures to ensure they are inclusive and support our mission.	1) Increase in tier 2/subcontracting opportunities reported by prime partners versus the previous period 2) Update and publish policies that encourage and support prime partners to utilize diverse businesses 3) Update and publish processes and procedures that encourage and support prime partners to utilize diverse businesses
3) **Increase response rate** of diverse businesses responding to bid opportunities.	1) Analyze response and win rate of diverse firms responding to bid opportunities.	1) Increase in number of diverse firms responding to opportunities versus previous period
4) **Increase win rate** of diverse businesses responding to opportunities.	1) Analyze response and win rate of diverse firms responding to bid opportunities.	1) Increase in number of diverse firms winning bid opportunities versus the previous period
5) **Increase capacity** of business owners.	1) Create training and FITD programs that support diverse businesses.	1) Increase in number of diverse firms that increase their business with the organization versus the previous period

FIGURE 10-2
A comprehensive supplier diversity plan.

GETTING CREATIVE WITH SUPPLIER DIVERSITY PLANS

Supplier diversity plans can come in many forms. There is no formal template or master plan to follow. This flexibility is great for you as the supplier diversity leader to formalize this task, bring structure to this process, and create something that works for you and your organization. To get started, think about your audience — who are you sharing information with? Next, consider what's most important for your audience to know. For example, in local government, many municipalities want to see metrics broken down by ethnicity and how many contracts are going to local businesses. Lastly, you'll want to include information that supports what you're doing but also gives you the ability to tell your supplier diversity story.

3

Supplier Development and Supplier Diversity

IN THIS PART . . .

Examine how to create inclusive procurement strategies and a business-centric program that puts small and diverse businesses first.

Uncover how to incorporate supplier development and capacity building that emphasizes business sustainability.

Chapter **11**

Creating an Environment that Puts Diverse Businesses First

Sometimes when managing the politics that can surround supplier diversity, people can forget what's important: connecting small and diverse businesses to opportunities within their organizations. Of course, because procurement is a contracting environment, organizations have to protect themselves from liability and risk at all costs. But if you think about it, you really don't have much of a program if the small and diverse business community isn't there.

In your haste to safeguard your organization, you can unwittingly create policies, processes, and procedures that are unnecessarily cumbersome. (I've even heard this scenario referred to as a small business tax.) This situation isn't conducive to creating a business-centric environment and can be a deterrent for doing business with you, which is counter to what you're trying to achieve.

In this chapter, I discuss creating an environment that puts small and diverse businesses first; nurturing a culture of trust, respect, and transparency (TRT); and managing supplier relationships.

Becoming the Champion for Diverse Businesses within Your Organization

I've worked in many organizations across several industries in a variety of roles in supplier diversity and small business development. While interviewing for a position, I asked the head of the department, "What is the one thing you'd like the successful person to have?" She thought about it for a minute and then she said she was looking for a person who would be a champion for small and diverse businesses.

I remember being pleasantly struck by the response. Not only was it the first time I'd heard this factor as a leading indicator for success, but it also demonstrated that small and diverse businesses were central to the organization's program.

Most organizations have good intentions for their supplier diversity programs. They don't deliberately set out to operate under a shroud of mystery. The truth is that regulatory/legislative issues and the organization's culture can make acting as a champion and still remaining unbiased a challenge. The role of a champion is to believe in what you're doing and to keep supplier diversity a priority, whether that means bringing it up in meetings or doing events when others have moved on. The champion is the one who finds paths to make supplier diversity happen in a way that benefits everyone.

In Chapter 5, I explain the role of supplier diversity within the organization, outlining the many hats supplier diversity professionals wear. I guess you can consider "champion" another hat. It involves keeping small and diverse businesses first without having colleagues questioning whose side you're on if you push or question a little too much.

REMEMBER

Being a champion in your organization doesn't mean you're on one side and your colleagues are on the other. You may cross a line between being a strong champion and going overboard to the point that you give the impression of favoritism or undermine your ability to be objective and effective. This kind of zealousness may call into question your entire process and program. Effective championing starts with understanding the principles that guide supplier diversity, working to remove obstacles, and pushing back on the status quo.

Perusing supplier diversity's key principles

REMEMBER

The principles of supplier diversity highlight the ethical duties required for supplier diversity professionals. Notice how they align closely with procurement:

>> Avoid the intent and appearance of unethical or compromising practice in relationships, actions, and communications

>> Demonstrate loyalty to your employer by diligently following the lawful instructions of the employer, using reasonable care and only authority granted

>> Handle confidential or proprietary information belonging to employers or suppliers with due care and proper consideration of ethical and legal ramifications and governmental regulations

>> Encourage all segments of society to participate by demonstrating inclusive support for diverse businesses

>> Enhance the proficiency and professionalism of the supplier diversity industry by acquiring and maintaining current technical knowledge and industry best practices and displaying the highest standards of ethical behavior

Focusing on removing obstacles

As a champion, one of your duties is to remove things that present a barrier for small and diverse businesses to successfully do business with your organization. The idea isn't that you remove rules that are there to protect the organization or are required by law. It does allow for removing policies that create an unnecessary burden and may not reflect the current business environment. I've frequently found some legacy regulations that were still in place simply because no one asked about updating or removing them.

TIP

With every new program activity you conduct, policy you create, or procedure you put in place, you should conduct the "how does this help businesses" test. If you can't answer yes to the following questions (or, at least, most of them), it may not be something you should spend your time doing. A few questions to consider before taking action:

>> How does this add value to our program?

>> Does this policy benefit or harm small and diverse businesses?

>> Does this connect businesses to contracts within the organization?

>> Is this an investment activity or will we see benefits immediately?

Another way to evaluate obstacles is by using a *win-win analysis*. Organizations want programs that allow them to contract with small and diverse businesses without exposing them to risk (that is, inferior goods and services, interruption in delivery of services, and so on). Businesses want programs and policies that allow them access to contract opportunities. A win–win analysis takes into account the benefit your policies and programs have on small and diverse businesses as well as the organization's tolerance for risk. In short, it measures how robust you can make your program so that it provides maximum benefit without causing harm to the organization.

To complete a win–win analysis, plot the risk to the organization and the benefit to small and diverse businesses on a graph like the one in Figure 11-1. Here are the possible outcomes:

>> **Win-win:** Low risk to the organization and high benefit (win) to the business community. Both parties benefit.

>> **Win-lose:** Low risk (win) to the organization and low benefit (lose) to the business community. One party benefits, but the other doesn't.

>> **Lose-win:** High risk (lose) to the organization and high benefit (win) to the business community. One party doesn't benefit, but the other one does.

>> **Lose-lose:** High risk (lose) to the organization and low benefit (lose) to the business community. Neither party benefits.

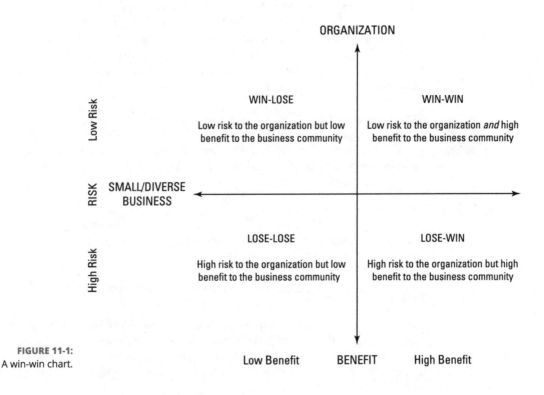

FIGURE 11-1:
A win-win chart.

REMEMBER

Unfortunately, many organizations operate from a win-at-all-costs perspective rather than win-win. As the champion, it's your job to find and encourage the happy medium.

Challenging the status quo

Organizational culture is built on the status quo, which can be good and bad. On one hand, that's how traditions are established, and it definitely works in certain industries or from a branding perspective. On the other hand, from a culture perspective, it doesn't always allow an organization to adopt new processes and move forward. Throughout this book, I've described supplier diversity as a change management function that requires forward, sometimes divergent, thinking in order to be successful.

A VP at one organization I worked in explained that organizations that have been around for a long time (such as the one where we worked) don't necessarily require innovation or new ideas as a condition for success. They *do* need people that can manage the status quo and keep things rolling along. In other words, don't spin your wheels trying to make change happen. Change takes time, and not everyone welcomes or even wants it. His insights gave me a valuable lesson in understanding organizational culture and taking a more measured approach rather than trying to enforce changes all at once.

Challenging the status quo can be a delicate process, especially in environments with an established hierarchy and long-standing processes. The tricky part is how to inquire and make suggestions without being perceived as annoying or intruding on someone else's turf (departments can be territorial). The key is to be informed, tactful, empathetic, and accepting of all perspectives.

TIP

Here are a few steps involved in challenging the status quo as a supplier diversity leader:

>> **Study and understand your process.** The more you understand about your organization, the more easily you can recommend and make lasting changes rather than short-term fixes.

>> **Ask questions about systems and processes.** Don't be afraid to ask questions. Sometimes change never happens because no one ever questions the process.

>> **Know industry best practices and do your homework.** You can't ask a question and recommend change without having a solution. You should be aware of what's happening in the industry, have examples of solutions that are a good fit for your organization, and know what's needed to implement them in your organization.

>> **Understand your selling point and unique value proposition.** Part of making recommendations and convincing leadership that what you're proposing is a solution it should consider is understanding the *unique value proposition,* or UVP, it delivers. Your UVP is a simple statement to convey why your proposal has value or is unique. Getting it approved may take a while, and you may have to repeat your pitch many times and to several groups.

>> **Know who your allies are.** Understand who else may be impacted by your recommendations and whether you need allies on your side to help push them through.

>> **Be patient.** You have to handle changing legacy systems and processes delicately. Getting them pushed through can take some time (maybe even a few budget cycles). If you believe in it and the benefits it will bring to the organization, be prepared for the long haul.

Fostering a Culture of Trust, Respect, and Transparency in Relationships

Relationship building is an essential part of the contracting process. The KLT (know, like, and trust) factor is so important in making decisions, but how do you get to really know, like, and trust a potential vendor? First, understand that some relationships are transactional, based on what your organization buys, how frequently you make purchases, the supplier's geographic location, and how complex or specialized the item is. Relationships with suppliers of items purchased frequently or with local suppliers can happen naturally and may only require minimal effort to build as interactions are more frequent. Check out the nearby sidebar, "Building business relationships one level at a time," for more on the relationship–building process.

REMEMBER

As the champion, setting the stage and building a program built on TRT is up to you. With TRT, small and diverse businesses will

>> *Trust* that they're a priority and that you'll advocate on their behalf

>> Know they'll be treated with *respect* within the organization regardless of their size or status

>> Be afforded a *transparent* environment that's equitable and fair

BUILDING BUSINESS RELATIONSHIPS ONE LEVEL AT A TIME

Andrew Sobel, noted author and expert on building business relationships, outlines six levels to this process:

- **Level 1: Contact**

  This initial level is part of the pre-client/relationship initial phase.

- **Level 2: Acquaintance**

  This next level is also in the pre-client/relationship initial phase, and it sets the stage for the next levels to occur. Supplier diversity plays a role in facilitating these two levels, but the entire team needs to pitch in for them to be successful.

- **Level 3: Expert**

  At the beginning of the relationship, some contacts and acquaintances become colleagues or even transactional suppliers whom you ask questions, almost in an exploratory way. Your organization has a problem you need solved, and the vendor may have the knowledge and experience to deal with it. Almost all relationships begin in this way. At this stage, the trust and mutual understanding that enable a relationship are starting, but the relationship hasn't deepened.

- **Level 4: Vendor or steady supplier**

  The expert is ready to move to the vendor or steady supplier phase. If they do a good job on the first engagement or transaction, you may probe to find out more about their ability to provide additional products or services. For now, they may not have access to senior management or part of the organization's inner circle, but you're providing them more face-time with procurement managers or lower-level buyers.

- **Level 5: Trusted advisor**

  Vendors earn this coveted role by demonstrating essential qualities that set them apart from the expert-for-hire or vendor. These attributes include personal trustworthiness, independence, judgment, big-picture thinking, and empathy. Trusted advisors are aligned with your organization's critical priorities and goals.

- **Level 6: Trusted partner**

  This level is the ultimate goal, especially for a firm: to be a trusted partner to your organization while becoming the go-to for helping to address your issues and challenges. Suppliers in this role have built a true partnership, helping to shape your organization's agenda and having relationships with a broad range of stakeholders. This high-touch role requires vendors to be attentive and accessible. But if a vendor can consistently perform at a high level, that partnership can last a lifetime.

(continued)

(continued)

Level 5 and Level 6 require the most time but also yield the greatest impact. Not every vendor reaches these levels, but increasingly, organizations have expressed interest in deepening their relationships and developing strategies that allow high-potential vendors to move into these levels. In their desire to focus not only on utilization but also on creating impact, having firms that are at these levels impact both their organization and the community.

Building trust

David Horsager, business strategist and author of the national bestseller *The Trust Edge: How Top Leaders Gain Faster Results, Deeper Relationships, and a Stronger Bottom Line*, conveniently outlines the trust–building process in his Eight Pillars of Trust. According to his Trust Outlook, the number–one reason people want to work for (or with) an organization is trust. Ahead of being paid more, having more autonomy, or working in a more fun environment, they want to trust their leadership. If a brand or the organization is trusted, revenue increases, and retention becomes greater. This correlation is also true in business relationships. When small and diverse businesses trust you, they're more willing to work with you and ensure your organization's success.

TECHNICAL STUFF

Trust is the most important leading indicator. When trust increases or decreases, the lagging indicator follows. If a leader is untrusted, satisfaction decreases.

Here, I highlight Horsager's eight pillars for building trust. For more information on his insights, go to https://davidhorsager.com/category/8-pillars/.

>> **Clarity:** Be clear about your mission, purpose, expectations, priorities, and daily activities. Follow the K.I.S.D. model — "Keep it simple, dummy" (with all due respect).

>> **Compassion:** Empathy (not pity) shows that you genuinely have someone's best interests at heart. Don't be a paper pusher. Do something to help others.

>> **Character:** Do what's right instead of what's easy. Develop a habit of doing what's right, even when no one is watching.

>> **Competency:** Know your craft. People have confidence in those who know their stuff.

>> **Commitment:** People believe in those who believe in them and are committed to their success.

- >> **Connection:** As humans, we crave connection. Connections drive relationships, and relationship build trust.

- >> **Contribution:** Focus on action and delivering results. Do what you say you're going to do.

- >> **Consistency:** It's all in the little things.

Garnering respect

Aretha Franklin's '60s hit "Respect" quickly became a rallying cry for anyone seeking to be recognized as a valued partner or contributor. Although it was just a song, it's still relevant today. Of course, respect in the business relationship is a two-way street. But sometimes, because of the haste to get through the day and small and diverse businesses' newness to some organizations, supplier diversity professionals may overlook that these businesses are entrepreneurs that are worthy of their respect.

REMEMBER

To foster an environment where mutual respect is a part of the process, you must

- >> **Remove judgement:** Everything may not be perfect in the beginning, but everyone has to start from somewhere. Remember, you aren't there to judge but to assist.

- >> **Actively listen:** Avoid using too much jargon and industry talk or being condescending. Also, take active steps to avoid giving short responses that may make you appear disinterested.

- >> **Remove implicit bias:** This step involves eliminating unconscious favoritism for or prejudice against people of a particular ethnicity, gender, or social group that affects your actions or perceptions.

- >> **Model the behavior you seek:** Nothing speaks more loudly about the culture of an organization than the leader's behavior. It influences employee action and drives organizational behavior. If everyone around them is doing it, including the boss, it's easy for employees to do the same.

- >> **Treat everyone the same:** Fair and equitable treatment for all is a tenet of supplier diversity and procurement.

- >> **Keep it professional, not personal:** Don't judge all businesses based on experiences with another vendor.

Cultivating transparency

Transparency is one of the most important principles in procurement and supplier diversity. An organization needs to ensure that the information related to any public procurement process is accessible to all procurement stakeholders — including suppliers, contractors, service providers, and the general public — at every stage of the process. (That is, except when circumstances require that it keep information confidential or in instances where discretion is required.)

Part of transparency is that you shouldn't keep any secrets about the business from your employees. Share everything you can with them and your investors so that you're all on the same page and they trust you.

Here are some ways to show transparency in your organization:

>> **Act with integrity:** Think about how you want people to treat others and make that an essential part of your business. You most likely want everyone to act with integrity and honor. Be consistent with those values for everything you do, from discipline to making new products to hiring new people.

>> **Don't hide behind processes and rules:** Selling is important, but it should not be the goal. Make spreading your core values throughout your team and in the world your goal.

>> **Stay open to questions:** Putting your company's opinions on social media is okay, but be aware that many people won't agree with them. Instead of shutting down people who disagree by removing their comments — or, even worse, posting a nasty one in return — stay open to discussion and respond politely.

>> **Be responsive to issues:** You should be there not only for your employees but also for your customers. When they comment on social media, give them an honest response (not a form response you've just copied and pasted) within a day. Providing clear and honest answers to people's questions and complaints goes a long way.

>> **Be receptive to feedback and suggestions for improvement:** When talking to your employees about underperforming areas in your company, don't just say "fix it." Talk with them to find solutions to the problem. This approach is more efficient in solving problems, and your employees will be happy to be included in the discussion.

TIP

In Table 11-1, I provide a few examples of the different types and levels of transparency to consider including in your program.

TABLE 11-1   ## Levels of Supplier Diversity Transparency

Level	Description
Solicitation transparency	Ensure that language is inclusive and clearly understood
Qualification transparency	Ensure that qualifications are fair and communicated to everyone
Process transparency	Ensure that everyone is aware of the process and that it's open and equitable
Award transparency	Ensure that the justification for award is clear
Performance transparency	Provide honest feedback on vendor performance on a contract or project
Relationship transparency	Be authentic about opinions and views towards the vendor

Chapter **12**

Building Capacity

I first heard the phrase "building capacity" in supplier diversity during the early 2000s. The term had actually been around since the 1990s in a social and economic development context, but in supplier diversity, it was a new term that grew in relevance as programs were focusing on making the business case for their programs and placing greater emphasis on small and diverse businesses.

Capacity building helps small and diverse businesses increase their management skills, responsiveness to changing market conditions, long-term sustainability, and overall effectiveness to their customer — your organization. You may think these are things businesses should work on themselves, but that can be a challenge because small and diverse businesses tend to have access to fewer resources.

REMEMBER

Although you may be the client, incorporating capacity building into your supplier development strategy can be essential for your program. Not only are businesses able to leverage your access to resources, expertise, and networks, but you can also develop firms according to the needs of your organization. This approach helps them become stronger vendors for *your* program and grow into sustainable businesses that have an impact in the community.

This chapter is all about building capacity: what it is and how you help vendors do it (and then assess the results), and which activities help businesses build capacity.

Getting a Handle on Capacity Building

Capacity is the facility or power to produce, perform, or deploy. Capacity determines how much business or how large a contract a supplier is able to realistically manage.

Capacity building is the process you use to help vendors gain this necessary capacity — obtaining, improving, and retaining their ability to produce, perform, and deploy the knowledge, experience, tools, and other resources required to perform on your projects. I've seen many entrepreneurs say they have everything in place and are ready for that dream contract or project, only to have something unforeseen happen or to find that the rigors of working with a large client are more than they anticipated. In these cases, the project can go south really quickly.

The goal of capacity building is to mitigate this risk not only by awarding contracts with small and diverse businesses but also by ensuring that they have the capacity or capability to successfully perform. This mindset is also reflective of the shift from relying solely on utilization. If a vendor is awarded a contract but can't deliver as expected, you may not get what you contracted for, ultimately costing you, the client, more time and money to fix it. The result for the vendor may be worse, causing irreparable financial or reputational harm. Such a failure can be devastating for the vendor and reflect poorly on your program and your efforts. In either case, no one wins.

Capacity building differs from other training and services you may provide. It's a systematic approach where each step builds on the next; it allows the vendor to grow gradually, performing on contracts that increase in value over time while looking internally at their business model and processes and ensuring that they develop accordingly. Without a strategy, a vendor will always be limited and may never have the ability to reach their full potential, no matter how qualified or skilled they are.

For example, if a vendor has historically completed contracts in the $200,000-to-$250,000 range, completing a project for $1 million may be a stretch (though not impossible). As contract amounts increase, so do the requirements, nuances, levels of scrutiny, and so on.

Take construction. Most construction projects over $100,000 may require some type of bond (such as bid, payment, or performance), which provides the client with assurances that the project will be completed free of defaults and defects and according to the terms and conditions of the contract and that all subcontractors will be paid. The ability to secure a bond is based on a number of factors such as credit score, financial stability, exposure to risk, relationship to the client, experience, successful past performance, and so on. In my experience working with a number of contractors, this area is usually one that prevents these businesses from progressing to bigger, more substantial projects.

The same is true with some professional services contracts. Contracts under $100,000 may not require any insurance, but for contracts over that amount, vendors may be looking at needing at least $1 million in professional liability insurance. Plus, some carriers may have restrictions on who can get that amount of insurance, which, again, presents a barrier to growing small and diverse businesses.

REMEMBER

It's unlikely that a new or unseasoned entrepreneur is going to win a substantial contract without vetting and comfortability that they can successfully perform. Capacity building follows a slow and steady approach that allows small and diverse businesses to methodically grow and scale. Capacity building supports the vendor's ability to gain access to capital to fund larger projects, get necessary bonding and insurance, refine their process for successfully ramping up on a project, or build their skills as a project leader. For your organization, this slow burn allows you to become comfortable with a vendor's ability to successfully perform on higher-level contracts. This isn't for every entrepreneur, but those that "trust the process" build longer term relationships with lasting business results.

TIP

Think about capacity building in terms of the relationship building process I cover in Chapter 11. The ultimate question is this: How do you move a vendor from a level 1 or 2 (acquaintance) to a level 6 (trusted partner)?

Covering Capacity Building Tasks

Capacity building includes the following five specific tasks:

>> **Assessing:** Assessing involves understanding vendors' present capabilities. This task also helps you determine which internal resources you should deploy to assist them.

>> **Strategic planning:** This task helps vendors understand their long-term visions for working with your organization. You're then able to help them find opportunities and partners, grasp the requirements, and establish the best path to achieve that goal.

>> **Networking:** Networking involves creating opportunities for vendors to meet and begin building relationships with key stakeholders within your organization. It also increases visibility, demonstrates the vendor's commitment to your organization, and encourages other small and diverse businesses to meet and potentially become collaborative partners.

>> **Measuring:** This task is the process you use to measure performance, determine whether the approach worked and what you and the vendors learned,

and get testimonials. The key here is building on *past performance,* or a history of successful performance on previous projects. You and the vendors can refine strategies that didn't work and use those that did to secure the next opportunity. If vendors are repeatedly bidding unsuccessfully, you can review to evaluate the gaps in their submissions. You can also use this task to determine whether the business is ready for the next stage or contract level.

» **Feedback:** This task may seem simple, but vendors don't always get the benefits of receiving feedback in a constructive way. Feedback is an important part of the development process and can help with understanding missteps and building confidence and competence. Without this type of guidance, the business may never progress.

Each task is designed to help you help vendors by getting to know them better, understanding their needs and gaps, finding and aligning them with the right opportunities and stakeholders, and creating a path to help them do business.

TIP

Before you get overwhelmed, remember that every business may not need a deep analysis. Also, as the relationship deepens and vendors' experience (and confidence) grows over time, they may need capacity building less. It's a bit like a bicycle: After vendors learn how to ride, the training wheels can come off.

Evaluating the Capacity of Businesses within Your Organization

The foundation of your supply chain is your vendor community. Having good working relationships with your suppliers and understanding where they are helps minimize costs, increase efficiency, guarantee quality, and encourage innovation.

As part of the supplier relationship management (SRM) process, many organizations regularly evaluate suppliers' performance to reinforce the relationship and determine growth opportunities or inefficiencies that may hamper growth. To be meaningful and add value to the supplier, evaluations are *holistic*, meaning that they take the whole business into account, and they are substantiated by qualitative feedback and quantitative metrics.

Capacity building takes evaluation a step further by peeling back the onion to understand the vendor's current capacities, technological resources, delivery strategies, and general business practices. You can ensure that your partners share your priorities and can then adjust their operations to your organization's competitive benefit.

Getting started

The decision to support and develop a supplier is just as important as the actions taken during the capacity building process. This means you should have an idea of what you want suppliers that go through this process to be able to accomplish once completed. For example, you might consider a program for existing, high-performing suppliers you already have a relationship with that are poised to go to the next level with direct coaching. Before you decide, determine what that next level is so that the investment of additional time and resources is worth it to both of you.

Once you've determine how the suppliers are selected and before evaluating them, you should establish guidelines for the relationship. For starters, emphasize that this assessment is a collaborative process to determine the best route to growing the vendor's business with your organization. For current vendors, it isn't intended to criticize or attack. For potential vendors, it isn't meant to discourage or dissuade. You should clearly articulate your goals so that the vendor fully understands the intention and can adjust their operations and systems accordingly.

Evaluations can be based on a number of factors. You can adjust your criteria based on your industry, your program's goals, and your organization's priorities. Here are a few basic elements you should include.

>> **Capability:** All evaluations should thoroughly review the supplier's strengths and weaknesses. A vendor who can't scale their operations in response to your needs may not be ready to move to the next level.

>> **Performance:** Ask as many questions as you need to determine whether a supplier can handle your typical functions. Relevant past and recent performance, experiences with projects of similar size and scope, knowledge of advances in the industry, and so on are good discussion topics.

>> **Exposure to risk:** Every business deals with risks, but vendors should be able to communicate how they work through risk to minimize their disruption to your organization. Reviewing performance metrics such as delays, response time, and corrective action/processes can help you understand the risks you may be exposed to with a vendor.

>> **Quality:** Although quantifying the quality of a product can be difficult, a conversation about technical ability and quality should always be part of a vendor evaluation. Some industry standards include BS EN ISO 9001:2000 certification, which indicates that the supplier excels in management responsibility; resource management; product realization; and measurement, analysis, and improvement.

Getting this certification requires a financial and time commitment, and not all products or services actually need it. Consider it an added bonus, not a requirement for doing business with you.

>> **Sustainability/environmental impact:** Sustainability has become an important focus, and having vendors and partners that agree is a valuable asset. As part of evaluation process, you can consider vendors' waste reduction/ management practices, materials procurement procedures, efforts to achieve energy efficiency, and safety protocols for handling harmful materials, equipment, and so on. For construction, certifications in green or LEED building can be helpful.

Measuring success

Regular vendor evaluations can be an invaluable tool for your organization to connect, proactively identify opportunities for growth, lower risks, streamline operations, eliminate unnecessary risk exposure, and bolster vendors' overall performance and service delivery. They also allow you and the vendor to monitor growth from the last evaluation period. I can't overstate these benefits, especially as organizations look for increased value and efficiencies from their supply chain partners.

Many companies can easily identify the criteria needed for supplier evaluation, but staying focused and remaining consistent so that evaluation is a tool to maximize results and not just another initiative that fizzled out can be a challenge. Evaluations should be comprehensive and informative without being time consuming or tedious. Creating a standard template can make the process simple for companies and suppliers alike. It allows each to better understand the other's expectations, strengths, and shortcomings (remember, no one has all the answers) while working together to build a stronger and sustainable partnership. Figure 12-1 shows an evaluation template.

Here are few ways organizations can stay focused and committed to this process:

>> **Create the process and schedule.** Clearly defining needed tasks and establishing deadlines for them ensures that everybody understands their responsibilities and will work to complete them correctly and promptly.

>> **Determine the criteria for the evaluation.** The questionnaire should request both factual and subjective responses, should only solicit necessary information, and shouldn't contain any questions that the respondent can't answer.

Contractor/Supplier Performance

Contract Number: _____

Contractor/Supplier: _____

Evaluator/Administrator: _____

Date Submitted: _____

Period of Evaluation   From _____   To _____

BASED ON THE FOLLOWING SCALE, RATE THE CONTRACTOR/SUPPLIER'S PERFORMANCE BY CIRCLING YOUR RESPONSE TO THE STATEMENTS BELOW:

1	2	3	N/A
Did Not Meet Expectations	Met Expectations	Exceeded Expectations	Not Applicable

Goods/Services were delivered in a timely manner	1	2	3	N/A
Goods/Services were of good quality	1	2	3	N/A
Business transactions with contractor/supplier were easy	1	2	3	N/A
Customer support from contractor/supplier was acceptable	1	2	3	N/A
Contractor/Supplier responded to questions/concerns quickly	1	2	3	N/A
Contractor/Supplier's resolution of issues was appropriate	1	2	3	N/A
Contractor/Supplier staff was courteous and professional	1	2	3	N/A
Estimate of goods/services was accurate to final contract expense	1	2	3	N/A

FIGURE 12-1: Vendor capacity building evaluation template.

>> **Take a visit to vendors' offices.** If allowed, a personal visit to your vendor can confirm information from the questionnaire and may paint a clearer picture of aspects the evaluation doesn't cover, which allows you to better advocate for a vendor and speak to their capabilities. However, you should consider visits optional and not a condition for doing business.

As a supplier diversity professional and a business coach, I have visited thousands of business offices, manufacturing plants, shipping distribution centers, showrooms, home offices, and so on. I have found that vendors love to show you where the magic happens. Visits also demonstrate that you recognize vendors as people and not just another box to check.

>> **Have the right people present.** The level and size of the vendor or the types of projects or services it provides can determine who should be part of the evaluation team. Who you send shouldn't be indicative of the vendor's value to the supply chain and your organization but more a matter of process.

Developing to Build Capacity

Supplier development is the last stage in the supplier development management (SDM) model that I lay out in Chapter 3, and it's essential because it focuses squarely on the suppliers. Supplier development, exactly as the name implies, is developing suppliers so that they're able to successfully respond to your organization's needs. One way to do that is through capacity building.

Organizations can implement any number of activities to help businesses build capacity. Make sure that you understand the regulatory environment and any local or state legislative statutes that may present any issues. For example, in order to designate contracts specifically for minority- and women-owned businesses, you may have to complete a disparity study, particularly in public procurement. (Head to Chapter 18 for more info on disparity studies.)

Here are a few of the more common activities you can implement:

>> **Rapid contracts:** These contracts are usually small, routine, and uncomplicated projects or services requiring responsive turnaround and quick performance. Their value is usually $10,000 and under. Procurement may maintain a list of vendors capable of performing on these contracts and may have a preapproved list that is routinely updated. Rapid contracts are perfect foot-in-the-door (FITD) contracts, especially for vendors that are new to the organization. There might be other contracts that are low risk where the buyer can accept problems should they arise. One of the biggest challenges with capacity building is that buyers are naturally risk averse. Thus, they're hesitant to take chances with new or smaller suppliers on mission-critical projects or purchases.

>> **Continuing services contracts:** *Continuing services contracts* call for periodic service provided by a list of preapproved vendors. Vendors are prequalified based on basic criteria. These contracts are usually for a specific period of time (two to three years) and are used for projects under $1 million. They're typically for routine services that don't require specialization, although they may require some expertise or experience.

>> **Sheltered market programs:** *Sheltered market programs* are a procurement process in which certain contracts are selected for businesses owned and

controlled by minorities, women, and people with disabilities on a competitive bid or negotiated basis. They're frequently used in public procurement.

» **Partnerships and teaming agreements:** Recommend and encourage partnerships or teaming arrangements with *prime* (tier 1) partners for large organizational contracts at the senior/executive level. Doing so allows vendors to gain experience at the senior level managing a large-scale project.

» **Goal setting and subcontracting:** Encouraging small and diverse participation on larger contracts. This approach allows businesses to get experience providing services on large, complex projects. Participation as a subcontractor is a precursor to direct opportunities. Chapter 1 has more on using goals to promote diverse utilization.

» **Networking and knowledge exchanges:** These options provide opportunities to meet with senior procurement leaders and target programs that address business knowledge gaps that may exist for small and diverse businesses.

» **Mentoring:** Mentoring programs partner small and diverse businesses with larger tier 1 partners or organization executives. These programs can be for 12 to 18 months and provide valuable insights focusing on business knowledge capital, navigating organizational structures, networking with experts in various parts of the organization, and so on. An example is Accenture's Diverse Supplier Development Program (DSDP), a formal mentoring program that matches selected minority-owned, women-owned, LGBTQ-owned, small, and other diverse businesses with Accenture executives to mentor and assist in developing and growing the capacity of their businesses.

» **Training and coaching:** This option provides more one-on-one training that assesses a vendor's business and helps develop a strategic plan. This requires the utmost discretion as you may discuss supplier's confidential information (be sure to stress that they are under no obligation to share information they are uncomfortable sharing). You may want to consider partnering with another local agency, such as a school or business development center, that may be able to provide these services at little or no cost.

TIP

There are a few national programs designed to support diverse businesses — Tuck Diversity Business Programs at Dartmouth, Kellogg ASCEND Business Growth Programs at Northwestern, and the Black Women's Entrepreneurial Leadership (BWEL) Program at Babson. The emphasis on these programs is to provide executive/managerial training to diverse businesses by covering pertinent business functions such as management, finances, operations, and so on. Diverse companies that are weak in any of these areas can limit their growth and development. While these programs can have a hefty price tag, there may be scholarships available through some of their national partners (or you may consider sponsoring your own candidate).

OTHER AREAS TO INCLUDE IN CAPACITY BUILDING

People often think of capacity as the ability to see, understand, and do. So when you're working to build capacity for entrepreneurs, you're working to make them more fluid and agile, which in turn makes them much more effective and successful for your organization. You can help entrepreneurs build capacity in many different ways, including through the leader, their people, and their processes.

- **The leader:** Focusing on leadership development is key because leaders have the primary role in making changes that allow their business to grow. Leaders need to focus on where they want the business to go but also whether they have the right resources and tools to get them there.

- **Their people:** Focusing on human resource capacity building is a great start because humans (their employees) always have the potential to grow. Some areas to consider include improving the capacity of their employees by providing them with greater access to resources, training programs, and consultations and creating new roles within the company and organizational development.

- **Their processes:** This area can include strategic planning, understanding their operational efficiency, introducing business development strategies, and networking opportunities.

4

Examining External (Community) Supplier Diversity Efforts

Get a handle on the stages of supplier diversity programs and which activities you should focus on for each stage.

Uncover how to build community partnerships to drive organizational results.

Chapter **13**

Highlighting the Stages of Supplier Diversity Programs

The best approach to supplier diversity is one that's measured and strategic. Many organizations aspire to create a world-class program, or at least one that yields results, overnight. The truth is that having all the elements fall into place at the right time takes time, patience, and planning. But with so many moving pieces, how do you know where to start to get everything moving in the same direction at the appropriate time? One way is by understanding the stage of your program.

Unless you have a large team, an unlimited budget, and endless resources, you're not likely to do everything at once. Each stage has minimum activities on which you should focus your efforts. This prioritization helps you avoid the urge to do too much at one time and therefore get overwhelmed. Success at each stage creates the foundation to move to the next stage.

In this chapter, I discuss how to identify the stage of your program — startup, growth, or mature — to discover the right activities for each phase.

Determining Your Program Stage and Dealing with Common Challenges

The stages of supplier diversity programs include startup, growth, and mature. In the startup stage, the program is new and in the introductory state. During the growth stage, program is growing and expanding. In the mature stage, the program is established and has a track record of results. Figure 13-1 illustrates the stages and the basics characteristics of each stage.

Startup	Growth	Mature
Program is new and in the introductory state	Program is growing and expanding	Program is established and has a track record of results
Limited resources and budget	Increased resources and budget	Has implemented all stages of the supplier diversity management model
Offers basic services	Offers more services and activities	
Usually 1–2 years	Usually 3–4 years	Usually 5+ years

FIGURE 13-1: Stages of supplier diversity programs

Depending on what your resources and capacity are, how quickly things move within your organization, and how enthusiastic the business community is, your program may be able to progress quickly from the startup stage to the growth and mature stages, where it can remain for years.

Programs can remain in a prolonged maturity state for years (think about programs that have been around since supplier diversity began). But sometimes organizations become complacent, running their programs on autopilot.

As a program matures, I recommend that you refresh it every few years to maintain its vitality and ensure that it continues to evolve to meet the demands of the community and the goals of the organization.

The following sections discuss each stage, including warnings about challenges your program may experience and how to overcome them.

Startup stage

The *startup stage* begins after the decision has been made to start a program. During this stage, your efforts to generate awareness for your program and build relationships are at a high. You likely invest quite a bit of effort and capital in communicating your program, being visible at community events, and recruiting businesses to engage with your program.

In this stage, you're beginning the relationship building process and getting to know the business community. You should be able to get a sense of how businesses are responding to the program and understand their needs, capacity, and interest in doing business with your organization. This part is an investment stage, and you should be prepared to forgo seeing results in the short term.

TIP

Avoid building a program based solely on tier 2 utilization. This practice appears to shift the responsibility to your partners. A good program has a mix of tier 1 and tier 2 opportunities.

WARNING

The following are some challenges you're likely to encounter in the startup stage:

>> **Limited awareness:** Like most people, business owners are busy. During this phase, small and diverse businesses may not even be aware of your program and of opportunities with your organization. You can't assume that just because you have intentions means businesses know everything you do.

Focus on building awareness by using lists of names acquired from events, free databases that list small businesses names (your state may have one of these), or other small business groups.

>> **Limited opportunities:** As you familiarize yourself with the business community and build relationships, you may have fewer or smaller direct opportunities available.

Familiarize yourself with all the things your organization buys and ask questions about how they're purchased. The more you know, the more you can inform businesses.

>> **Limited resources:** Most programs suffer from a lack of resources during this phase, requiring the program manager to be the most resourceful. Understanding the activities in which you'll engage helps you determine exactly what resources you'll need.

Your budget is what it is. Asking for more is likely an uphill climb, especially if you haven't delivered any real results. Focus on what you can do within your initial means. Then look for alternative means, whether that's through partnerships, sponsorship, in-kind, or some other avenue.

>> **Investment:** During this phase, the investment of time and resources may be disproportionate to the results you experience.

The only way to overcome this hurdle is time, patience, and a keen focus on delivering results.

Growth stage

During the *growth stage*, small and diverse businesses are fully engaged with your programs. Your activities are working and you're seeing positive results in connecting businesses to opportunities within your organization. As your investment into the program increases, so do your results.

In this stage, you should continue the relationship building process. Your programs are working, and (hopefully) you have some vendors that have been able to secure contracts, whether with your organization directly or as a subcontractor. As a result, your utilization numbers are increasing. You have a clear vision for your program and where you want it to go. You should continue to fine-tune your program offerings.

WARNING

A common challenge in this stage is becoming overextended. As the program grows and you start making progress, it's easy to incorporate more activities, which results in getting overstretched and overwhelmed.

To avoid overwhelm, follow the activity recommendations I lay out for each stage in the later section "Identifying the Right Activities for Each Stage." If you'd rather create your own list of activities, reduce your tasks to the four or five most important. Take some time to think through things clearly; if something doesn't align with your goals and objectives, you may want to forgo doing it for now.

Mature stage

Programs in the *mature stage* (also called the *legacy stage*) have been around for at least five years. They may even date back to the inception of supplier diversity itself. Mature programs have a track record of utilization and deploy an active slate of activities.

At this point, you have to consider creative ways to keep your program fresh and engagement and momentum high. Here are some common challenges to watch for and deal with during the mature/legacy stage.

>> **Complacency and arrogance:** When a program reaches maturity, it may not generate as much activity as it once did. Just because a program is mature doesn't mean it's still effective. After a while, organizations can slip into a routine, and they may not have the same level of enthusiasm as they had during the startup and growth phases. Departments may start to fall into their old ways and not actively look for small and diverse businesses.

To overcome this obstacle, revitalize your efforts every few years, as I note earlier in the chapter. Also, reconnect with your goals to become more energized and excited.

>> **Small and diverse business availability:** As these businesses gain experience and grow their capacity, they may secure contracts in other areas, making them less available to you. (This outcome is a good one, though.) These success stories demonstrate the viability of your program and the results a business can expect by working with your organization.

To overcome problems with business availability, you should continue to build awareness and recruit businesses into your procurement pipeline.

>> **Fighting diversity fatigue:** Even when everyone agrees that diversity is important, you may run into collective exhaustion from the debate and discussion that may arise over supplier diversity processes.

Make sure supplier diversity is relevant to everyone in the organization by using a soft touch approach rather than a heavy hand.

Identifying the Right Activities for Each Stage

When you know which stage best describes your program, directing and focusing your efforts becomes easier. (You can find out more about the stages in the earlier section "Determining Your Program Stage and Dealing with Common Challenges.") This precision helps you avoid overextending yourself and your program and not achieving your desired results.

The activities in the following sections represent the minimum set of undertakings on which you should focus your efforts. Depending on your particular variables, you can go as fast or as slow as you need to. If your organization is motivated, providing all the necessary resources, and you have an enthusiastic business community, you may be able to incorporate all the startup activities within a short time, allowing you to quickly progress to the growth and mature stages.

REMEMBER

Ultimately, the goal is to create a strong program that delivers results for your organization and has a lasting impact on your community and the small and diverse businesses you work with.

REMEMBER

Specific activities define each stage. As I mention earlier in the chapter, each stage should provide the foundation to move your program to the next. For example, during the startup phase, you should look at the systems you have or will have in place (such as the vendor registration portal, which is one of the first points of contact for vendors).

Also, you should be able to identify the opportunities that exist within your organization (what you buy) and understand your process for procurement (how you buy) so that you can clearly communicate them and not waste time engaging with businesses where you have no mutual connection. Take, for instance, a potential vendor who sells dried flowers. If dried flowers are something your organization routinely buys, you can guide this business through the process. But if your organization has no need for those, having that vendor engage in your programs doesn't make sense because they have no hope of your becoming a customer.

Startup stage activities

The following are some of the basic activities you should focus your efforts on during the startup phase:

>> **Vendor registration portal:** This system is the initial onboarding step and is usually necessary in order for a vendor to get paid. It typically includes pertinent information about the business, including its socioeconomic/demographic information. Most organizations have upgraded to an electronic portal where businesses can register at any time.

To better manage the massive amounts of data that can accumulate in these databases, some organizations limit registration to those that have a pending contract in place. You can determine what's best for your organization. Whatever you select, the system needs to be easily searchable so internal users looking to make purchases can find the appropriate small and diverse businesses. Check out Chapter 6 for more on the importance of the vendor portal.

WHY UNDERSTANDING YOUR PROGRAM STAGE IS IMPORTANT

For each stage of a supplier diversity program, I have outlined a sequential pattern of activities and expectations. As your program moves through each stage, you're able to develop greater competency and a deeper and wider understanding of the needs of small and diverse businesses you work with, resulting in increased effectiveness in your program.

>> **Creating/understanding your process:** The number of supplier diversity professionals who don't fully understand how the contracting process works at their organizations is always surprising. Telling vendors to register in your portal and wait for opportunities to be emailed to them doesn't work. Understanding what you buy and how you buy it helps you direct businesses to the shortest and fastest path to doing business with your organization.

>> **Understanding/analyzing the opportunities within your organization:** You should be able to articulate what opportunities exist within your organization. To keep it simple, focus on the low-hanging fruit: those immediate opportunities that are transactional and not complex. You should also look at opportunities to increase spend with any existing small and diverse vendors you may already do business with.

>> **Direct (tier 1) spend tracking:** At a minimum, you should be able to track the *direct* or *tier 1 spend* with small and diverse vendors (the amount spent directly with the business) by using your existing systems. Doing so not only tracks your basic utilization but also helps you assess areas like your contracting portfolio and procurement methods to determine ways to increase direct spend, such as creating small purchase programs, signing fewer contracts with large customers in select categories, or creating preapproved vendor lists.

>> **Networking events:** This activity may include opportunities to meet and engage with organizational stakeholders, internal departments, or your *prime partners* — businesses that have large contracts and require subcontractors to complete.

Growth stage activities

The growth phase should incorporate all the activities in the preceding section with these tasks:

>> **Benchmarking:** You should actively look at programs whose efforts and results you want to model. Although gravitating toward large, mature

programs that have been around for a while is great, you should also examine programs at organizations comparable to your size, industry, location, and so on. These provide the best barometer of what you're likely to achieve. You can always adjust up or down based on what's best for your organization.

» **Communication program:** Your communication plan is your chance to build awareness for your program, keep stakeholders informed on what you're doing, and advise small and diverse businesses on upcoming events and opportunities. It helps you build a case and be a bridge to what's happening within your organization. I discuss communication in more detail in Chapter 15.

» **Basic supplier development workshops:** These may include introductory workshops that focus on doing business with your organization, understanding your systems, and knowing how to best market themselves for opportunities. These programs are largely driven by your availability to conduct or facilitate.

» **External outreach:** Not every business will come to you, so you should have an active plan to meet viable firms that are a good fit for your program. Your outreach may include attending and exhibiting at local, state, regional, and even national events that small and diverse businesses attend.

» **Multi-tier spend tracking and compliance:** This activity tracks small and diverse business utilization on projects awarded to your prime partners. That is, you track how many small and diverse businesses your prime contractors use for their subcontracting. You then add this spend to your direct spend to create your total overall spend. In modern procurement, because subcontracting makes up a large portion of total spend, organizations have come to rely on it to supplement their direct spend while allowing their philosophies to trickle down to their partners.

» **Cross-departmental/community collaboration:** This task involves partnering and collaborating with internal and external stakeholders to help augment your programs.

» **Internal in-reach program:** *In-reach* describes your efforts to reach internal departments that purchase goods and services. It includes keeping them informed on upcoming activities and events where they can meet small and diverse businesses and conducting departmental workshops to help them become more familiar with your program. If your organization has a government affairs department or receives funding from government agencies, you can advise those groups on how your program assists in fulfilling federal business utilization requirements.

Mature stage activities

The mature phase should include all the activities in the preceding two sections in addition to the following:

>> **Advanced supplier development program (M.O.D.E.):** This comprehensive form of supplier development includes mentoring, outreach, development, and education. M.O.D.E. is designed to touch every aspect of the vendor's business in order to boost sustainability within your organization and as an entrepreneur. You can read about M.O.D.E. in Chapter 23.

>> **Advanced supplier development workshops:** Topics for these workshops can include accounting, insurance, securing bonding, and so on. You may bring in industry experts or professional speakers/partners to facilitate.

>> **Compliance program:** In this activity, you monitor large contracts for compliance with your diversity utilization goals. It may also involve serving as mediator when problems arise between the prime partner and the subcontractor on a project.

>> **Dedicated personnel for program management:** This task involves expanding the team to include an analyst who monitors projects for compliance and compiles various reports.

>> **Personnel certifications and thought leadership:** Certifications help distinguish you as an expert in the field. As the industry has sought to define higher standards for expertise, certifications have increasingly become a preferred requirement for job listings on job boards with top organizations. Major industry certifications include the Certified Professional in Supplier Diversity (CPSD) issued through the Institute for Supply Management and the ASDP certification issued through the Alliance of Supplier Diversity Professionals.

Another activity you may be asked to engage in is speaking at industry events, panels, and discussions to share your thoughts on the industry and your program efforts.

» Identifying the importance of collaboration

» Determining how to engage with various stakeholders

» Seeking out community partners at a variety of levels

» Recognizing the benefits of supplier diversity councils

Chapter **14**

Cultivating Community Partners to Drive Supplier Diversity

Supplier diversity's impact on the entrepreneurial ecosystem in local communities is undeniable. This intentional business arrangement between two or more entities to create and share to provide value creation for an audience is present in every local community. More and more supplier diversity programs are looking at collaborative partnerships to help drive results.

TIP

You may be asking, "Where's this entrepreneurial ecosystem in my community?" Well, it's not a formal group that holds meetings or memberships. Rather, it's an informal collective of agencies with the same mission. To get started, think about organizations and agencies in your community who work to help small and diverse businesses — chambers of commerce, colleges of business, city/county economic development offices, supplier diversity colleagues at other organizations (private or public). Or consider the local and regional offices of federal resources such as the SBA, small business development centers (SBDC), or minority business development agencies (MBDA). Then, there's any number of independent advocacy groups that may target by demographic group, experience, and so on. This shared mission makes them the perfect partners for your supplier diversity efforts.

As the African proverb says, "If you want to go fast, go alone. If you want to go far, go together." Effective partnerships leverage the strengths of each partner and apply them strategically to support the mission. It may take more work, and it may take longer, but strong partnerships build the relationships, shared understanding, and collective focus to make lasting change.

In this chapter, I discuss creating partnerships, engaging those stakeholders appropriately, finding the right partners at all levels, and forming councils to support your mission.

Building Allies and Alliances through Collaborations and Partnerships

Collaborations and partnerships are indispensable for quality decision making on strategic initiatives and economic development issues. The ability to successfully bring people together for a common cause represents the pinnacle of leadership in modern society. It can be the most challenging yet rewarding and effective tool you can use to help you create policy and drive change. The challenges with supplier diversity can be complex and exist at a wide range of scales. Increasingly, partnerships represent the solution for issues that involve many stakeholders or require many tasks to address.

Every business ecosystem has collaborators, partners, stakeholders, and allies you can consider. Not only can they provide insights and awareness about the business community, but they can also help you activate your programs and activities. This factor is extremely helpful in extending your reach and giving you the ability to provide services, especially if you don't have the bandwidth or expertise internally.

Partnerships and collaborations are strategic tools that allow organizations to combine forces with other entities so that they can have a greater impact than they can on their own. In order to use them effectively, it's important to understand the differences between them.

Using partnerships

Partnerships are based on relationships between willing entities formed to address shared objectives. Partnerships usually consist of two or more parties who join forces to achieve common goals. They work best when the common goals are better achieved together rather than separately and there's a tangible benefit to all partners.

You may consider a partnership with a local business school to provide low- or no-cost consulting to business owners. The business school wants to increase its community engagement, and you're able to provide valuable business training. Or, you may even consider a partnership with an internal department (yes, you can have internal partnerships) to conduct weekly virtual sessions on upcoming procurement opportunities. The department can ensure that their message gets out to the community, and you're able to ensure that small and diverse businesses get access to the information they need.

Using collaborations

Collaborations are based on processes. They allow you to leverage the collective expertise of collaborators to find solutions to challenges or problems. They tend to be more formal arrangements and focus on the long term. Participants can represent a broad range of backgrounds and interests and maintain their independence but still have the same goal as you.

You may consider collaborative ad-hoc committees that quickly address a short-term issue and then disband shortly thereafter. Or you may form a committee to take on a larger challenge, developing operating guidelines and creating comprehensive strategies to support and advance your goals. You may also consider a standing arrangement, where you frequently meet to discuss long-term issues on an ongoing basis.

Reasons to consider partnerships or collaborations (or both)

Working with a variety of organizations has tremendous value, one of the most important aspects being understanding the community landscape and its behaviors (see the nearby sidebar for an example of how I experienced this one). The following are some other reasons to consider collaborations and partnerships:

>> **Active engagement:** They function best when all participants actively engage.

>> **Variety of perspectives:** They encourage input and understanding from a number of perspectives.

>> **Learning through listening:** People learn a lot when actively listening, even when — especially when — opinions and ideas challenge their own.

MEETING THE COMMUNITY WHERE (OR WHEN) IT IS

I remember planning to hold a networking event to meet the small and diverse businesses and business leaders in the community. At most places I've been, I'd hold events in the evening to accommodate attendees' schedules, so I planned this one accordingly. But as we got closer to the event, I noticed that the RSVPs weren't coming in as I'd hoped. I began to get alarmed; we'd sent invites to over 100 people and had only received about 20 responses.

When I asked a colleague at one of my partner agencies what was happening, he chuckled and advised that many of the larger businesses preferred to do events during the day rather than after 5 p.m. He explained that by that time, most people were headed home to their families. He reassured me that they may eventually come around, but it'd take some time.

I ended up doing the event with few people in attendance. (I like to call it an intimate event.) But he was right. In a few months, as I got to know more people in the community and their comfort level grew, they eventually started coming to evening events. I also made adjustments in how we coordinated events so that we had evening events once or twice a year only. Having a family of my own, I understood the desire to be with them after a long day.

>> **Growth:** Partnerships offer new opportunities to build relationships; learn about new tools, resources, and programs; and expand your network. Speaking of which . . .

>> **Network expansion:** Partnerships help you gain champions and allies that can work on your behalf, even when you're not in the room.

REMEMBER

Collaborations and partnerships rarely emerge on the fly. They're the result of time and careful consideration. Those two factors bookend a series of other key elements to ensure that they're effective:

>> **Leadership:** Community partnerships are leader collectives. My colleague wrote that "leadership is to communities as chocolate chips are to cookies: the more the better." If that's the case, then partnerships are the batter holding the chips in place.

>> **Aligned vision:** Each participant must be pursuing the same essential goal. This alignment doesn't mean they're committed to the same outcomes, approaches, values systems, and the like. In fact, disagreement about these

can be healthy for the group. But the partnership must be moving in the same general direction — your direction.

>> **Roles, responsibilities, and accountability:** Identifying clear roles for participating members and their responsibilities reduces confusion and clarifies the group's effectiveness. Additionally, pinpointing clear roles and responsibilities helps with accountability. When partners understand how their contributions add value and can see whether others are meeting their roles, it creates opportunities to provide accountability.

>> **Framework for culture and values:** Developing a framework for how you'll work together is crucial, especially for partnerships tackling a bigger, longer-term issue. Roles and responsibilities can fall here, but the framework generally covers items like meeting ground rules, decision making, behavioral expectations, conflict resolution, and overall goals and purpose. A poorly managed partnership is the fastest way to damage your credibility and get people to disengage from what you're doing.

>> **Communication:** Strong and consistent feedback keeps the wheels of understanding and progress turning. It's also one of the easiest things to achieve, especially today with the availability of smartphones, social media, and so on.

Planning for Engagement

With your partners, you have to spend time mapping and planning your engagement strategy, communication plans, and how much support you may need. The time you spend on this planning stage directly impacts your overall success.

Through positive engagement with your collaborative partners, you should be able to improve the quality of your outcome because stakeholders can provide important and often unknown information as well as support after communication takes place instead of putting obstacles in the way of progress.

WARNING

If you don't identify and manage/engage the correct stakeholders effectively, they may not be aware of all the things you're doing and assume that your program isn't yielding results. This breakdown can lead to the worst possible scenario: that your program is considered a failure.

TIP

Partner or stakeholder mapping provides a useful project management tool for understanding your relationships. The aim is to make the best possible use of partnerships to further your business aims. One way to manage engagement is through a tool called Mendelow's Matrix, which identifies stakeholders' value according to their power, influence, and interest in the organization.

The first step is to create a list identifying the stakeholders you need to engage with and identify their power and interest levels (let's face it, although we're passionate about what we do, not everyone has the same level of enthusiasm). This list can include community leaders, supplier diversity colleagues, internal departments, senior leaders within your organization, the small and diverse business community (check out the sidebar below for more on building a database), and new small and diverse businesses.

Next, to manage stakeholders, map them according to the matrix (see Figure 14-1). Identifying those with both the highest power and highest influence shows you the relationships to focus on. These may be partners that provide financial support or are critical to provide services or training. You want to keep these high-value stakeholders fully engaged and on your side. In contrast, those with low power and low interest aren't worth exerting a lot of energy on. Keep them engaged, but use a minimum effort.

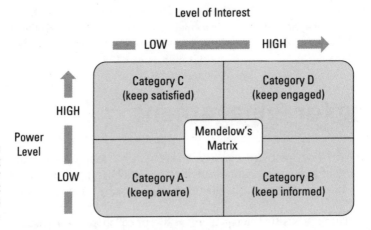

FIGURE 14-1: Managing stakeholder engagement using Mendelow's Matrix.

How you engage a particular stakeholder depends on where in the matrix they fall:

>> **Category A (low power, low interest):** Keep in touch with stakeholders in this quadrant from time to time and ensure that they're aware of what you're doing, but don't go wasting too much energy on them.

>> **Category B (low power, high interest):** These stakeholders can become a distraction. Keep them informed, but don't show them too much attention. Otherwise, you risk wasting effort that's unlikely to bear much of a result.

>> **Category C (high power, low interest):** The idea is to keep these stakeholders satisfied but not hassle them too much. Their low interest levels mean that they may quickly become bored with you or your program.

>> **Category D (high power, high interest):** These stakeholders deserve the most attention. Your aim is to keep them fully engaged. Your business success depends on them!

REMEMBER

In all cases, you should monitor stakeholders to see whether their power or interest levels rise or fall. Adjust your strategy accordingly.

Finding the Right Community Partners: Local, State, Regional, and National

Gathering partners for your program depends on what you're planning to do and what type of support you need them to provide. A good strategy is to have collaborators from every level — local, state, regional, and even national. Identifying all procurement and supply chain stakeholders at the beginning helps you understand impact at each stage in the process. The key to managing these stakeholders is building relationships and doing your homework on the function, needs, and wants of both groups.

Your partners may also vary by function:

>> An *upstream partner* is engaged at each point in the process. For supplier diversity, your upstream partners are the agencies, prime (tier 1) partners, subject matter experts, internal departments that you collaborate with to deliver your programs and events, and so on.

>> The *downstream partner* receives services. Your downstream partners in supplier diversity are the small and diverse businesses or internal departments that receive services or training from you.

REMEMBER

Classifying partners this way is likely a minor part of your supplier diversity big picture, but it may help you determine what type of support you need and make your pitch a little stronger as you approach partners at each level.

The following sections outline some of the community partners to consider at each level. *Tip:* The local level provides the most resources and potential partners for you. It's also likely to allow you to create the greatest impact. Nonetheless, I list the others as information and potential sources.

Local

Local stakeholders are broadly divided into two categories: internal or external. *Internal stakeholders* include departments and senior leaders. *External stakeholders* refer to those outside the direct employ of the organization, including the following:

>> Small and diverse businesses

>> City/county governments

>> Local businesses (non-diverse/prime)

>> Chambers of commerce (Black, Hispanic, Asian, LGBTQ, veteran)

>> Economic development authorities

>> Higher education institutions/colleges of business

>> Advocacy agencies such as women's centers and veterans' centers

>> Grassroots organizations and nonprofits focused on small and diverse business development

>> Other organizations

State, regional, and national

Stakeholders in the state group are a broader group, from the suppliers of materials and services to delivery, logistics, and customers and consumers. The regulations of government and local bodies and the actions of competitors also make them connected stakeholders in this process.

Managing regional and national stakeholders is more complex and may require some innovative communication and collaboration techniques, such as the following:

>> State, regional, and national branches of economic development agencies:

- Small Business Administration (SBA)

- Small Business Development Center (SBDC)

- Minority Business Development Agency (MBDA)

- Service Corps of Retired Executives (SCORE)

>> Third-party advocacy groups

Creating and Using Supplier Diversity Councils to Drive Efforts

A *council* is an assembly of stakeholders specially organized to act in an advisory or administrative capacity to provide consultation, deliberation, or advice. Unlike a collaboration or partnership, which helps with implementing and activating your programs, a council can be an effective resource to provide input and recommendations on strategies to help your program. You can think of them as an informal board of directors directing your program at a high level.

The following sections discuss a few ways to use councils. You may choose to have one and then add other councils as your program grows. Having a joint council should be a long-term goal because it brings together everyone for the good of your program's success.

Internal councils

Internal councils may consist of colleagues and senior leadership. They can help determine policies that can be implemented to improve responsiveness to small and diverse businesses. These councils can also help you gain support for your program within the organization. Internal councils may include representatives from procurement/facilities, finance, DE&I, corporate communications, and, if you can manage it, someone from the senior leadership team.

External councils

External councils may consist of small and diverse businesses, community leaders, prime partners, and resource partners to help you understand the needs of the business community.

It's perfectly fine for external councils to meet, at a minimum, twice a year. They should include high-level decision makers, community entrepreneurial and economic development leaders, and "mature" diverse business owners who can see their roles on this council as going beyond their narrow business interests with the company.

Joint councils

As your program progresses, you may choose to have a *joint council* comprised of both internal and external members to help maintain and expand your efforts. Your council makeup may depend on what your needs are at the time. For example, if you need internal support, you may have more internal participants. If you need more external resources, you may opt to have more external participants.

REMEMBER

The benefits of creating a cross-functional team are that each group gets to understand the perspective of the other. Sometimes hearing it from someone other than yourself can help to get the message across, even if they're just reiterating what you've likely been saying.

SOME QUICK (AND FREE) WAYS TO BUILD A SMALL AND DIVERSE BUSINESS DATABASE

Following are some quick (and free) ways to build a small and diverse business database:

- Check your state's Department of Transportation list.

- If applicable, check your state's Office of Small Business Diversity for certified names.

- Get cards from events and add them to your database.

- Create an "opt-in" option on your website.

- Check with supplier diversity colleagues (you can also send information to them to share with their networks).

5

Using Technology and Compliance to Enhance Supplier Diversity

Chapter **15**

Telling the World About Your Supplier Diversity Efforts

Increasingly, organizations are recognizing communication skills as a leadership and management imperative. Employees and stakeholders demand a greater sense of purpose and meaning from the organizations they align with. Communicating a strong story is part of that. It tells the story of where an organization has been, where it's going, and what its challenges are. Storytelling isn't just pushing out facts or entertaining; it's an opportunity to engage and empower.

Communication is an essential skill just like the ability to get buy-in, round up stakeholders, plan, organize, and make decisions for the program, and it provides the foundation for you to do those things. As both the leader of the program and the head change agent (one of the hats of supplier diversity I discuss in Chapter 5), you have to use the power of narrative to set out your series of program actions. Because of this imperative, successful programs are placing a higher value on interpersonal communication skills.

This chapter discusses why telling supplier diversity's story is so important and how to develop a communication plan.

Understanding Why Communication Is Crucial in Supplier Diversity

Communication plays a crucial role in all aspects of a business. Organizations have traditionally used public relations teams who pushed out scripted information that painted the organization in a positive light or passed on what the organization wanted people to know. As consumers and the public grew weary of the PR spin, organizations had to rethink their communication process, and they began to embrace storytelling as a part of their communication strategy.

In supplier diversity, communication is crucial for two reasons:

>> **Relationship building is an essential part of the supplier diversity management (SDM) model.** Communication and business storytelling are necessary vehicles to help build rapport, create understanding, and remove barriers. Having positive business relationships enables you to be more collaborative and more productive at work, creating relationships that have a desirable effect on the bottom line. See Chapter 3 for details on the SDM model.

>> **As the saying goes, if you don't tell your story, someone else will.** Imagine someone without your knowledge about supplier diversity or your relationships with the small and diverse business community being able to make decisions about your program or influencing your outcomes. Whether securing buy-in or organizational support from senior leadership or coordinating collaborations with stakeholders and departments, telling the story of the small and diverse businesses you're working with builds empathy and reiterates why supplier diversity is an important part of your organization's strategy and your community's entrepreneurial ecosystem.

I remember getting a call from an organization looking for help increasing engagement with small and diverse businesses. During our initial meeting, the company prepared an elaborate presentation outlining all the events it participated in and the programs it conducted. It seemed committed to its supplier diversity program and was taking active measures to engage with the small and diverse business community. The presentation was actually very impressive.

The company's concern was that it wasn't getting the response it'd hoped and that the program wasn't growing fast enough. Its efforts weren't landing with businesses for many reasons. The organization clearly had a lot of activity, but I asked the representatives two questions that seemed to change their whole perspective: "How do people know what you're doing, and what incentive do they have to engage?"

I told them to think about how hard staying in the loop about everything that goes on in their city or even within their organization was for them. Small businesses are inundated with invitations to bid, information sessions, everyday minutiae — anything that's going to give them an advantage and help them grow. During the COVID-19 pandemic, the messages increased tenfold to include barrages of invites to sit in on endless Zoom sessions promising to help their businesses. If you're a small business, how can you attend sessions when you have to work? After a while, the constant messaging becomes counterproductive. Instead of feeling empowered, businesses feel overwhelmed and exhausted.

It was then — ding ding ding — that the light bulb went off. (I love this moment.) They could clearly see why a communication plan was necessary to develop messaging that resonated with small and diverse businesses and deliver it in the most efficient way possible, leaving those businesses feeling like the opportunities with their organization were worth investing their time and energy.

Developing a Supplier Diversity Communication Plan

Communication can be internal or external. With internal communication, you're dealing with departments, collaborative partners, and senior leadership. With external communication, you're dealing with small and diverse businesses, external stakeholders, and resource partners. You may have different goals and messaging for each:

» Internal

- Get buy-in and support

- Inform stakeholders of activities

- Introduce departments to businesses, capabilities, and so on

- Tell the stories of your program and small and diverse businesses

» External

- Inform businesses and stakeholders of your program, activities, events, and so on

- Communicate business opportunities

- Build engagement and community

- Establish your program as an entrepreneurial resource

Your communication plan may look different depending on what you're doing, what you want to achieve, and who you're targeting. Whether it's promoting an event or just keeping stakeholders informed on what you're doing, your plan and the tactics you use may vary.

Whether you're outsourcing your communication or doing it internally (see the nearby sidebar), you can find many articles that provide numerous steps to create a communication plan. But I like to keep things simple, so I've narrowed it to four steps:

1. **Establish your goals.**

2. **Identify your target audience.**

3. **Determine your message.**

4. **Create a tactical plan/method.**

The following sections cover each of these steps in more detail.

Establishing goals

Think about the goals for your communication plan. What do you want to convey, and how do you want it to be received (that is, do you want the recipient to take a specific action).

To establish communication goals, start by breaking them into shorter frequency timelines — daily, weekly, monthly/quarterly, and annually. How frequently do you want to communicate with your audience, and what mediums will you use? I usually do something like the following table. Then I can create a plan for each level of frequency.

Daily (short term)	Monthly/quarterly (long term)
Goals: Build awareness; inform	Goals: Inform; increase partnerships
Weekly (short term)	Annual (long term)
Goals: Build engagement; inform	Goals: Inform; get buy-in and build long-term support

Defining target audiences

After you establish your goals (see the preceding section), you want to define your target audience for each.

When defining your target audience, use your discretion to determine who needs to receive communication. The object is to make sure that the audience stays informed and engaged, not overwhelmed.

How frequently you give an audience information depends on what you're communicating. For example, you probably don't need to inform senior leadership of every workshop you conduct or event you attend. However, a report that summarizes activities, utilization results, program highlights, and so on for the quarter may be more appropriate. I talk about this a bit more in the later section "Creating a tactical outreach plan."

Daily (short term)	Monthly/quarterly (long term)
Goals: Build awareness; inform	Goals: Inform; increase partnerships
Audience: Small and diverse businesses; anyone	Audience: Internal departments; community stakeholders; senior leadership; collaborators/partners
Weekly (short term)	Annual (long term)
Goals: Build engagement; inform	Goals: Inform; get buy-in and build long-term support
Audience: Small and diverse businesses; prime partners	Audience: Senior leadership; internal departments; community stakeholders; small and diverse businesses; prime partners; collaborators/partners

Identifying key messages

Think about the actual messages you're communicating to each group. What messages are going to resonate most strongly with your key audiences? This can be an upcoming event, an outreach meeting, a bid opportunity, an information session, a networking or matchmaking event, or a program awareness campaign.

TIP

In determining your key messaging, stick to messages that are important to the audience at that time.

Daily (short term)

Goals: Build awareness; inform

Audience: Small and diverse businesses; anyone

Messaging: We are a resource to help you; upcoming workshops, outreach events, bid opportunities, and opportunities to meet key purchasers; entrepreneurial resources and information

Monthly/quarterly (long term)

Goals: Inform; increase partnerships

Audience: Internal departments; community stakeholders; senior leadership; collaborators/partners

Messaging: We are a resource to partner and collaborate with; upcoming events; quarterly utilization reports; awards and recognitions; vendor spotlights

Weekly (short term)

Goals: Build engagement; inform

Audience: Small and diverse businesses; prime partners

Messaging: We are a resource to help you, and here's how we help you; upcoming workshops, outreach events, bid opportunities, and opportunities to meet key purchasers; entrepreneurial resources and information; opportunities from prime partners; bid opportunities from partner agencies

Annual (long term)

Goals: Inform; get buy-in and build long-term support

Audience: Senior leadership; internal departments; community stakeholders; small and diverse businesses; prime partners; collaborators/partners

Messaging: We are a department that delivers results for the organization; annual utilization reports; summary of performance; awards and recognitions

Creating a tactical outreach plan

Your *tactical*, or *activation plan* is where you put things into action and answer key questions like how you get your messages to your audiences and what materials you need to develop to do so. As you move from daily to weekly communication, the goals change, and the messages become more targeted. With your daily communication, your audience may be more generalized, and you're using social media to build program awareness and inform about your program, upcoming events, and so forth. With your weekly communication, your audience is more targeted and may include businesses that are already in your database or that you've met at outreach events. Here, you're providing more specific information that may be of benefit to them.

REMEMBER

Today's supplier diversity programs should have an active and engaged social media presence. Most entrepreneurs these days get their information from social media, word-of-mouth, or targeted campaigns. They aren't reading ads in the paper or waiting on faxes to get information. In fact, by the time they see that information, it's likely yesterday's news.

The digital environment provides a number of tools to take advantage of to reach small and diverse businesses, such as email automation, social media scheduling, and design templates, that can help you create professional, polished materials. Your outreach and materials should be a reflection of your image and brand as a professional department. They should convey to vendors and other stakeholders that you're a professional and a relevant business resource and to your senior leadership that you're a department worthy of continued investment.

Daily (short term)	Monthly/quarterly (long term)
Goals: Build awareness; inform	**Goals:** Inform; increase partnerships
Audience: Small and diverse businesses; anyone	**Audience:** Internal departments; community stakeholders; senior leadership; collaborators/partners
Messaging: We are a resource to help you; upcoming workshops, outreach events, bid opportunities, and opportunities to meet key purchasers; entrepreneurial resources and information	**Messaging:** We are a resource to partner and collaborate with; upcoming events; quarterly utilization reports; awards and recognitions; vendor spotlights
Medium: Social media	**Medium:** Email blasts
Weekly (short term)	**Annual (long term)**
Goals: Build engagement; inform	**Goals:** Inform; get buy-in and build long-term support
Audience: Small and diverse businesses; prime partners	**Audience:** Senior leadership; internal departments; community stakeholders; small and diverse businesses; prime partners; collaborators/partners
Messaging: We are a resource to help you, and here's how we help you; upcoming workshops, outreach events, bid opportunities, and opportunities to meet key purchasers; entrepreneurial resources and information; opportunities from prime partners; bid opportunities from partner agencies	**Messaging:** We are a department that delivers results for the organization; annual utilization reports; summary of performance; awards and recognitions
Medium: Email blasts	**Medium:** Email blasts; digital magazine; annual reports (printed and digital)

UTILIZING PUBLICATIONS THAT SPECIALIZE IN SUPPLIER DIVERSITY

In addition to efforts in your local community and using advocacy groups (if you're a member), there are several national magazines and websites that specialize in supplier diversity. They can be very helpful to get messaging out to suppliers and to demonstrate to senior management that you're connected to industry resources.

MBE Magazine (https://magazine.mbeforyou.com/)

Supplier Diversity TV (YouTube) (https://www.youtube.com/c/SupplierDiversityTV)

Diversity Inc. (https://www.diversityinc.com/)

Diversity Plus (https://diversityplus.com/)

Supplierty News (https://suppliertynews.com/)

Chapter **16**

Establishing Supplier Diversity Metrics, Benchmarks, and KPIs

"That which is measured improves. That which is measured and reported improves exponentially."

—KARL PEARSON

As organizations have begun to pay more attention to the supplier diversity function, the importance of tracking, reporting, and compliance to help tell the story has become front and center. In this age of continual improvement, adopting formal processes to monitor and manage this portion of supplier diversity was only a matter of time.

This attention created a small but growing industry focused on technology-based supplier diversity solutions. These systems oversee program results and automate a number of functions and tasks, which, as Karl Pearson's famous quote indicates, allows you to make decisions to continually improve and expand your program. The introduction of technology has simplified the process and has definitely been a boon for the supplier diversity industry as a whole.

In this chapter I discuss the role of technology in monitoring program metrics, benchmarks, and key performance indicators (KPIs).

Understanding the Importance of Metrics, Benchmarks, and KPIs

Throughout this book, I discuss the importance of evaluating program effectiveness from a holistic, 360-degree perspective, considering the value your program delivers rather than looking only at utilization. However, you can't completely disregard quantifiable metrics to gauge your program results.

Metrics measure activity, performance, or results. They provide straightforward information about what your organization is spending with small and diverse firms. The right metrics support your program and your story. (I talk about this later in the chapter.)

TIP

If you don't measure a process, you don't have a benchmark for what constitutes "better" or "worse."

The quote at the beginning of the chapter gives a high-level outcome from measuring performance. But measuring supplier diversity results is a necessary function for far more compelling reasons:

>> Serves as an early warning system and allows you to be proactive

>> Helps you understand drivers of successes and failures

>> Help you make decisions

>> Confirms your results and leaves no doubt about what you've done

>> Helps you sell your ideas and gain allies

>> Can be the basis of process or continuous improvement plans

>> Allows you to compare yourself to a tangible standard

>> Helps you set individual and team objectives

>> Presents results in a way organizations understand (the universal language of business in dollars and numbers)

REMEMBER

Without metrics, your results are just your opinion. Opinions are great during brainstorming, but organizations can't make long-term decisions based on them.

Establishing Metrics, Benchmarks, and KPIs

The following sections take a look at some things to consider when establishing metrics, benchmarks, and KPIs. If your program is new, you may want to stick with basic metrics. Then, as it matures, you can add in benchmarks and KPIs to really understand how efficiently you're using your resources to achieve results.

Metrics

Metrics are basic points of information to understand whether the organization is achieving supplier diversity program objectives. The most common is spend/utilization. Table 16-1 covers some common metrics.

TABLE 16-1 **Common Supplier Diversity Metrics**

Metric	Description
Spend/ utilization	Tracks how much your organization spends directly with small and diverse suppliers. Calculated as a percentage of your total spend (for example, if total organizational spend is $1 million and small and diverse spend is $100,000, small and diverse business spend is 10%).
Risk	Looks at the depth of diverse suppliers by spend category and evaluates opportunities to increase spend with diverse suppliers. Also looks at spend categories where you may have too many suppliers *(overindexing)*.
Impact	Involves measuring the impact your program has on the long-term sustainability of diverse businesses in your community.
Trends	Includes looking at positive growth trends in utilization as a result of your efforts.

Benchmarks

A *benchmark* is a standard or point of reference you can compare or assess things against. Benchmarks can be internal or external. In supplier diversity, they can include comparing and modeling your program after that of another organization of similar size/industry or examining how another department is able to encourage engagement across the organization. You need to determine which benchmarks are most meaningful to your organization. The questions in Table 16-2 can help.

TABLE 16-2   **Generating Meaningful Supplier Diversity Benchmarks**

Benchmark	Questions
External	**By industry:** How do our program policies, activities, results, and so on measure against other programs in our industry?
	By program length of time: How do our program policies, activities, results, and so on measure against other programs that have been around as long as ours?
	By community: How do our program policies, activities, results, and so on measure against other supplier diversity programs in our community?
	By organization: What organization/programs do we want to model ourselves after? What organization/program has the results we want to achieve?
Internal	How do our internal in-reach and engagement efforts compare to those of other departments?

KPIs

Key performance indicators (KPIs) are measurable values (quantitative or qualitative) that determine how effectively a team or organization is achieving its business objectives. In supplier diversity, you may use KPIs to understand whether you're utilizing your time, budget, and resources on the right strategies, tasks, and tools to achieve your program goals. You can also establish KPIs for each step in the supplier diversity management (SDM) model, as indicated in Table 16-3. (See Chapter 3 for details on the SDM model.)

REMEMBER

KPIs are different from metrics (see the preceding section) in that KPIs look at your overall efficiency to achieve results rather than at just the result itself.

KPIs can differ depending on the organization. I like KPIs that start with actionable verbs — words that require physical action to accomplish and complete. This approach is also more specific about what needs to get done. Using the SDM model, Table 16-3 shows a few sample KPIs to consider for your supplier diversity program.

TABLE 16-3   **KPIs for Supplier Diversity Objectives**

KPIs	Description
KPIs for internal processes	Review the number of new diverse businesses registering in our system
	Access the number of diverse businesses that respond to solicitations and do win/don't win
	Review utilization increases/decreases in each of our spend categories
	Evaluate the number of diverse businesses procurement personnel meet with on a monthly basis

KPIs	Description
KPIs for external processes	Examine the engagement of diverse firms participating in the program
	Access the number of new diverse firms participating in the program
	Review the number of new partnerships with external organizations
	Review the number of new programs created and events held
KPIs for supplier development	Assess the capacity of businesses versus the previous year
	Review the number of diverse businesses that win/lose contracts after receiving training
	Review the number of introductions to key decision makers within the organization
	Review the number of new diverse businesses participating in programs and events
KPIs for compliance and reporting	Review the number of diverse businesses at the tier 2 level
	Review engagement of stakeholders in the program: prime partners, senior leadership, community collaborators, and so on
	Review the impact/value the program has delivered to the diverse business, organization, and/or community

Seeing How Software Can Help You Manage Your Program

Ask anyone working in supplier diversity about their most dreaded function and they'll likely say reporting. In the past, generating monthly or quarterly reports required poring over mountains of data from legacy systems that weren't implemented with supplier diversity reporting in mind and then piecing the data together to create a semblance of a cohesive report that accurately told the story about what was happening in your program. This required you to be a whiz at Microsoft Excel and could take weeks of your time to decipher. It never took into account lag indicators or changes, and you were never sure whether the information was correct (because of how businesses were labeled, what constituted a diverse business in your system, and so on, but I digress). The bottom line is that if it sounds miserable, believe me, it was.

Thankfully, as every aspect of people's work and personal lives have become tech-enabled, software to manage most phases of the SDM model has improved tremendously, making this process less cumbersome and tedious and more efficient, accurate, and immediate.

Using technology can help you effectively manage your supplier diversity program. Many providers have created tools to help with everything from supplier onboarding, certification management, and sourcing other qualified diverse suppliers to event management dashboards and supplier relationship management (SRM) integration. Technology provides real-time visibility into each supplier's performance criteria.

With supplier diversity, you have three ways to adopt and integrate software:

>> Making it part of the existing procurement enterprise resource planning (ERP) system

>> Creating a custom supplier diversity tracking system

>> Getting an off-the-shelf system that interfaces with the existing system

Some of the most common procurement ERP systems, such as Jaeggar or SAP, have added supplier diversity modules because of the increased demand for supplier diversity analytics. Most organizations don't have the time or in-house capability to create a custom program. That leaves the off-the shelf options. Though many of these are cloud-based and require an ongoing financial commitment to maintain, the advancements and functionality they provide make them a worthwhile investment. Of course, this investment depends on your organization's commitment, budget, and program needs.

Here are a few software options focusing on various functions within supplier diversity — reporting/analytics, matchmaking and research, and consulting and training. I also added a new category: reporting transparency, which has been a hot trend in supplier diversity. The website listed is the only one that tracks organizational program results.

>> **Software for data analytics and compliance**

- Coupa (www.coupa.com)

- SupplierGATEWAY (www.suppliergateway.com)

- Supplier.io (www.supplier.io)

- B2G Now (www.b2gnow.com)

- Quantum SDS (www.quantumsds.com)

>> **Software for matchmaking and supplier sourcing**

- Hire Ground (hireground.io)

- Supplier.io Supplier Explorer (www.supplier.io/supplier-explorer)

>> **Software for research, consulting, and professional training**

- The Hackett Group (`www.thehackettgroup.com`)
- Supplier.io (`www.supplier.io`)
- Supplier Diversity Training Institute (`sdti.co`)

>> **Software for reporting transparency**

- Tapinda (`www.tapinda.com`)

Using Metrics to Tell Your Story

In Chapter 15, I talk about telling the world about your supplier diversity efforts. In addition to what you're doing from a supplier development perspective, your metrics give a more complete picture of how effective your efforts are.

What's your organization's story?

Your supplier diversity story is one that validates that your program works! Using metrics, you can demonstrate that your program gets results when compared to peer organizations and even industry leaders or best-in-class programs. You want to show that your program is worth continued investment and that it's having the desired impact on the diverse business community.

Table 16-4 illustrates an example report. It looks at basic metrics I cover in Table 16-1 earlier in the chapter — spend/utilization, risk, impact, and trends — and compares how an example program ranks versus a peer organization and the industry leader or a best-in-class program.

TABLE 16-4 **Sample Metric Comparison Report**

Metric	Reporting company	Peer	Industry standard
Spend/utilization	30%	20%	50%
Risk (category saturation which indicates room for growth)	10%	5%	20%
Impact (growth of diverse businesses)	25%	10%	30%
Trends (growth year versus prior year)	10%	5%	20%

Here are the example program's metrics:

- **Spend/utilization:** $300,000 spent with diverse business/$1 million total procurement spend = 30%

- **Risk:**
  - Goods and services: $90,000 spent with diverse firms/$200,000 total spent on goods and services = 45%
  - Professional services: $10,000 spent with diverse firms/$100,000 total spent on professional services = 10%
  - Construction: $200,000 spent with diverse firms/$700,000 total spent on construction = 29%

This company is overindexing on construction and goods and services and underindexing in professional services. This discrepancy represents room for growth. The company may want to consider doing more to analyze the situation and the available opportunities (the number may be low for many reasons). Then it can identify a target utilization goal and create programs to achieve the goal.

The risk applies when you look at the number of firms the company is utilizing in each category. Take professional services . If one firm represents the entire 10 percent, the company's utilization in that category becomes zero if something happens to that firm (it goes out of business, gets acquired by a non-diverse firm, or whatever). Ideally, you want to spread your utilization among several firms, not just one or two representing the majority of your diverse spend.

REMEMBER

The totals for all your categories should add up to the total amount spent with diverse businesses in your spend calculation. In this example, $90,000 + $10,000 + $200,000 = $300,000, which matches the total spend in the previous bullet.

- **Impact:** Here, you may consider what's happening with the businesses individually by comparing the current period with the previous period. Look for any changes in activities, contracts awarded, contract amounts, bonding capacity, hiring (full-time, part-time, and independent contractors), and so on. This is a multi-step process and will require you to get information from each business individually in order to get an aggregate or collective number. In the following example, you can see the impact that one additional contract (whether direct or as a subcontractor) can have on a business:

Business XYZ	2021	2022	Change
Contracts awarded	2	3	+1 or +50%
Contract amounts	$100,000	$200,000	+100%
Bonding capacity (if applicable)	$150,000	$250,000	+67%
Hires/Total employees	2	3	+1 or +50%

Note: I realize doing this for every vendor is a time-consuming proposition. You may consider doing this for firms you've identified as long-term partners or as part of a coaching program.

>> **Trends:** Again, compare the current period with the previous period (I recommend month or quarterly). Look for any changes in activities and so forth that may have contributed to the difference. If you see an increase versus the prior period, keep doing what you're doing. If you see a decrease, consider changing your tactics. You can calculate using a trend analysis model like this one:

Percentage change = Current year amount − Base year amount

TIP

Comparing your organization's performance to peer industries helps you make the case for why your program should continue to exist and what value it brings.

What story are you telling?

Almost every organization today has some form of storytelling on its website, whether that's blogs, articles, whitepapers, webinars, or something else. It's another method of stating your facts and figures in a way that's interesting and relatable and that motivates people to take action. Organizations have embraced this tool as a way to authentically craft their own narratives rather than wait for others to put their spin on them.

REMEMBER

In supplier diversity, you tell many stories to different audiences. Whether you're telling stories about your organization to the public or telling the stories of diverse businesses to internal departments, your ability to use metrics to convey these stories is an essential part of your communication plan.

I remember taking a storytelling course for business professionals around the time when storytelling as a business tool was becoming very popular. I realized I could apply all the makings of a great novel — identifying the hero, creating the main plot, and crafting the plot twists, key messages, and the ending — to supplier diversity:

>> Hero = Diverse business; organization

>> Main plot = Problem

>> Plot twists = Challenges

>> Key messages = Solutions; efforts

>> Ending = Result/outcome

In the preceding section, I mention that the right metrics should support your program and your story. Well, your stories should also support and validate your metrics. Metrics provide evidence — not just anecdotal observations — about your performance, which helps reinforce your story ending or result. In Table 16-5, I look at which metrics to include in your report based on what story you want to tell and which audience you're telling it to.

TABLE 16-5   **Metrics for the Story You Want to Tell**

Audience	Key takeaway or outcome	Story focus	Performance Metrics to Include
Diverse businesses	Engagement and inspiration	How diverse businesses can succeed with your program	Trends (businesses growth versus previous year) Contracts received
Internal departments	Utilization of diverse businesses; collaboration	Impact on diverse businesses Impact on the organization	Spend Impact Trends
Community stakeholders	Collaboration	Impact on diverse businesses Impact in the community Organization's commitment to diversity and economic equity	Impact Economic impact in the community (may require additional resources for research)
Senior leadership	Support and investment	Impact in the community Organizational impact (increased sales, lower cost of goods sold, increase in innovation, and so on)	Spend/utilization Risk Impact Trends

Are your metrics getting in the way of the story?

Before getting started, think about your audience, what you want to communicate, and what action you want/need from the audience after it receives this information. Table 16-5 in the preceding section gives you a quick breakdown of some of these options.

Make sure that your story is high-level (try not to get too far in the weeds) yet still informative. Too much information overwhelms, and you may lose people's interest. Too little information leaves them confused, which causes inaction. Find the right balance. Try to avoid using industry jargon and acronyms, but if you must, make sure that you have the appropriate explanation.

TIP

Here are some questions to ask yourself when you're using metrics in your reports:

>> Are you using both the positive and negative aspects of data to make your business case?

>> Are you using metrics to paint the "true picture" for your team's performance?

>> Do you have the basic foundation to give management high confidence in your team's ability to perform at industry standards?

>> Are you highlighting key best practices your team has incorporated?

- » **Tackling the tiered procurement system**

- » **Recognizing your role in mediating subcontractor relationships**

- » **Working with tier 1 vendors to encourage diverse utilization**

- » **Identifying why tier 2 data is so important**

Chapter **17**

Understanding Tier 2/Subcontracting Spend

"Do what you do best and outsource the rest."
—PETER DRUCKER, MANAGEMENT CONSULTANT, EDUCATOR, AND AUTHOR

Procurement and contracting can be complex and complicated. It's a necessary environment that supplier diversity professionals have adapted to as the supply chain has become more dynamic and global. At the end of the day, no matter how intricate it is, procurement is tasked with finding the required goods and services at the best price.

For small and diverse businesses, this environment doesn't always allow opportunities, particularly high-dollar contract opportunities, to organically occur. Sometimes you have to get creative. That's where subcontracting comes in. Subcontracting, or *tiered procurement,* has become one of the most important tools to create opportunities, increase utilization, and build capacity for small and diverse businesses. Yet it remains one of the most confounding and underutilized tools to track and report spend by organizations.

This chapter explains subcontracting/tiered spending and its importance to supplier diversity.

Tracing the History of Subcontracting

Subcontracting is the practice of bringing in an outside company or individual to perform specific parts of a business contract or project. Your organization awards contracts to *prime* contractors/partners. They subcontract a portion of a project, usually very specific tasks, in order to complete it. On large projects, subcontracting can provide access to professional expertise, allow you to realize better pricing, ensure that projects are completed in a timely manner, and introduce new vendors to your organization. It has become a standard process across public and private procurement, especially on large, multitasked projects. Yet, as I mentioned at the opening of this chapter, it remains a tremendous challenge and one of the things I get asked about the most when consulting with organizations.

Supplier diversity began focusing on subcontracting as a tool to drive diverse business growth during the late 1970s and early 1980s. Businesses were ready to scale from the smaller contracts that they had been relegated to, prompting organizations to study the barriers that prevented diverse businesses from winning larger, more substantial contracts and getting ahead. Looking at contracting vehicles, they focused on the construction category for a couple of reasons:

>> **Construction represented the largest category for most organizational procurement spend.** Although it accounted for only a few projects a year, it made up for that volume in total dollars spent, awarding millions upon millions in new building construction, renovations, and so on and eclipsing other categories by miles.

>> **The tasks involved in construction made it a perfect environment for subcontracting.** Construction consists of very specific tasks that smaller tradespeople had the expertise to complete but for a long time were closed off from opportunities to do.

Despite the desire to work on larger projects, most diverse businesses lacked the connections, financial footing, and experience on large construction projects required to win contracts. Organizations realized breaking down projects to be small enough for diverse businesses to participate would be a project management and procurement nightmare and wasn't the most cost-effective or efficient way to build and manage a large project. Further, most organizations didn't have the in-house expertise or bandwidth to manage several small contracts in a fast-paced construction environment all at once.

This realization occurred around the time construction management was becoming more popular, especially in public procurement. *Construction management,* or CM, is the management of a construction project on behalf of the owner. The CM replaces the general contractor and is paid a fee. In turn, the CM competitively bids or submits a proposal. They're awarded the project and paid a fee to hire and pay subcontractors to perform the work, creating a tiered model (head to the following section for more on those tiers).

This new format was embraced as a new way to build construction projects across the country. Solicitations were updated looking for construction management firms with experience managing the entire building process, not just constructing the building itself (although most construction management firms have people that hold general contractor licenses). Many general contractors began rebranding their companies as construction management firms in order to compete and respond to this new model.

For organizations, it was a win. They could get experts to build and manage their projects according to their budget specifications. They could also heavily influence their conditions to award. For supplier diversity program leaders, this was the perfect time to advocate for the inclusion of diverse businesses. And passing this task on to the prime contractors made sense: It let primes do the heavy lifting, and then supplier diversity practitioners could work collaboratively with them to enforce and ensure compliance. This system became a game-changer and ushered in a whole new era of policies around inclusion. It also gave diverse firms the opportunity to get their feet in the door on large construction projects.

REMEMBER

Subcontracting only works when the project scope is large and has distinct tasks that can be performed by another business without impacting the quality or final cost while still being profitable for a subcontractor to perform. Some organizations have created tiered programs around other procurement categories such as professional services, usually with mixed results.

The things that make subcontracting a great option also create a challenge. As you add a tier, you add another firm to the mix, inserting another level of responsibility and liability. In order to gain some control over the subcontracting process, some organizations put rules in place. The level of oversight and the guidelines really depend on your organization. Rules vary from limiting the percentage of the project that the prime contractor can self-perform to reviewing subcontractor bids to ensure that they're competitive and the organization is getting the best pricing. They may even prohibit selling the contract or subcontracts to another firm without prior approval. You usually see this level of oversight with public procurement agencies where taxpayer dollars are involved or on a high-profile project.

Stepping through the Levels: Tier 1, Tier 2, and Beyond

As I discuss in the preceding section, the advent of subcontracting introduced the tiered system of procurement. The tiers represent the supplier's proximity to the client or end user. Thus, the contract flow is between the organization and the prime contractor (tier 1) to manage the project. Contracts between the prime contractor and the respective trade contractors or suppliers performing the work are considered tier 2 and are independent of the organization. These tiers can go down several rungs.

The following sections take a look at each of the tiers and their relationship with your organization. Figure 17-1 also provides a visual overview of the common tier 1 and tier 2 setup.

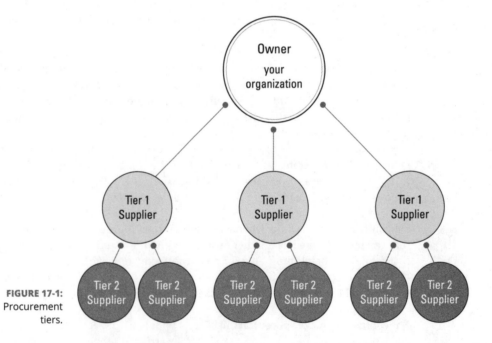

FIGURE 17-1: Procurement tiers.

Tier 1 suppliers

Tier 1 suppliers are partners, or primes, that you work, contract with, and pay directly. This category constitutes the largest part of your spend. Tier 1 supplies can be anything that you buy directly from a supplier such as promotional items, office supplies, financial services, training, or catering.

Tier 2 suppliers

Tier 2 suppliers are those that perform work or sell supplies to a tier 1 or prime partner. Tier 2 suppliers provide tier 1 suppliers with their prices to perform work or provide services in support of a project or contract.

REMEMBER

Because tier 2 can count toward diverse business utilization, your organization may set rules outlining how the tier 2 subcontractor is used, such as how it acquires materials or whether it's actually performing the work. With materials, the question is whether the supplier is an authorized reseller or distributor that's been approved to resell items or an intermediary or *pass-through* (a diverse business put in place to facilitate or "front" the transaction, allowing goods and services to be passed through its business). It works the same with services, although depending on the services provided, suppliers may find limited opportunities to subcontract to another firm.

Many organizations count only utilization performed by diverse firms that are certified, verification issued by an approved third-party provider that the supplier is at least 51-percent owned by a person representing a historically underutilized demographic. A number of certifications are available. Ensure that there's a standard for certifications and that everyone is accepting and tracking the same thing.

Tier 3 suppliers

Tier 3 suppliers may be hired as a subcontractor by tier 2 suppliers to perform work. This becomes a contractual arrangement between tier 2 and tier 3 and is one step further removed from your organization. They follow the same guidelines as tier 2 suppliers (see the preceding section), and their utilization can be tracked and reported to tier 2. A tier 3 supplier might be hired by a tier 2 supplier if, for some reason, the tier 2 is not able to perform the work. The tier 2 supplier is still responsible for making all payments and ensuring timely delivery and quality of work performed by the tier 3 supplier. This utilization can count toward diverse spend; however, it gets a bit tricky (see the warning in the next section).

Tier 4 suppliers and below

Tier 3 suppliers may also hire subcontractors — *tier 4* suppliers. That contractual arrangement is between tier 3 and tier 4 and is yet another step further removed from your organization. Tier 4 can contract tier 5, and so on.

At this level, things get a bit gray for both sides.

>> For organizations, the project becomes harder to manage, and the quality of work and data may become questionable. Some organizations may frown upon tiers going down past tier 4 or prohibit selling the contract to another supplier.

>> For the supplier, very little profitability may be left by the time you get to tier 4. The vendor may feel taken advantage of or exploited, not only by the contractor that hired them but also by your organization. Even though it's not your contract directly, it can become an issue for you if things go wrong.

For instance, suppose client A is planning to build a new office building for $20,000,000. They award prime contractor A (tier 1) the contract and set a 20 percent goal, which means that at least 20 percent, or $4,000,000, of the contract should be awarded to diverse firms. Prime contractor A awards several subcontracts to build the project. They award a subcontract for $2,000,000 to subcontractor B (tier 2) to perform work. The contract with subcontractor B represents 10 percent of the total contract and 50 percent of the total designated spend. Each month, the prime contractor reports this information to client A to let them know the subcontractors they've awarded contracts to, how much they're being paid, and so on. Unfortunately, by the time the project gets to his scope of work, subcontractor B is working on another project and his team is not available. Rather than cancel the contract, subcontractor B looks for another team to perform the work. They contract with subcontractor C (tier 3). If, for some reason, subcontractor C is unavailable, they can either cancel the contract with subcontractor B (tier 2) or subcontract it to another firm, subcontractor D (tier 4), and so on.

The upside for the client is that the work continues to get done, but at what cost? As you can see, as you add tiers, subcontractor manageability is more challenging. For the supplier, as they go further down the tier, the less profitable the project becomes. From a reporting perspective, your reports rely on receiving good information from your prime (who is now relying on getting information from subcontractors). I'm not saying it's all bad, but as suppliers go further downstream, there's very little incentive for them to be meticulous about every detail, including making sure that you have good data. (Head over to Chapter 19 where we discuss reporting in detail.)

Subcontracting only works when the project scope is large and has distinct tasks that can be performed by another business without impacting the quality or final cost while still being profitable for a subcontractor to perform. Some organizations have created tiered programs around other procurement categories, such as professional services, usually with mixed results.

Managing Subcontractors and Tiered Procurement

Although a contract between a prime contractor and a subcontractor doesn't directly reside with you, that doesn't mean that you can't assist and advocate on the subcontractor's behalf if issues arise. In fact, your advocacy doesn't necessarily end after a vendor gets a contract with a prime contractor, especially if that vendor is new to the process.

Depending on the type of contract, issues always come up — delayed payments, poor treatment on the project, unjust termination — that may need a third party or unbiased ear to come in and mediate. Although you're the owner/client, in this instance, you're also that third party. Your goal is harmony on the project so that it can be completed in a timely manner. If subcontractors are unhappy, that may disrupt the project and impact your outcome. Further, it sends a message that you don't support diverse businesses working on your projects (you're the bigger fish here). You've heard the saying "bad news travels fast?" Well, whether the issue is your fault or not, disgruntled subcontractors can be bad for your project and your program. By no means should intervening be construed as coddling or patronizing. You're there to ensure transparency and, again, that the process *and* the experience are equitable and fair.

Some organizations have mixed feelings about intervening and mediating in these situations. They feel that the contract is between the prime and the subcontractor, not them. I've worked in organizations where this mindset was the norm and the approach to settling disputes was hands-off. I've also worked in organizations where I was encouraged to intervene if situations couldn't be resolved at their level. In my experience, mediating is part of the advocating process. It's an opportunity for all parties to feel heard and to resolve their issues. I see it as a means to help keep the peace and keep projects moving along.

Because subcontracting and tier 2 programs have become such a big part of organizational procurement process and an important component in your overall supplier diversity strategy, turning a blind eye and not assisting with resolving issues is almost impossible. It's also a necessary part of the compliance process. You're not only monitoring the project for compliance (ensuring they're meeting your utilizing goals) but also making sure that subcontractors are treated fairly. Fortunately, this outcome is the one everyone is working toward. But it's also good to know that as long as diverse businesses are working with your organization, your advocacy can extend as far as it needs to.

Your organization may want to see that primes have programs in place to mitigate problems such as prompt payment clauses, stipulations that prohibit a subcontractor's removal without an explanation of just cause or your approval, or even their own diversity person to act as a liaison with you.

Influencing Your Prime Vendors to Use Diverse Suppliers

Subcontracting and tiered procurement has many benefits all around and can be an important part of your overall supplier diversity program. Your prime partners are your best allies, and getting their support and buy-in for this phase is key.

The benefits of getting your prime partners involved include the following:

>> Provides another layer of opportunities for small and diverse businesses.

>> Allows them to mirror your commitment to supplier diversity by creating subcontracting opportunities for small and diverse businesses.

>> Strengthens and expands the pipeline of subcontractors able to compete on projects.

>> Provides mentoring support for subcontractors.

>> Increases the capacity of small and diverse firms, which drives business sustainability.

>> Creates opportunities for diverse vendors to enter into partnership or teaming arrangements, which helps strengthen relationship building.

>> Facilitates joint-venture projects to create a record of past performance on projects of increasing size, complexity, and so on. (**Note:** These are long term arrangements and may require legal input.)

Many organizations provide incentives for prime partners that can demonstrate and articulate their commitment to supplier diversity and diverse business development in their proposals. You may consider giving bidding priority points to those that can show their past performance and future commitment to this effort. When prime partners know that's a priority for you, they'll make sure that you know it's a priority for them as well.

A strong tier 2 program starts with working collaboratively with your prime partners. The more time you're able to spend mapping and planning an engagement strategy and communication plans for vendors, the more successful you'll be in impacting your overall success.

Because lack of access to information is one of the areas that supplier diversity tries to address, coordinating events that provide as much information as possible is crucial. One thing that has worked in making this information available is coordinating joint events such as a "pre" pre-bid for subcontractors to discuss the project and hear about opportunities specifically for smaller vendors. Vendors are able to ask questions that they may not want to discuss in a room full of seasoned contractors.

Another program, if you have enough time, is a project-specific accelerator. These are in-depth learning programs that go over everything a vendor needs to get qualified to work with the prime partner. Many multinational primes that work all over the world have programs such as this.

Knowing the Importance of Tracking and Utilizing Tier 2 Data

Reporting tier 2 data is an important part of capturing your overall spend, but it can also be a tricky one. That's likely because you're depending on the reporting of other people — prime contractors — to get this information. What you're able to put out depends on what you put in. Think of it like running a marathon. You're not likely to do well if you load up on pizza, burgers, fries, and soda the week before. Just like with your own systems, if your prime partners don't have the right systems in place and you're collecting the wrong/inaccurate information from them, you end up preparing incomplete or flawed reports that add no value to what you're doing and don't capture the full story of your efforts. Without good data, you can't optimize your program and convince stakeholders to support you.

REMEMBER

Every organization has goods and services it buys in order to operate. But the nature of your business and what you buy determines the type of vendors you require. This may create fewer opportunities for smaller vendors to enter your procurement pipeline directly. Here are some reasons tracking this data is important for your program (and why every organization needs to have a tier 2 program):

>> Helps supplement your program, especially while you're working to increase direct opportunities within your organization

>> Provides a truer picture of the real impact your program has within the community

>> Provides additional opportunities for vendors

>> Builds hands-on experience in preparation for direct opportunities

You can read more about developing a tier 2 tracking and compliance plan in Chapter 19.

Chapter **18**

Getting a Grip on Goal Setting in Supplier Diversity

S etting goals is a fundamental function of business, and it requires intentional thought, emotion, and behavior. In supplier diversity, the goal is the specified utilization with small diverse firms. *Goal setting,* which is usually expressed as a percentage of total spend, has become the industry-wide standard for measuring utilization and compliance.

In this chapter, I cover the importance of goal setting, how organizations set goals, and how a disparity study can play into the process.

Aligning Supplier Diversity Goals with Procurement Strategies

Organizational supplier diversity doesn't happen in a vacuum. It starts in procurement, but increasingly organizations are connecting it to other parts of the organization, such as diversity, equity, and inclusion (DEI) or community relations. Wherever supplier diversity is housed, its goals should first be aligned with the strategic goals of procurement because of those departments' interdependent nature.

Looking back at the purchasing department of yore

Purchasing departments have always been around, but unlike the procurement department of today, they originally were primarily there to get other internal departments what they needed in order to do their jobs for the organization. Over time, purchasing became a bureaucracy. Its practice was to go to the regular sources, get what it needed, keep the departments happy, and never shut down because of a lack of some critical product or service. Negotiating price was often secondary to assuring supply.

During the 1990s, things began to change as globalization increased competition and reduced organizations' ability to simply pass on cost increases to consumers, who now had more choices. Without the ability to raise prices more easily, companies had to generate greater profitability by becoming more efficient through technology, particularly information technology and the (then new) Internet, as well as by rethinking key functions. Purchasing was ripe for change.

Working within the strategic sourcing model: It's all about the bottom line

Globalization increased competition and put downward pressure on prices (as I explain in the preceding section), but it also allowed organizations to source goods and services globally, often for significant savings. The realization that supply chains can become more efficient through globalization confirmed for senior leaders that purchasing departments can become a source of profitability and not just an internal service bureaucracy. This is how strategic sourcing was born.

Strategic sourcing is an approach that allows a supply chain manager to use information other than price or cost to make decisions to align purchasing strategy to business goals. When strategic sourcing was introduced, it was a dramatic redesign of the stodgy purchasing department into an organization that can generate a measurable increase in an organization's profitability.

The key differences between strategic sourcing and purchasing are in expectations and in relationships. As strategic sourcing developed, corporate procurement wasn't just expected to buy what internal customers needed; it now had to buy products and services that met the requirements of internal consumers at the lowest possible prices. The old saying that a penny saved is a penny earned made the potential to increase profitability a reality even when compared to the sales function. Organizations began to look at procurement and purchasing through a very different lens, with a new expectation that procurement would focus on generating profits.

REMEMBER

When a company increases sales by one dollar, only a fraction of that dollar makes its way to the bottom line because of cost. But when a company reduces its cost by one dollar, all that reduction can make its way to the bottom line.

The relationship between procurement and its internal customers began to change. Effective strategic sourcing that generates profitability now got a seat at the table and was no longer considered overhead. In fact, organizations are now known for the quality of their supply chains, which are the result of this focus on strategic sourcing.

REMEMBER

Strategic sourcing has had a major impact on supplier diversity. Organizations have shifted the focus from just transactional purchasing to procurement and strategic sourcing, specifically tasking procurement to make money through cost savings. Some of these cost saving techniques have put significant pressure on all suppliers but particularly diverse suppliers.

Historically, suppliers sent their invoices to their customers and offered those customers terms so that if the organization paid the supplier within 10 or 30 days of receipt of the invoice, the supplier would offer a discount off the bill. Now organizations are dictating terms to their suppliers. Forget 10, 30, or even 90 days; strategic sourcing companies routinely put their contracts in 120- to 180-day terms. In effect, many companies with these extended terms have made and sold the product before paying the suppliers. Essentially, their suppliers are financing their customers.

Strategic sourcing also works on the premise of forcing suppliers to compete for the business. Suppliers of many corporations are expected not only to give the most competitive pricing now but also to lower their prices over the life of a contract. Some companies expect buyers to save amounts of money multiple times — even ten times — their salaries. In these situations, supplier diversity professionals find themselves in an environment of intense cost saving pressure.

REMEMBER

Supplier diversity goals in this environment must acknowledge the dominance of strategic sourcing in the company. This fact means that you as a supplier diversity professional may have multiple goals. You must increase the amount spent with certified diverse businesses while also saving your organization money in the process. These twin goals of growth in diverse supplier spend and saving money mean that you have to successfully communicate to the diverse supplier community that being diverse simply isn't enough. Successful suppliers must also be cost competitive, as I explain in the following section.

Helping diverse suppliers become more competitive: A win for everyone

TIP

One way to accomplish the competing goals of supplier diversity I lay out in the preceding section is to help potential diverse suppliers fully understand their own competitive environment. Suppliers often lose more bids than they win. When diverse suppliers lose bids, debrief them to let them know why they lost. If it's pricing, the diverse supplier now knows it has to "sharpen its pencils" the next time around. And perhaps more importantly, it now has valuable market information that can lead to changes in its company — changes to its strategy, supply chain, technology, production processes, or management. Well-managed diverse suppliers will take this information and become stronger competitors.

REMEMBER

The goals you set must be consistent with the goals of procurement/strategic sourcing, or you — and perhaps the entire supplier diversity department — will be shut down or ignored. Having reasonable but aggressive supplier diversity goals given the culture and goals of procurement is the only way you create sustainable relationships with your procurement colleagues.

Setting Goals with a Disparity Study

Ever since the landmark *Croson v. Richmond* case in 1989, state and local governments that establish supplier diversity goals, preferences, and (in some cases) quotas must demonstrate that those programs are necessary because of laws and practices that had a *disparate impact* on (discriminated against) the beneficiaries. Otherwise, white-owned firms can successfully sue the states and cities and stop these programs on the grounds that *they're* being discriminated against. The only counter for these reverse discrimination claims is data that shows harm to diverse businesses.

As mentioned in Chapter 2, with the *Croson* decision, states and cities across America began a mini-industry of companies that conduct disparity studies. The goal of the *disparity study* is to inform the state or city whether a disparity exists between the utilization of diverse businesses and the potential utilization of diverse businesses. The more specific the study, the better.

Corporations or private entities don't have the same level of judicial scrutiny that those in the public sector do. Most corporations can buy from whomever they want. One major exception is companies with federal contracts — for example, Department of Defense (DOD) contracts for products that must have American content. Contractors can't build submarines for the U.S. Navy using steel made in China, no matter how inexpensive that steel is.

But although private corporations don't have to conduct disparity studies for legal protection, some may use them to measure how well they're doing given market conditions. As the supplier diversity professional, you can conduct private internal disparity studies, which can be powerful tools as you make analytical decisions. This internal document can show how many diverse suppliers are in particular commodities, how many of those diverse suppliers your organization is using, and which products or services it's most likely to source with diverse suppliers. A disparity study may also help you create a valuable dashboard that you can share with procurement professionals and others. An understanding of these market conditions helps put goal setting into perspective.

A well-designed disparity study first includes an identification of the market. This market identification is both geographic and commodity-/service-specific. It determines the number of potential diverse suppliers that can compete for public sector contracts. Obviously, the bigger the geographic market, the more diverse suppliers it has. But the geographic size of the market must reflect how particular industries operate. For example, the market for plumbers is local. Most plumbers don't drive 100 miles in crowded urban markets for business unless the contract offers exceptional opportunities. Software companies, however, may be national or global. These differences are important to determine the number of viable diverse businesses that can compete for public sector contracts.

A second component of a well-designed disparity study is a review of the organization's policies and practices to see whether actions and activities are inherently biased against diverse suppliers. These practices may include things like only speaking to trade groups that don't have diverse representation or only sending out RFPs (request for proposal) to the local chamber of commerce or other organizations that may not have good diverse business representation. These policies and practices are things that you'll likely change if the disparity study shows disparities do exist because of these biases.

The results of the disparity study show where disparities are by race, ethnicity, and gender and for which categories of goods and services. For example, it may reveal that Black carpenters are underrepresented and show evidence of past discrimination against this group. The same study may also show that Hispanic carpenters aren't underrepresented. These results may lead you to establish goals and preferences for Black carpenters but not for Hispanic carpenters.

DISPARITY STUDIES IN ACTION

Harold Washington, the former mayor of Chicago, made the development of minority businesses a priority for his administration. It may be urban legend, but the story goes that when he was elected, he established very aggressive set-asides for Black and Hispanic businesses. He was told that without a disparity study, the City of Chicago would be sued. His response was that a lawsuit would take time, and during that period he was going to create scores of Black and Hispanic millionaires.

Well, he was sued and was forced to change the city's program. The new, redesigned program established local preferences that the courts didn't consider to be unjustified racial preferences. Most states, counties, and cities don't want to get sued, so they're inclined to conduct disparity studies to avoid being dragged to court like this.

Setting Goals without a Disparity Study

Corporations don't have to conduct disparity studies to create preferential programs (see the preceding section), but their supplier diversity goals still have to come from somewhere. Most corporations set their supplier diversity goals based on historical data and more anecdotal factors such as their perceptions of market opportunities for diverse suppliers and where they think firms in their industry are with their own goals:

>> **Current utilization:** One of the first things you should do when considering goals is to conduct a baseline analysis to determine your organization's current utilization of diverse suppliers. If the company is spending 2 percent of total spend with diverse suppliers without the support of a supplier diversity program, a realistic goal may be to grow that to 5 percent over some specified period. If the company is starting at 5 percent, 10 percent may be a good target.

>> **Perception of market opportunities for diverse suppliers:** After analyzing current purchasing activity, you may realize that some categories of spend that don't utilize diverse spending easily can. This type of analysis, often called a *spend analysis,* can be very helpful as you establish corporate supplier diversity goals.

>> **Competitor analysis:** When one organization is successful in supplier diversity, other companies in the same industry want that same success. The *Billion Dollar Roundtable* (BDR) is one example of this idea in supplier diversity.

The BDR is a national organization made up of the leading corporations in supplier diversity, each spending at least $1 billion annually with certified diverse suppliers. It began with fewer than 10 companies, but as of this writing, it has 28 companies, who spend a combined $115 billion with diverse suppliers. At this time, some industries are very well represented. The automotive giants GM, Ford, Toyota, and Honda are members, and several other large automakers have stated corporate goals to join.

REMEMBER

Many, if not most, U.S. corporations with supplier diversity programs never become members of the BDR because their total spend is simply not large enough. However, that doesn't stop companies from competing with each other to achieve success in supplier diversity. Advocacy organizations like the National Minority Supplier Development Council (NMSDC) and the Women's Business Enterprise National Council (WBENC) provide ample opportunities for corporate supplier diversity professionals to come together to compare notes and share information. The NMSDC has industry groups whose expressed purpose is to share best practices that grow diverse business spend with their members. This cooperation and competition create an environment where companies learn how to establish supplier diversity goals without formal disparity studies.

Meeting Utilization Goals versus Adding Value

Organizations judge supplier diversity professionals on their ability to accomplish the goals of diverse business utilization alongside the organization's strategic sourcing goals. When you can do both, you unquestionably add value. If you do neither, you probably aren't going to survive the next round of corporate cost-cutting. But other, secondary goals can help you add value for your company.

REMEMBER

Being an ambassador for the company can be a source of significant value. In the process of doing your job, you're networking with stakeholders outside the company's walls. Supplier diversity professionals are often asked to serve on the advisory boards of supplier diversity organizations. These roles are opportunities for the company to change consumers', competitors', and the government's perceptions of it and increase its presence in the market.

This is particularly true when problems come up that put the company in a bad light. Dr. Fred McKinney, a leading authority and historian on supplier diversity, shared a poignant story about the power of adding value during an unlikely situation:

I remember as president and CEO of the Greater New England Minority Supplier Development Council, I had a corporate member in construction management. They had an incident on a worksite where a white worker hung a noose from a beam near where one of the Black workers was stationed. The incident made the front page of the paper. I got a call from the company's supplier diversity professional asking for my assistance. Together we planned a public response that included the CEO of the company who flew into town to announce an appropriate response but also to share with the community the commitment to supplier diversity. In the press conference, the company could give concrete examples of diverse suppliers who were part of their supplier diversity program who were working on the site. After this, I often told corporate members that having an effective supplier diversity program can be a powerful insurance policy when faced with negative public information.

Another way to add value is to facilitate access and exposure to other senior corporate leaders who come together to discuss supplier diversity. In a meeting with leaders in the automotive industry, the CEO of Johnson Controls spoke about how his supplier diversity leader had tried to get him to attend a meeting of an automotive industry group within the NMSDC. When he (reluctantly) arrived at the meeting, he was surprised to realize that many of the chief procurement officers of his largest customers were part of it. He quickly began to view the supplier diversity professional in a different light because of the value and insights gained from meetings such as this one.

WARNING

You need to constantly look for opportunities to add value to the organization beyond the goals of utilization and cost savings. But make no mistake: If you don't meet utilization and strategic sourcing goals, these other valuable activities aren't enough to sustain you or the program.

Chapter **19**

Tracking, Measuring, and Reporting Metrics in Supplier Diversity: It's All in the Numbers

racking, measuring, and reporting on the work you do is the last part of the supplier diversity management (SDM) model and provides a window into supplier diversity, especially to those who don't work with you every day. (I talk about the SDM model in Chapter 3.) You know how people say the devil is in the details? Well, the numbers tell the tale. Your numbers tell the story that confirms what you've been evangelizing and advocating. Even if the news isn't great, it should still provide you with the information you need to move forward.

In this chapter I discuss methods for assessing both diverse spend and the impact it has on the larger community, issues that often come with reporting, and what and how you should communicate with senior leaders and community stakeholders.

Tracking Diverse Spend

Tracking diverse spend is an important function for supplier diversity professionals. Without measuring what your organization buys, who you're buying from, and how much you're spending, you can't determine whether your efforts are effectively accomplishing one of your primary and most visible goals of supplier diversity.

Using certifications to identify diverse businesses

REMEMBER

The ability to accurately track diverse spend starts with knowing who your suppliers are and whether they fall into the designated categories (that is, diverse or non-diverse). To get started, most organizations use *certification*, a process that verifies whether a business is minority owned, managed, and controlled through intensive vetting, document review, and personal/on-site interview. The certifying agency sets the criteria.

Before third-party certifying organizations like the National Minority Supplier Development Council (NMSDC) and the Women's Business Enterprise National Council (WBENC) started, organizations allowed businesses to self-certify that they were diverse. That meant that no matter who they were, if they checked the box (even accidently) that said they belonged to an underutilized group, they were likely going to be in the system as such. Organizations soon realized that relying on businesses to be forthright may not be the most reliable method to confirm their diversity status, especially when the supplier diversity business model hinges on whether a firm is truly diverse.

As supplier diversity programs began formalizing their efforts and putting policies in place that yielded tangible results, businesses learned how to use certifications to gain a competitive advantage and saw real value in being certified. This evolution led to the rise and dominance of third-party certifying agencies.

Today, these agencies provide a valuable service to the supplier diversity community by establishing a set of uniform rules that define what classifies a business as diverse. Certification from NMSDC (for ethnic and racial minorities) and WBENC (for women) centralizes this function for the corporate world, which means a business doesn't need to get certified by each organization it may work with. Although certifications can vary by industry (corporate or government), each uses the same standard to define a diverse business. Can you imagine if every organization had its own definition of what qualified as a diverse business? That's a door best left closed.

Third-party agencies target mainly organizations and help them identify diverse businesses that want to sell to them. Unfortunately, NMSDC and WBENC certification doesn't work for most government organizations (although WBENC recently partnered with the Small Business Administration [SBA] to offer an interagency certification for women-owned businesses). States, cities, counties, and the federal government's Department of Transportation require different certifications to prove diverse status. For example, diverse businesses must show NMSDC and WBENC certification to private organizations, Disadvantaged Business Enterprise certification for state Department of Transportation contracts, state certification for state contracts, and municipal certification for city and county contracts.

On the one hand, the fact that diverse businesses commonly have several certifications with a number of agencies helps them expand their businesses by becoming more competitive and appealing to a wider range of clients, which is good thing. But it's also ironic and inefficient because 99 percent of the information required by these various public and private certifying bodies is the same. A universal certification accepted by all organizations would be so much simpler. I guess that's what they call the cost to be the boss.

Organizations often find out which of their suppliers are diverse by asking all suppliers to register in databases on their organizational websites. These databases collect certification information and other business details so that when those suppliers are awarded contracts, their spend can be identified by their certification status. Some of these organizational databases allow uncertified businesses to attest that they're minority owned, operated, and controlled in lieu of having third-party certification, but organizational members of NMSDC and WBENC don't generally accept this practice when they request reports from these large organizational suppliers.

REMEMBER

Organizations require spend data on diverse businesses because they want to know, but they also collect this information because others want to know. Many times those others are other organizations who are customers or potential customers. Organizational contracts often ask organizational bidders on large contracts to report to the potential buyer information about their supplier diversity programs. This is known as tier 2 spend, which I cover in more detail in Chapter 17.

Large organizations doing business with all levels of government are often asked to report on their spending with diverse businesses. This demand for data is another major reason organizations track diverse spend. Depending on the priorities of the administration in office, the federal government pays close attention to how much large prime federal contractors spend with diverse businesses. Contractors who don't meet the company's and agency's established objectives can lose business with that agency or face other sanctions.

Identifying diverse spend based on accounts payable reporting

When you understand the why of tracking spending with diverse businesses, you need to understand the how.

Tracking diverse spend should be based on payables to diverse suppliers. Seems like a simple enough definition, right? But companies often contract with suppliers, both diverse and non-diverse, for unspecified times and amounts. For instance, I currently have a contract with a large company that commits to pay my firm up to several thousand dollars at an agreed upon hourly rate for my services. I've had the contract for several months, and it's good for several years, but I haven't received one purchase order yet. I suspect some companies are counting such contract values as spend, although I'd argue they shouldn't be.

REMEMBER

Spend occurs when a business submits an invoice to the corporation and a payable is created, not when the business signs the contract, particularly a contract like the one I've just described.

Most large organizations have sophisticated enterprise software programs that link purchasing with accounts payable. These systems track purchases by individual sourcing managers/buyers; commodity; the number of contracts with a particular supplier; and race, ethnicity, gender, and other characteristics of the supplier. As the supplier diversity professional, you should have diverse spend data accessible to you on demand so that you can generate reports on demand for organizational customers and government clients. Systems that are set up with this need in mind save a lot of manual work in the future.

Because many organizations set up their enterprise systems without thinking about supplier diversity, many of them use third-party companies to review a company's supplier database so that the company can identify diverse suppliers within its supply chain. Some of these third-party diverse supplier database companies also offer spend analysis when they have access to a corporation's accounts payable systems. But because organizational accounts payable data is sensitive, most large companies don't outsource this function, which means you get to do the spend calculations.

TIP

The best time to build supplier diversity identifiers into the database is when your company is changing enterprise software or updating existing software.

Measuring the Impact/Success of Supplier Diversity Efforts

When organizations started their supplier diversity programs, the primary measure of success was total spending with diverse suppliers. This is still the most recognized measure of organizational success in supplier diversity, but it's no longer the only measure. Today, organizational leaders also want to know what impact their supplier diversity efforts are having on society at large.

Looking at economic impact

As companies get more experience with supplier diversity, they learn that a dollar spent with one diverse supplier doesn't have the same effect as a dollar spent with another diverse supplier. Economists use the term *value add* to measure how much effort goes into transforming inputs into outputs. If one diverse company just slaps its label on a product that it sells to a corporation, the economic impact of that transaction is very different from the same transaction with a diverse company that actually manufactures a similar product. Both transactions may show up as spend with diverse suppliers, but the first may have only a small impact on local or diverse employment, particularly if the product is manufactured offshore.

For this and other reasons, supplier diversity success should go beyond spend and look at the real economic impact of the transactions a program engages in. In my view, economic impact determines success. *Economic impact* (EI) is measured by the effect that dollars spent with diverse suppliers have on employment, tax revenues, tier 2 transactions with diverse and non–diverse suppliers, and general consumption. When a diverse supplier sells to large organizations (or any consumer), it's then able to hire more workers, increase its taxable income, buy more from other suppliers, and have a generally positive impact on the local economy. Organizational supporters of supplier diversity want to be able to point to these impacts as well as the total amount spent with diverse suppliers.

Knowing the importance of context in reporting total spend

Reporting total spend without providing context for that spend can create a problem. Two large companies may have the same total diverse spend but with very different effects depending on whether that spend is concentrated with a handful of large diverse suppliers or over scores of diverse suppliers. One method isn't inherently worse than the other, but they're different.

Concentrated spend with a few diverse suppliers may contribute to the development of larger diverse businesses. However, it may not impact as many diverse entrepreneurs or communities. Dispersing spend with many diverse suppliers spreads the wealth, but it may not be enough to develop larger-scale businesses.

REMEMBER

Well-designed supplier diversity programs should recognize that some of what they spend requires scale and some doesn't. Where you need scale, you may want to have a concentration strategy. Where scale isn't an important competitive factor, you can use the talents of more but possibly smaller diverse suppliers.

Being Aware of Problems in Reporting

Creating a perfect supplier diversity report can be a challenge. No matter your challenge, know that you're likely not alone. Some basic issues, such as inconsistent formatting or styling, can likely be fixed without too much effort. Other issues may require a bit more thought or tools like creating a dashboard and report navigation. To create better, more meaningful reports, you need to know where the problems are and identify the issues that can be holding you back.

Garbage in, garbage out

The old saying "garbage in, garbage out" can be used to describe reporting supplier diversity spend and other measures of success. If your organization doesn't have a good handle on the characteristics of its suppliers, your reported spend can be off by a lot.

A conversation with a colleague demonstrates how certification can impact reporting:

> "I worked with a large healthcare company recently and asked to see a list of its largest diverse suppliers. I knew most of the suppliers on the list and had to inform my client that several of its largest 'diverse' suppliers weren't eligible for certification as minority-owned or woman-owned. The client called the suppliers to 'see for themselves.' And, yup, you guessed it, they were not eligible to be certified. Rather than leaving things as they were or sweeping this issue under the rug, the client ended up removing those suppliers from the list of diverse suppliers and taking a significant hit to their overall total spend numbers. But, they now have a solid baseline to build on."

Counting "self-certified" suppliers

Organizational reporting of supplier diversity spending sometimes counts companies that are "self-certified" or are certified by organizations whose certification processes don't meet any kind of established certifying guidelines or capture companies that shouldn't be certified. A recent client told me that an entrepreneur who was visibly minority didn't feel the need to go through the certification process, but as an alternative he would provide a letter from his lawyer stipulating that he owned, operated, and controlled the business. My client rejected this alternative on the grounds of having no way to know whether the lawyer was being honest.

WARNING

Don't include spend with self-certified diverse businesses in reporting data. Not only does it cause potential headaches, but it's also fundamentally unfair to diverse businesses that went through the process.

Changes at the top that affect eligibility

Businesses change ownership and control, and these changes can hurt or help total spend depending on what (if anything) they mean for diversity certification.

Unfortunately, diverse suppliers don't always admit to these changes, particularly if they come at the risk of losing business. This situation is where systems can be very helpful: to catch when suppliers' certifications expire. Third-party certifying organizations generally require diverse suppliers to prove annually that they haven't had significant changes in ownership that would make the company ineligible for certification. Well-managed supplier diversity programs automate the recertification process to eliminate this problem.

Industry-specific reporting issues

Every industry is a little different in its certification and reporting. The following sections cover three big ones: construction, hospitals, and the government.

Construction

In construction, construction management companies are responsible for interacting directly with the owner of the project (usually large public- or private-sector organizations). Owners usually want diversity on their projects and require that of the construction manager. But often the construction manager doesn't work for the company doing the actual construction. The construction management company frequently hires a general contractor who does some of the work and subcontracts other work to trades (plumbers, carpenters, electricians, painters, masons, and so on). Significant diverse spending on the project often depends on the relationships the general contractor has with diverse firms.

WARNING

Construction projects have a lot of room for slippage in reporting diverse spend if the construction management firm doesn't strongly monitor them. If your company is about to start a major construction project, you need to specifically state to the winning construction management firm what the supplier diversity goals are on the project and which trades they need to use to achieve those goals. You can read more about goal setting in Chapter 18.

REMEMBER

The project owner is usually the one held accountable for diverse supplier participation on big construction projects, even though the owner doesn't pay the diverse suppliers directly or decide which suppliers to use.

Hospitals

Hospitals have an antitrust exemption that allows them to use the services of *group purchasing organizations* (GPOs) — large buying organizations that have hospitals and hospital systems as clients. The GPOs negotiate prices on behalf of clients so that hospitals can lower their costs.

All GPOs have programs that are designed to register certified diverse suppliers that their hospital members can then use. The GPOs make some of their money by charging suppliers a fee based on a percentage of a contract the supplier has with a member hospital. Hospital supplier diversity professionals need to be vigilant about measuring diverse spend that their GPO provides them. Tell the GPO which certifications your hospital accepts and which it doesn't.

Hospitals aren't prohibited from buying outside the GPO. Many smaller, local diverse suppliers may not want to work with the GPO because of the administrative fee. Hospitals now have two ways that diverse suppliers can get into their supply chains: one through the GPO and the other directly. You have to be diligent about managing this complex relationship between the GPO, the hospital, and the diverse supplier so that you're counting all the spend you should be counting (and only the spend you should be counting).

Government

REMEMBER

The federal government's program is really a small business program layered on top of a diverse business program. This setup is different from third-party certifying organizations, which certify diverse businesses regardless of their size.

Therefore, some spend with very large diverse businesses may not be eligible to be counted on federal contracts, even if the businesses are otherwise certified, because those businesses exceed the federal definition of small. Additionally, the federal government doesn't recognize all third-party certifications as of this writing. Some of your suppliers who you encouraged to get certified may now need to register with the federal government in order for your spend with them to be counted.

Large organizations with significant federal contracts need to keep one set of diverse suppliers for the federal government and another for their nonfederal commercial business. This dual system can be extremely frustrating for buyers and category managers who are hearing two very different messages from you, the supplier diversity professional.

Reporting What Matters: Creating an At-a-Glance Dashboard

I'm a firm believer that supplier diversity professionals should create a dashboard that captures the most important measures of supplier diversity success. Every company's dashboard may be different, but here are some of the variables I recommend most companies be able to track by just turning on the computer:

>> Total organizational spend by major category

>> Total diverse spend by major category

>> Total diverse spend by major racial, ethnic, gender, and other demographic

>> Total local business spend by category

>> Total procurement by business unit

>> Planned business spend over the coming six months by category

>> Number of diverse suppliers in the supply chain

>> Number of diverse suppliers registered with the company

>> Total employment of diverse suppliers in the supply chain

>> Ranking of diverse suppliers by quality

REMEMBER

If you can track these variables on demand or daily, you're prepared to report your performance to customers, government, and senior management.

Reporting to Senior Leaders and the Community

As I explain throughout this book, supplier diversity professionals need to be excellent communicators. Two of the most important audiences for this communication are senior leadership and the outside community.

Keeping senior leaders informed

Senior leaders are often in situations where they're caught off guard. They may have a general idea of how the company is doing with supplier diversity, but they don't have a level of detail that demonstrates mastery of the subject when asked a question about it. Senior organizational leaders are expected to know sales, profitability, and strategic initiatives almost as second nature, but organizational supplier diversity isn't on that list (yet).

You need to fully understand the organizational structure within your company because that informs how your information about the program flows up to the

CEO and other senior leaders. Supplier diversity professionals often report to the head of procurement, who typically reports to the head of finance. But now this reporting is often also provided to the head of diversity, equity, and inclusion (DEI), who's often reporting to senior vice presidents or the CEO directly.

REMEMBER

Although senior leaders want to know what's going on, they usually want the condensed version. This is where a dashboard like the one I describe in the earlier section "Reporting What Matters: Creating an At-a-Glance Dashboard" can be very helpful in organizing communications to senior leaders. It's a quick way to see what's taking place. A short quarterly memo summarizing activities and developments with screenshots of the dashboard is a way to organize and prepare for the informational demands of senior management, and it demonstrates a level of professionalism that they'll appreciate and respect. This system ensures that you can address any request immediately with information that's no more than three months old.

Presenting to the public and other supplier diversity professionals

As a supplier diversity professional, you're also expected to report and communicate with the public, including others in your field.

TIP

Opportunities to speak to the community are great opportunities for you to show your talents. You only get one chance to make a first impression. Often these presentations are the first impressions the community or senior leadership have of you. How well you present, how organized you are, and how compelling your story is not only makes the presentation better but also positions you positively for other professional opportunities within the company and with other companies. Supplier diversity covers serious activities, but it's a performance art.

The general public

I recently worked with a large construction company that was bidding on an energy construction project. The energy company was a public utility that reported to a public utility commission. I worked with my client and the supplier diversity team at the company to prepare a presentation for the public utility commission and the team that would make the decision. This setup isn't uncommon.

TIP

Develop a template presentation for public presentations. Think of it as your program's elevator speech.

Generally speaking, your presentation should include the following:

>> A short history of the company

>> Your time/tenure with the company

>> Your professional background

>> Your knowledge of the community

>> Your role in supplier diversity

>> The company's supplier diversity goals

>> The company's supplier diversity successes with examples

The other aspects of your communication depend on who's in the room. Do your homework before speaking to community organizations. I've seen these meetings become volatile and unmanageable. Neither you nor the company wants to be caught up in a food fight.

WARNING

I recommend that you keep community presentations short and guard against being overly salesy. If the community wants more, you have more than information and experience to give them more. A presentation that feels like a sale may come off as disrespectful and insensitive to the realities of the audience, who may not have a "big organizational job."

Supplier diversity professionals

Presentations for other supplier diversity professionals are often very supportive environments that include others in the field who are also trying to develop their skills and expand their networks.

In these situations, your audience often wants an insider's view, demonstrating how you overcame a challenge. I think these presentations should be built around a real case. Of course, you should remove the names, but your colleagues are looking for examples of how you overcame a challenge — and the more wicked the challenge, the better.

6

Building a Career in Supplier Diversity

Examine the education path and skill requirement to become a supplier diversity professional.

Explore the supplier diversity certifications and continuing education programs available. Understand the benefits of investing in career development.

Chapter **20**

Becoming a Supplier Diversity Professional

Supplier diversity can be an enjoyable and fulfilling career. Because of the field's increased visibility and value to the organization and supply chain, supplier diversity professionals can work in almost any sector, including the federal government, local/state government, and corporations. You can find these jobs in any corner of the United States and the world as global markets look to increase diversity in their procurement channels. Supplier diversity's connection to the community and close involvement with stakeholders make it a good career path for young people looking to make a difference in their communities.

This chapter gives you an overview of jobs in supplier diversity, what's required to establish a career, and how the jobs vary by industry. You also get some tips for how to make yourself as attractive as possible to potential employers.

ADVICE FOR NEW PROFESSIONALS INTERESTED IN SUPPLIER DIVERSITY

I often talk to colleagues on their journeys to getting into the supplier diversity industry and their recommendations for new professionals interested in a career in supplier diversity. I had a chance to speak with Dr. Fred McKinney of BJM Solutions. Here's what he advised for new professionals to get started:

"I'm currently consulting with a client that asked me to help them create a position of Supplier Diversity Manager, including writing the job description and showing how this person fits into the existing organizational chart. Professionals interested in a career in supplier diversity should attend supplier diversity conferences, participate in local and national council events, attend supplier diversity professional training programs, get the necessary certifications, serve on boards, get a mentor (preferably one who has been in the industry for a while), and take the time to understand entrepreneurship from a small and diverse business perspective. The industry has done a lot to formalize the process and encourage professionals to consider this industry as a career. They should take advantage of them and use becoming a supplier diversity expert as their north star."

Understanding Job Titles and Job Descriptions

Figuring out how to get started in a career in supplier diversity can be tough. Even professionals who are already working in supplier diversity can find getting the information they need to properly plan a career trajectory challenging. Like most careers, finding the right path starts with three questions:

>> What can you see yourself doing?

>> What are you skilled to do?

>> Will someone pay you to do that?

Just because you choose one thing now doesn't mean you'll do it for the rest of your life. According to career change statistics, in today's fluid job market, the average person changes careers five to seven times during their working years.

Job titles

Supplier diversity jobs and job titles can be confusing, which can make the career planning process a bit of a maze. Even though business inclusion has been around since the 1960s, the term *supplier diversity* is relatively new. Over the years, organizations have adopted many different terms to describe this function so that it's more reflective of what the role is within their companies:

>> **What supplier diversity represents to the organization:** Small business versus economic opportunity

>> **Where it's housed:** Within procurement or in a stand-alone department

>> **What industry they're in:** Federal or corporate

Over the years, I've worked in a number of industries, housed in a variety of departments, each with a different title.

Job description

Job descriptions can make the career planning process a bit cloudy. Earlier in the chapter, I explain how important the job description is in establishing clarity and expectations in the role. Organizations often merge supplier diversity with another title or job function, essentially combining two jobs into one — for example, Supplier Diversity and Inclusion Manager or Supplier Diversity and Sustainability Manager. As I discuss throughout the book, supplier diversity requires more than enough tasks to build an effective program without the pressure of additional responsibilities. However, whether you're comfortable with this structure and accountability is a personal decision.

TIP

Know the keywords or phrases that also signify a job in supplier diversity: *small business liaison, vendor diversity, business opportunity, vendor inclusion.* You may not see the same positions available in every organization.

Looking at Department Structures and Job Functions

Because supplier diversity means different things to different organizations (see the earlier section "Job titles"), the structure of your supplier diversity department and the job functions it entails may vary from one company to the next. The following sections break down these important aspects of supplier diversity as a profession.

Department structures

How supplier diversity departments are structured can depend on whether supplier diversity is a stand-alone department or part of another department. Being part of another department, such as procurement or diversity, equity, and inclusion (DEI), may limit how much support is available for you. In addition to managing the program at the macro level, you may also be responsible for performing all the micro level functions as well. This scenario is when your relationships and collaborative partners are critical to help with carrying out all your programming functions.

As a stand-alone function, you're more likely to have a supporting team, even if it's a lean one (but don't be surprised if you're still a solo act). Supplier diversity never has the same depth or breadth found in other departments. (In fact, in addition to the type of structure, the size of the supplier diversity department can depend on the size of the organization, the size of the market, the types of contracting opportunities with your organization, the availability of small and diverse firms in the market, the level of support needed for supplier development programs, and so on.)

Depending on the job, you may need to do some cross-functional work within the department, such as being a marketing coordinator who's able to write articles, manage social media, and coordinate events or an analyst who can conduct training or assist with events. And if you're at a conference or outreach event, it's all hands on deck. You can see a sample supplier diversity department structure in Figure 20-1.

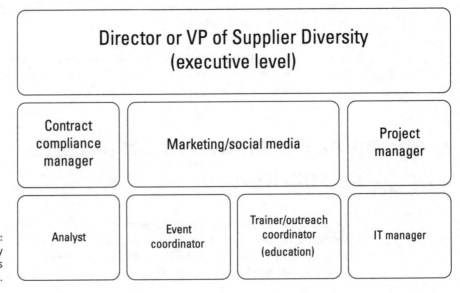

FIGURE 20-1: Supplier diversity careers framework.

Of course, all these factors vary by organization, and you may not be privy to the reasons behind why the structure is what it is. But if you're managing an existing program, understanding how to structure your program can be helpful if you're asked what type of support you need and an opportunity exists to restructure.

Job functions

To make sense of supplier diversity careers, you need to understand the types of jobs that may be available. Here are the job categories most directly related to the tasks involved in supplier diversity:

>> Analyst

>> Marketing/social media coordinator

>> Event coordinator

>> Trainer/outreach coordinator

>> Contract compliance manager

>> Associate director

>> Program manager/director/VP

Other job functions that are also important to supplier diversity include the following:

>> Project manager

>> IT manager

The following list describes what's involved with each of those earlier job categories:

>> **Analyst:** Collects data and prepares reports on diverse supplier utilization and spend.

>> **Marketing/social media coordinator:** Coordinates all internal and external marketing communication efforts and ensures that target audiences are aware of program activities and events, especially the small and diverse business community. This includes website management, marketing materials, newsletters, event management, social media, annual/end-of-year reports, presentations, and so on.

- » **Event coordinator:** Coordinates internal events and external outreach events, including exhibit setup/breakdown, exhibit management, and material delivery.

- » **Trainer/outreach coordinator:** Creates education training schedule and prepares and facilitates in-house training and workshops; coordinates speakers and subject matter experts as needed. Works with small and diverse suppliers to explain the process and opportunities with the organization.

- » **Contract compliance manager:** Manages subcontractor participation on projects. Works with vendors to ensure they're in compliance.

- » **Associate director:** May be the senior position depending on the structure (see the preceding section). Usually found if supplier diversity falls under procurement or another department.

- » **Program manager/director/VP:** Senior position in supplier diversity. Manages all efforts of the program and team. Establishes the strategic vision and goals (in alignment with the organization), finds collaborative partners, and establishes strategic relationships. Interfaces with senior leadership and community stakeholders and works with internal departments on in-reach efforts.

  Note: Some organizations have a Global VP, Senior VP, or National VP of Supplier Diversity, but they're usually large, global organizations with many divisions around the world. Under this structure, they may have regional supplier diversity managers who are responsible for a specific territory or region. Many have a CDO or chief diversity officer, but it's usually a DEI position. However, as the industry continues to evolve and supplier diversity gains increased importance, maybe one day you'll see a CSDO (chief supplier diversity officer). That role would require some experience; a degree in business, public relations, supply chain, or a related field; and maybe even a certification in supplier diversity.

- » **Project manager:** Manages special projects as needed.

- » **IT manager:** Manages IT efforts, including department website, vendor portal (with procurement), and special projects.

REMEMBER

Regardless of the position you were hired for, the more skills you're able to contribute to improve your program and department and raise the professionalism of supplier diversity, the more valuable (and possibly promotable) you become, whether with your existing organization or with another organization.

Supplier Diversity by Any Other Name: Examining Industry Terminology

An important part of understanding supplier diversity jobs and job descriptions is understanding the industry in which you're looking. Different industries use different terminology to describe this function. This section describes each of the sectors and the jobs you may see in them.

These distinctions are important to know because supplier diversity with public agencies can be different from working in private corporations. Some professionals have worked across both public and private sectors, and some prefer working solely in one over the other. Understanding how each differs and identifying the keywords helps you decide which industry best suits your professional needs.

TIP

Look for keywords to describe where the job is. The use of the words *DBE liaison, small business,* or *MWBE* can be an indicator for the industry that the job is in.

Federal government

The federal government is the founding industry for economic inclusion for business. It doesn't use the term *supplier diversity* to describe its programs or positions, but practically every agency within the federal government has an office that focuses on connecting small and diverse businesses to economic and contracting opportunities within the federal government. Some titles you may typically see are these

>> Small Business Liaison Officer

>> Disadvantaged Business Enterprise Officer

>> DBE Liaison Officer

The public sector

Jobs in the public sector include local/state government, higher education institutions, K–12 schools, airports, and some hospitals. Like the federal government in the preceding section, the public sector doesn't necessarily use the term *supplier diversity*. Rather, it focuses on the services it provides or the audience it serves, such as the Office of Business Opportunity or the Office of Minority and Women-owned Business Enterprises (MWBE). Here are some typical titles:

>> Business Opportunity Manager

>> MWBE Program Manager

>> Small Business Relations Manager

>> Small Business Services Manager

Corporations

Today, almost every corporation has a supplier diversity program. You may see a number of different positions or titles to describe the senior level position; the following are some typical ones:

>> VP of Supplier Diversity

>> Director of Supplier Diversity

>> Supplier Diversity Program Manager

Landing a Job in Supplier Diversity

Check any job board, and you can find a slew of jobs in supplier diversity across a number of public agencies, institutions, and private corporations. This abundance is great for supplier diversity because it sends a strong sign that organizations are increasingly making it a central strategy.

As the supplier diversity industry continues to expand, the field becomes more and more competitive, requiring professionals to have specialized skills and the ability to deliver results quickly.

Whether you're already working in an organization, applying for a new position, or transitioning into a new career, the steps to getting your break into the industry can vary. When I began working in the industry, my previous related experience was working for a diverse construction firm on a large project and working as an entrepreneur. I didn't necessarily have tons of experience in supplier diversity, but my experience did frame my thinking around working with entrepreneurs and what they needed, making me a great person to advocate for them to gain access to opportunities.

Now, this was many years ago, and standards have changed quite a bit. But, like any job, the goal is to make yourself as attractive a candidate as possible. This step may include having the appropriate educational background and certifications (I discuss these in Chapter 21), the right interpersonal skills, and relevant industry relationships. Depending on your situation, the following sections discuss ways to make yourself a strong candidate and land your next job in supplier diversity.

Already working in an organization

If you're already working in an organization and you want to transition into a supplier diversity role, your value is your institutional knowledge. You should have a strong grasp on how your organization works and know the internal stakeholders. You should be able to navigate fluidly and continue to build support.

REMEMBER

If it doesn't interfere with your current duties, consider doing some or all the following:

>> Begin working with the team to learn as much as you can about the inner workings of supplier diversity. This can be working on projects, volunteering for events, and so on.

>> Focus on your knowledge of the organization, which gives you the ability to ramp up quickly and deliver results.

>> Become familiar with the small and diverse business community and external stakeholders.

>> Attend workshops or take courses to learn more about supplier diversity.

>> Think about getting certified.

Applying for a new position

If you're considering a new opportunity with an organization, your value is different depending on whether you have previous industry experience. If you're an experienced professional, you may want to focus on your knowledge of supplier diversity, any quantifiable results achieved with your last organization, and your ability to implement an action plan fairly quickly.

If you don't have prior experience, you want to focus on your understanding of small businesses, relationships with community groups and stakeholders, and knowledge of entrepreneurial resources and concepts (such as access to capital, networking, procurement processes, marketing to institutional customers, and so on).

Other things you can consider include these

>> Research the organization to get a sense of what it has done in the past.

>> Think about getting certified.

Transitioning into a new career

I frequently get calls from professionals looking for tips on how to break into supplier diversity. They usually want the one thing that can help them. But finding just one thing that can give you a definite advantage is hard. If you're looking to make a career change and choosing supplier diversity, the value you bring is your passion for helping small and diverse businesses. This motivation and enthusiasm will buoy you to do everything you can to ensure that you're successful.

If you're looking to change your career path and transition to a career in supplier diversity, you should

>> Attend workshops or take courses to learn more about supplier diversity

>> Get familiar with small business advocacy groups and community stakeholders

>> Think about getting certified

>> Talk to industry experts

>> Read this book!

» Finding ways to fulfill continuing education requirements

» Examining a range of educational opportunities

Chapter **21**

Supplier Diversity Certifications and Continuing Education

L ike most careers, if you want to advance and get recognized as a professional, you probably need a combination of degrees and certifications, along with online learning and continuing education. This chapter provides information about the most popular supplier diversity certifications from professional associations. It also discusses degrees and other credentials that you can earn from colleges and universities and introduces you to new and emerging online learning options for supplier diversity professionals.

Checking Out Certification Programs

Credentials like certificates or certifications tell your boss, colleagues, and recruiters that you're knowledgeable about what you're doing. As the supplier diversity industry continues to refine itself and establish more stringent and rigorous programs, the following sections introduce some of the most popular and widely recognized industry certifications.

Certified Professional in Supplier Diversity (CPSD)

The Institute for Supply Management (ISM) is the first and largest not-for-profit professional supply management organization worldwide. Founded in 1915, ISM has over 50,000 members across 100 countries. It has impacted supply management and the purchasing profession through education, certification, leadership development, and research.

ISM offers two certifications:

» Certified Professional in Supply Management (CPSM)

» Certified Professional in Supplier Diversity (CPSD)

The CPSD is the leading certification for supplier diversity professionals (I've been certified since 2015). I previously served on the CPSD Task Analysis Committee, which established standards for the supplier diversity function and the exam.

The CPSD exam consists of two parts. The first covers central principles in supply management, and the second deals with critical supplier diversity topics. Here's the test breakdown:

PART/EXAM 1: Supply Management Core

Sourcing: 50 questions

Category Management: 10 questions

Negotiation: 14 questions

Legal and Contractual: 21 questions

Supplier Relationship Management: 43 questions

Cost and Price Management: 10 questions

Financial Analysis: 9 questions

Total questions: 180

Total time: 3 hours

PART/EXAM 2: Essentials in Supplier Diversity

Policies and Planning: 37 questions

Sourcing/Supplier Development: 32 questions

Finance/Budgeting: 18 questions

Metrics/Oversight: 12 questions

Training and Development: 11 questions

Advocacy/Marketing/Outreach: 10 questions

Total questions: 120

Total time: 2 hours

You have five hours to complete both parts. You receive your score immediately after completing the first part and must pass that part in order to move on to the second. So if you fail part one, your day is done; you can't proceed to the second.

TIP

Both the CPSD and CPSM use the same Supply Management Core test, and your passing score for part one of the CPSD can also count toward the CPSM exam. So if you wanted to take it a step further and get that certification as well (like many do), you'd be halfway there. You have to meet education and practitioner experience requirements to qualify to take the CPSD exam.

TIP

You can take the exam at an authorized testing facility, but you also have the convenience of doing it at your home or office through online proctoring. A live proctor monitors you through the webcam on your workstation to provide a secure exam experience.

You can prepare for the exam by studying on your own, taking classes, or using online study tools. You get a discount on the materials if you're a member of ISM. If you want to take an instructor-led class, check with your local ISM chapter or contact the national office to see where the closest training may be held or whether virtual trainings are available. For more information, go to www.ismworld. org/certification-and-training/certification/.

Certified Supplier Diversity Professional (CSDP)

Founded in 2003, the Alliance for Supplier Diversity Professionals (ASDP) is a nonprofit that educates and offers professional development for people in the field of supplier diversity and small business liaisons. As the name indicates, the ASDP focuses on one area — supplier diversity — and offers one certification: Certified Supplier Diversity Professional (CSDP). You can find more information about ASDP at asdp.us/.

TIP

Trying to decide between the CPSD with ISM or the CSDP from ASDP is like trying to decide which school to go to for an MBA. The curriculum and information are likely going to be similarly matched, but the experience may be different. I would recommend researching both to see which one offers what you're looking for. Also, look at job descriptions to see whether organizations are asking for a specific supplier diversity certification. Like an MBA, they may not specify a school, they just like to see that you have an MBA, or in this case, supplier diversity credentials.

Compliance administrator certifications

The American Contract Compliance Association (ACCA) began in 1986 as a non-profit. Their mission was to ensure equitable employment and contracting practices. Today, it provides training, standardization of practice, networking, and support to the many affirmative action, contract compliance, equal employment, and human rights workers across the country. It offers three certifications:

>> **Certified Compliance Administrator (CCA) Certification:** If you have two years of professional experience, complete the CCA program requirements, and receive at least 42 hours of ACCA training, you can receive ACCA's certification as a Certified Compliance Administrator

>> **Master Compliance Administrator (MCA) Certification:** Complete the MCA program requirements and get at least 84 hours training through ACCA, and you can receive its certification as a Master Compliance Administrator. This one requires four years of professional experience.

>> **Executive Certified Master Compliance Administrator (ECMCA) Certification:** But wait! If you graduate from the MCA program in the preceding bullet and complete the ECMCA program (at least 20 hours of ACCA training), you also get its certification as an Executive Certified Master Compliance Administrator. *Note:* The ECMCA has a leadership/executive focus, preparing people for senior positions in supplier diversity.

TIP

You can find more information at accaweb.org/.

Staying Current with Continuing Education

Continuing education is another great way to demonstrate that you're on top of your game and a leader in the field. It's also a requirement for many of the certifications I cover in the earlier section "Checking Out Certification Programs." Supplier diversity is still very green when it comes to the breadth and depth of educational resources available. However, the offerings continue to grow every year, and the situation is much better than it was. The following sections show you a few organizations that offer continuing education and training.

TIP

Many of these programs were offered in person but shifted to virtual during the COVID-19 pandemic. This makes them more readily available than ever.

Alliance of Supplier Diversity Professionals

In addition to offering the CSDP certification, ASDP also provides training that you can take separately or as a precursor to taking the certification exam. Flip to the earlier section "Certified Supplier Diversity Professional (CSDP)" for more on this group.

American Contract Compliance Association

ACCA's comprehensive training program focuses on vital issues facing the supplier diversity industry. ACCA provides continuing education units (CEUs) from Morgan State University to participants who complete 21 hours of training.

Institute for Supply Management

In addition to offering exam prep workshops for its certifications (see "Certified Professional in Supplier Diversity (CPSD)" earlier in the chapter), ISM offers training and education on topics that cover every aspect of supply management. Although these subjects aren't specific to supplier diversity, many of them are still applicable to that field, including the following:

>> Business acumen and leadership

>> Category/commodity management

>> Corporate social responsibility/ethics

>> Cost and price management

>> Financial analysis

>> Legal and contractual

>> Logistics and materials management

>> Negotiation

>> Project management

- >> Quality management
- >> Sales and operations planning
- >> Sourcing
- >> Supplier relationship management
- >> Supply chain strategy
- >> System capability and technology

TIP

These trainings are offered in person and virtually (live online, self-paced). You can access ISM's extensive education calendar at www.ismworld.org/certification-and-training/training/education-calendar/?page=1&rr=&q=&from=&to=&zip=&dist=10&s=date&so=asc.

National Minority Supplier Development Council

The National Minority Supplier Development Council (NMSDC) is the nation's leading minority supplier development and business advocacy organization. NMSDC partnered with Rutgers University to develop a seven-week online supplier diversity course. It's a self-paced, three-tiered course that covers best practices for planning, implementing, and assessing your company's diverse supplier development process. It's open to NMSDC members (national and local corporate members) and nonmembers (corporations, supplier diversity professionals, and supply chain, procurement, and government professionals). You can find more information at www.nmsdc.org/wp-content/uploads/SDOnline.pdf.

Supplier Diversity Training Institute

The Supplier Diversity Training Institute provides advanced training to develop supplier diversity professionals and stakeholders for the future. The institute includes a comprehensive two-day training program offered twice a year. As of this writing, it has plans to expand the program and offer virtual workshops on additional topics throughout the year. You can find more information at sdti.co/.

National Association of Educational Procurement Supplier Diversity Training Institute

The National Association of Educational Procurement (NAEP) is a nonprofit professional association primarily dedicated to serving higher education purchasing officers in the U.S. and Canada. With over 800 colleges and universities as members, NAEP's mission is to facilitate the development, exchange, and practice of effective and ethical procurement principles and techniques within higher education and associated communities through continuing education, networking, public information, and advocacy.

NAEP conducts the Supplier Diversity Institute for supplier diversity professionals in higher education. (I was a member of the planning committee for several years.) This program is for procurement professionals who want to develop or grow a supplier diversity program. It's available on demand so you can work at your own pace.

TIP

You can find more information at www.naepnet.org/page/Institutes.

Regional/industry specific programs

A host of smaller organizations offer local and regional training for supplier diversity professionals. These aren't as widely known as the national programs but may still be a good, less costly option.

Another option is to do an Internet search for "supplier diversity continuing education" and include your region. You may have to do a little digging, but they're out there.

National conferences

Many national conferences offer workshops and continuing education. The certifications I cover in the earlier section "Checking Out Certification Programs" sometimes accept attendance at these conferences to fulfill the continuing education requirement. Although the COVID-19 pandemic has forced many organizations to cancel their national conferences as I write this, their education is still available through virtual programming.

Digging into Degrees, Diplomas, and Other Education Options

The best way to prepare for any career is with a formal degree or diploma. Picking the right school and selecting the right major depends largely on what you think you may want to do.

Unfortunately, supplier diversity has no clear path to a career. As of this writing, no academic programs offer degrees in supplier diversity. The best way to prepare is to look at skill set. Supplier diversity jobs require business, public administration, and supply chain management skills. When you consider the degree options, thinking of how you can develop in all three of these areas may be helpful, whether that's through internships or some other opportunity. Because of the contracting nature, I've seen these positions filled by professionals with a *juris doctor* (JD) or law degree.

In order to increase the pipeline of supplier diversity professionals, some organizations have created internships and fellowship programs, which provide an opportunity for young professionals considering supplier diversity to really see what it's like.

Undergraduate degrees

Even though no programs offer an undergraduate degree in supplier diversity as I write this, you can still adequately prepare yourself for a professional career. Most schools offer programs in business, public administration, or supply chain management. Undergraduate programs in supply chain management have become very popular and are offered in business schools at colleges and universities around the country. I frequently speak to college students about careers in supplier diversity.

Graduate degrees

As you continue to move up in your career, you'll probably need an advanced degree. Many professionals choose to get an MBA or an MPA (master of public administration) if they plan to work in government. You may also consider a graduate degree in supply chain, although these tend to focus on the engineering or industrial side and are usually geared toward careers on the logistics side of the house. I've also seen professionals in this role with terminal degrees such as a PhD or JD, although a terminal degree isn't required.

Online education

Online supplier diversity education can range from free videos to certificate courses to full-blown graduate programs. Although these programs aren't likely to replace traditional degree programs, they're making supplier diversity education cheaper and more accessible. Putting industry information into more hands is definitely a good thing for the industry. Here are a few online programs that offer courses on supplier diversity.

Udemy

Udemy is a for-profit, open online course platform aimed at professional adults and students that allows instructors to build online courses on their preferred topics. Courses are offered at a minimal price, and anyone can create a course.

Coursera

Coursera is an online learning platform that allows universities to share their courses online. It offers supply chain management classes from a few schools. The prices for courses vary, and learners pay a monthly subscription to access the library of content.

LinkedIn Learning

LinkedIn Learning is an online library of thousands of courses taught by university professors and subject matter experts. You can buy classes individually or through a subscription to LinkedIn Learning. Instructors have to get approval to create courses for the platform, which ensures a higher quality of materials. *Tip:* One of the benefits of completing a course on LinkedIn Learning is that it's automatically posted to your LinkedIn profile.

YouTube

This resource is the least formal available and is largely self-directed. It may include interviews with supplier diversity professionals or content from universities or any of the organizations I mention throughout the chapter. Even though it's unlikely to fulfill any continuing education requirements, it can be a great source of information.

7

The Part of Tens

IN THIS PART . . .

Find out how to become an impactful supplier diversity leader with longevity.

Get tips for building a world-class supplier diversity program.

Explore ten myths about supplier diversity.

Chapter **22**

Nearly Ten Ways to Become an Effective Supplier Diversity Leader

For many years, supplier diversity efforts often stalled because of lack of senior leadership involvement, disinterest or rejection at lower levels, or just plain confusion about what to do. As more organizations were motivated to embrace supplier diversity, champions emerged who focused on outcomes and results — the impact their efforts would have on small and diverse businesses. They pushed their organizations beyond the status quo to encompass the intent of supplier diversity.

In a world where business moves fast and everyone must show their worth, simply conducting activities has no value. It has to be about impact. Unfortunately, many confuse effort with impact. If I'm making an effort, it must be having an impact, right? (This mindset may be an organizational culture thing.)

As I discuss throughout this book, supplier diversity is a multilayered function. Depending on the audience, it requires you to wear many hats. At a high level, supplier diversity leaders develop the policies, processes, and procedures that ensure that small and diverse business have access to procurement opportunities within an organization. But to become effective, the focus should on be how these activities translate into achieving the organization's goals. In other words, do your actions help small and diverse businesses connect to opportunities within your organization?

In this chapter, I discuss the traits effective and impactful supplier diversity leaders embrace, the knowledge they need to have, and the actions they must take.

Be the Champion within Your Organization

Supplier diversity leaders set the stage for change management to occur. By convincing senior leadership to embrace supplier diversity as a true management function rather than an optional or philanthropic initiative, you transform the culture of the organization and change the tone from a nice-to-do to a must-do. This actively demonstrates to internal employees and external stakeholders that supplier diversity isn't just something you all do but rather who you are.

Be an Influencer

Nowadays, supplier diversity leaders are influencers and strong change leaders whom other employees know and respect and whose input they value. The best influencers are able to have an impact across their organization's chain of command. Interestingly, influence is one of the traits people indicate they most want to become better at.

Having influence is all about getting things done without having to exert authority. You're able to gain support for your ideas from your colleagues and peers in other departments, and your input is valued by senior leadership or during important strategic meetings.

REMEMBER

The basis of being a good influencer is building relationships, being a good communicator/listener, being authentic, and being transparent.

Be an Advocate

Advocacy is any action that speaks in favor of, recommends, argues for, supports or defends, or pleads on behalf of others or a cause. Supplier diversity leaders advocate for the utilization and the success of small and diverse businesses within your organization. Some of these activities can include reviewing your 4 P's (people, policies, processes, and procedures; see Chapter 6) to ensure that they're as inclusive as possible or making recommendations on an award.

Advocacy can be tough and may require pushing back on long-standing institutional policies or going against popular decisions. I recall many times when I had to go against colleagues when I felt decisions weren't in the best interests of small and diverse businesses and we had the ability to make a change. Many times I won, and sometimes I didn't, which happens in advocacy (you have to know which battles to fight). Friendly discourse is common among colleagues, and as long as your advocacy is rooted in data and facts, you should be able to make your argument (which also helps with increasing influence; see the preceding section).

Be a Collaborator

Collaboration is a necessary function in supplier diversity for creating purposeful connections, both internally and externally, to achieve goals or solve problems. Collaborating allows you to share varied skill sets, strengths, and perspectives. Supplier diversity leaders need to build collaborative relationships with internal champions to ensure that the message stays top of mind and to work with external partners to help boost and support the needs of the small and diverse business community.

Know How Your Organization Works

I'm a firm believer that part of your due diligence as the supplier diversity leader is knowing how your organization works. This requirement means two things:

>> Knowing what the organization buys, how it buys it, when it buys it, and who makes the buying decisions

>> Understanding the entire supplier diversity life cycle: the development phase; the solicitation phase; the award phase; and the completion, payment, and evaluation phase

I know it sounds like a lot, but because you're a gatekeeper to opportunities within your organization, information is a valuable commodity. The more insightful information you can provide, the more easily small and diverse businesses can successfully navigate your system and avoid pitfalls.

All it takes is one misstep during any phase in the process to give the impression that a company isn't ready, which can derail or delay access to an opportunity.

Know What to Ask For

Part of your internal analysis involves knowing what to ask for, whether it's budget support, personnel (analysts, marketing, administrative, interns, and so on), or even a public show of endorsement from senior leadership to gain support. Assess your program to know exactly what support is required. And you want to be certain that whatever you ask for is going to be the thing(s) to get your program going and allow you to achieve your goals. Nothing is worse than making an ask and then still not meeting your goals; that may undermine your authority and how others perceive your knowledge of your program.

You'll likely get one time to make an ask, so make it count!

Know the Needs of Your Business Community

You're an integral part of your community's entrepreneurial ecosystem, so you should not only know the businesses that make up your small and diverse business community but also their needs and how they drive results with your organization. This knowledge helps you shape your efforts, offer programming that's responsive and relevant to their needs, and connect them to contract opportunities within your organization.

Focus on Impact, Not Activities

To work smarter, prioritize impact over activity. This doesn't mean that you won't conduct activities and events; on the contrary, they're the foundation of supplier diversity and the backbone of relationship building.

One concept that has come to the forefront as a result of the COVID-19 pandemic is reevaluating how we work. Futurists have been touting this idea for years, eschewing the traditional models of work and challenging what being productive really means. You need to focus on what allows your program to have the greatest impact, not just what gives the appearance of being busy for the sake of being busy.

Delivering effective programs comes down to three things: analyzing the situation and needs, gathering the right resources, and executing according to those needs. If your resources are slim, your management of them has to be spot on.

Focus on Driving Results

When you're just starting a program or are new to the supplier diversity role, having some anxiety as you try to figure out what you should be doing is natural. You may be tempted to just mimic what other organizations are doing with their programs with the hope of achieving similar results or chasing big headlines of organizations vowing to spend billions of dollars with small and diverse business over the next few years. You know the outcome, but do you understand how they're planning to do it?

Though you never fully know the inner working of an organization, what you do know and have to consider are the dynamics involved that guide its decisions and factors into its results. Think about the following:

>> **Type of industry:** The type of industry greatly impacts results. For example, businesses in the retail and entertainment industries can simply buy more products or content from small and diverse businesses or creators. But service-based businesses or specialized industries (such as manufacturing) may find spending diversely a bit more challenging because of what is or isn't available. Creating a product line or writing a script presents fewer barriers to entry than building a manufacturing facility does.

>> **Discretionary spend:** Organizations with expansive spend budgets have many opportunities for engaging and including small and diverse businesses, causing little disruption to their supply chains. Organizations with smaller spend budgets and a tighter supply chain have to be more intentional about engaging or switching vendors. Any change can cause a major disruption, and organizations may not be ready to fully commit to that.

>> **Development investment:** This area looks at how much the organization invests to scout, educate, and train its vendors in order to achieve its spend and utilization results. Development includes information workshops, trainings, events, outreach, mentoring, and sponsorships, among other things. The larger the organization and the longer the program has been in existence, the more efficient its development investment becomes. For example, larger organizations tend to have more money to put toward coaching and providing the necessary time and resources to help small and diverse suppliers ramp up quickly. Thus, these suppliers are able to position themselves for contract opportunities and win them much faster.

>> **Ability to attract vendors:** Access to, or the ability to attract, vendors is another factor that can impede results. As customers, large organizations with brand name recognition have a slight advantage over smaller organizations. The obvious lure of having a large, big-name client (financial rewards, prestige, and so on) may be too hard to resist. As much as organizations prefer that businesses have multiple customers — they don't want to make up the bulk of a vendor's business — these clients can be so demanding and time consuming that they may leave little time for other clients. A business fulfilling orders and being responsive for a large, multinational retailer may not have the capacity to sell to another customer.

REMEMBER

Looking at another program, or benchmarking, sounds great and can provide a baseline of things to aspire to, but it doesn't always take into account the things that make your organization unique. As I discuss in Chapter 6, take time to evaluate and understand your organization before you rush to do what everybody else is doing. Your execution plan should be based on the stage of your program, your circumstances, and what success looks like for your organization. You want to create an action plan that focuses on getting those specific results, not a generic model of supplier diversity.

Chapter **23**

Ten (Plus One) Ways to Create a World-Class Supplier Diversity Program

L
ike most things, you have no one route to achieve success in supplier diversity. Ask any supplier diversity leader the secret to their success, and you'll likely get a different response from each one. But if you look at their programs, you'll definitely see some common things across all of them.

This chapter provides elements necessary to create a world class supplier diversity program, or, at a minimum, a program that meets the needs of your community while achieving the goals your organization has established. Now, you don't have to do all of them at once. You still have to remember your organization's culture and appetite for change. I remember one of my first meetings with my new VP at a particular organization. I was bursting with questions and ideas. He listened patiently and then gave me some crucial feedback: He told me my ideas were great and that leadership loved my passion and enthusiasm. But he cautioned me that people there had been doing things a certain way for a really long time and that instituting change would take time. He didn't want to see me get frustrated and burned out when change didn't happen at the pace I wanted.

It was sound advice that I never forgot. It was also one of the first times I really had to think about culture as a part of this process. I had to reframe my thinking to create an internal program that educated departments on supplier diversity. Did I implement everything I discussed in that meeting that day? Of course not. But we did have some great wins, and I see that the company maintained some of the programs I started. It's always great to see your work have a lasting impact on an organization.

Connect Program Deliverables to Organizational Goals

I mention the importance of this point many times throughout this book. Connecting your program functions and deliverables to organizational strategic goals allows you to position your program as a long-term strategic endeavor rather than a short-term initiative. As I discuss in Chapter 7, doing so helps you make a stronger business case for your program, get buy in from internal champions and stakeholders, and support the change management process.

Develop Your 4 P's to Be Small and Diverse Business-Centric

In Chapter 6, I explain the importance of the 4 P's (people, policies, processes, and procedures). As you look to build your program, consider solutions that are business-friendly while minimizing exposure to risk. You've probably heard "It's not personal; it's business" many times to justify certain actions or measures. But when you build relationships and work with a vendor for a number of years, business becomes personal. Yes, organizations need to protect themselves, but sometimes the policies, processes, and procedures they use are so complex and cumbersome that they deter small and diverse businesses rather than encourage them.

Focus on Connecting Businesses to Opportunities

Supplier diversity management (SDM) focuses on building a program that includes *all* aspects of the system to maximize benefits, deliver value, and create impact. Events like luncheons and workshops may give the impression that you're busy, but if you can't satisfactorily answer crucial questions like "How many small and diverse businesses are getting connected to opportunities?", your program probably doesn't have the impact you'd hoped.

REMEMBER

At the end of the day, if your program isn't connecting businesses to opportunities, it's not likely going to be around for much longer. Every activity you do should reinforce getting businesses closer to opportunities within your organization.

Establish Your Place in Your Community's Entrepreneurial Ecosystem

The nature of supplier diversity makes it a valuable and relevant contributor to the success of small and diverse businesses. You connect actual businesses to real opportunities within your organization, which builds the small businesses in your area. Because of this, your organization and your program are a vital part of your community's entrepreneurial ecosystem, which I talk about in Chapter 10. Your thought leadership and expertise are just as important as those of economic development agencies, start-up incubators, business development assistance centers, and so on.

REMEMBER

You should be a contributor to every conversation, initiative, or event impacting and improving the outcomes for small and diverse businesses in your community.

Become Self-Sustaining: From Limiting to Limitless

This topic is one many supplier diversity practitioners don't think enough about. Most supplier diversity departments have to operate within the confines of a (generally modest) budget. They usually don't have a lot of wiggle room to do many programs, including many mentioned throughout this book, limiting their ability to be as impactful as they want. (This is where partnerships and collaborations are important.)

REMEMBER

Many supplier diversity practitioners make the mistake of thinking their programs would be successful if they had a bigger budget. I learned many years ago during my days in marketing and brand management that you can argue for more money, but then you have more scrutiny and greater (sometimes unrealistic) expectations. However, when your program is self-sustaining and you're able to create your own resources and revenue without being cost prohibitive to small and diverse businesses, your program potential becomes limitless.

When I was a practitioner, I was able to create and produce a number of successful events and programs. Some events grew to become the biggest and most anticipated events for diverse and small businesses in the region and/or the state and generated thousands of dollars in revenue annually that supplemented my original budget. Believe me, putting on events at this level was a monumental task and took up a considerable amount of time each year in planning, and I was fortunate to have teams in place to support this effort. They became central to my programs, not just because of the revenue they generated (which meant I didn't have to ask for a budget increase every year) but also because they gave me the ability to be creative and deliver programs that provided access to even more small and diverse businesses. These events were successful because I focused on adding value to the sustainability of their businesses, whether through the speakers presenting, the topics discussed, or the valuable networking opportunities facilitated.

REMEMBER

A good program adds expertise, value, or revenue. A great program adds all three.

Invest in Analytics to Help Manage Your Program

The idea that what gets measured improves is a common tenet. Like most business operations, supplier diversity has to continually evolve in order to grow as a strategic asset. One way to do so is through data-driven insights.

Analytics are now an essential part of the total SDM infrastructure. In Chapter 19, I talk extensively about how much better and more efficient data enriched programs perform. Analytics allow practitioners to make informed decisions about program performance, programming, and compliance and make adjustments as needed. And the robust tools that are available allow this data to flow to senior management quickly, which keeps it informed and able to communicate results to stakeholders as needed.

Cultivate a Supplier Development Program Using M.O.D.E.

Organizations looking to create lasting impact have to look beyond basic metrics of utilization and spend, as I detail in Chapter 6. Supplier development has become the game-changer for many programs' time and resource investment. I coined the term M.O.D.E. (mentoring, outreach, development, and education) years ago to look at all the elements involved in developing suppliers into sustainable, contract-ready candidates.

Today, entrepreneurs can take advantage of many resources to sharpen skills in their business toolkits. However, M.O.D.E. is relevant because it also includes elements to prepare them for the nuances and rigors of doing business *with your organization*. Businesses that engage with you may not need all that your program offers. Businesses that have gone through your program and have developed into successful vendors may even become collaborative partners and advocates for your program.

REMEMBER

At the end of the day, supplier diversity is a two-way street. No matter how advanced your program is or how much attention you pay to the 4Ps, if your small and diverse vendors aren't ready to leverage your resources and successfully perform on contracts, your program will never achieve its goals.

Don't Be Afraid to Try New Programs

I love the role that innovation plays in supplier diversity. When you look at the major shifts that have occurred over the years in supplier diversity (which I outline in Chapter 2), innovation and disruption have always been at the forefront.

According to Howard Schultz, chairman and former Starbucks chief executive officer, "Innovation must be disruptive. And by disruptive, I mean *disruptive*. You gotta fracture and break the rules and disrupt." He provides three ways that organizations (or programs) can infuse innovation into their operations:

>> **Business-model innovation:** Looks at the business model for places to implement innovative solutions — processes, strategy, mission statement, technologies they use, and businesses that they partner with

>> **Industry-model innovation:** Looks at the industry model for places to innovate — industry they currently work within and what potential industries they can transition to

>> **Revenue-model innovation:** Looks at the revenue model for places to innovate the products and services offered, prices of their products and services, and the customers they target

Put a Compliance Program in Place

If what gets measured improves, then what gets measured and reported improves dramatically. When you're establishing your policies, your contracts, especially long-term contracts, need to outline how vendors are managed and how you monitor their compliance with your terms.

Contract compliance is a form of contract management that ensures that organizations and their prime/tier 1 contract holders are complying with the contractor's goals regarding spend with small and diverse businesses. Because of the size and scale of contracts with large organizations and government agencies, they can be a significant source of unfairness if small and diverse businesses aren't able to fairly compete or participate on these projects. Contract compliance promotes using small and diverse businesses and assures that prime contractors know that this important element is being tracked.

Compliance plans may include provisions that businesses must solicit and accept bids for contract work from small and diverse businesses, including minority-, women-, and veteran-owned businesses. The process involves periodic reviews, usually monthly or quarterly, of existing contracts to determine whether contracts are utilizing small and diverse businesses.

Get Your Prime/Tier 1 Partners Involved

The relationship between supplier diversity and its prime/tier 1 partners is a special one, as I explain in Chapter 12. Strong programs are able to get their partners involved in a variety of ways, whether supporting them as subject matter experts or mentors, encouraging them to sponsor events and programs, or inspiring them to start their own supplier diversity programs within their organizations.

Get out from Behind That Desk

If you think you're going to build a program sitting behind a desk all day, you're mistaken. Whether meeting with small and diverse businesses, collaborating with external partners, or working with internal stakeholders, supplier diversity practitioners should have their ears to the ground and balance internal responsibilities. This role is very *intrapreneurial* in that it requires you to behave like an entrepreneur while working within your organization. Get up, get out, and make some connections!

» **Failing to recognize supplier diversity as a specialized discipline**

» **Having the wrong mindset and expectations**

Chapter **24**

Ten Myths about Supplier Diversity

From organizations to entrepreneurs, supplier diversity is on everyone's mind. Despite its popularity, many people still have misconceptions about supplier diversity that are generally based on entrenched mindsets rooted in unconscious bias, misinformation, and just plain ole bad habits. They prevent companies from using supplier diversity as a strategic tool for competitive advantage, which then prevents small and diverse businesses from leveraging supplier diversity to drive their business growth.

In this chapter, I highlight ten myths that continue to bind supplier diversity and have negative impacts on your efforts.

Supplier Diversity Will Increase How Much We Pay for Things

This myth derived from *prime* contractors (tier 1) that didn't like being forced to use small and diverse businesses as subcontractors (tier 2) by their clients. They'd report that they'd made a "good-faith effort" but couldn't find any vendors.

When they did find them, those vendors prices were too high. If the client wanted them to use these businesses, they'd have to be willing to pay the higher price. Because clients hear only one side of the story, this myth has been able to prevail for years.

In reality, a number factors cause gaps in estimating prices (small and diverse businesses aren't the only ones guilty of this). This area is where supplier diversity professionals have an opportunity to shine by working with these businesses to understand why their pricing is high and how it prevents them from being competitive. You can then develop or recommend programs or training that can help them improve.

REMEMBER

As the supplier diversity professional, you should be able to counter this argument by showing prime contractors that there are lower-cost alternatives in the market.

Supplier Diversity Doesn't Add Value Because It Doesn't Generate Revenue

Because supplier diversity is largely community-facing, people always debate about the value it delivers to the organization. Supplier diversity isn't usually a revenue-generating function (although I discuss incorporating revenue generation in Chapter 23), but depending on how you define *value*, monetary gain paints only a partial picture.

Today's organizations, governments, and community ecosystems are intertwined. Across the country, each relies on the other to address the many economic and social challenges people are faced with. Many corporations have philanthropic foundations that give millions of dollars each year to support countless social causes for which they reap no economic return outside of a tax break. They do so because, as a major economic engine, they have a responsibility to ensure that the community is healthy, whole, and vibrant. Sure, they may hope their efforts create enough goodwill to capture a sale or two. However, few organizations are going to base their entire sales strategies on goodwill generated by donations.

REMEMBER

Organizations need small businesses to provide goods and services that are necessary for them to operate their businesses. They have a responsibility to obtain these goods and services equitably and inclusively so that any interested business has the opportunity to compete, not just portions of the community. You need to be able to explain the intrinsic value that the organization receives by supporting supplier diversity. You can also make the case that effective supplier diversity and a diversified supply chain reduce risks (look at what happened to supply chains too heavily reliant on China during the pandemic). I talk more about making the business case for supplier diversity in Chapter 7.

Supplier Diversity Is Just a Feel-Good Initiative

As I discuss in Chapter 2, the motivations behind supplier diversity have evolved over the years from following a federal initiative to doing the right thing to embracing a true strategic management endeavor that organizations can use to gain a competitive advantage. Classifying this pursuit as a philanthropic or charity measure couldn't be further from reality.

Supplier diversity provides an opportunity for small and diverse businesses to get a foot in the door. After they get there, they're required to compete and successfully perform in order to win and sustain contracts just like everyone else. In fact, the scrutiny on these businesses can sometimes be greater, with dire consequences for less-than-stellar performance. Organizations are able to leverage the agility, expertise, and enthusiasm these firms bring to the table and likely don't have to pay a premium to get it.

Supplier Diversity Is Too Confusing

As a supplier diversity champion and lead advocate, your existence is to steer organizational change and ensure that supplier diversity stays top of mind. However, without the work I lay out in Chapter 7 (such as doing proper analysis, establishing a compelling vision, and communicating clearly to secure buy-in), the organization is left confused by the whole thing. The impulse is then reactive: to do something, anything, to give the impression that it's happening and progress is being made. This mindset results in focusing on activities — meaningless workshops or endless community events that don't add value or create impact.

WARNING

The problem with building a program based on activities rather than strategy is that it's not designed to bring real change but only to give the appearance of being busy. Because of this confusion, poor planning, and execution, supplier diversity becomes another failed initiative (it never really made it to an actual program) that's over in a few months or, worse, never quite gets off the ground.

Supplier Diversity Doesn't Impact Our Bottom Line

For most organizations, getting necessary materials is vital to keeping operations running smoothly. Procurement provides access to materials (or resources or services), which can have a significant impact on daily operations and the balance sheet; materials make up the second largest expense category for organizations, behind HR and human capital expenses. Because supplier diversity is a procurement function, the benefits derived from procurement can also be felt through the inclusion of small and diverse business.

REMEMBER

Because the role of procurement is to find suppliers, any suppliers, that can provide materials at the best price, savings achieved from reducing the cost of goods results in an increase in profit margin, thus impacting the bottom line. Supplier diversity can impact the bottom line if it has real power in procurement.

Supplier Diversity and DEI Are Close Enough

As I explain in Chapter 4, supplier diversity and DEI are closely related, are often collaborative partners, and use some of the same tactics to drive results. But that's where the similarities end. DEI is an HR function that focuses on culture and targets internal employees. Supplier diversity is a procurement function that focuses on business processes and targets the external business community. Because their audiences are different, each has different outcomes and expectations and distinct metrics to measure success.

WARNING

Organizations that are new to the diversity conversation often make the mistake of lumping all their diversity efforts together. Over the years, I've seen many different scenarios, whether it's supplier diversity housed under DEI or it's one, all-inclusive superposition: Supplier Diversity, Equity, and Inclusion Director. (At least it's at a director level.) Sometimes when you ask organizations about their diversity efforts, they're quick to discuss their hiring practices, their employee resource groups (ERGs), and their culture (what they do to make employees feel included). These are all great things every organization should have, but they have nothing to do with getting small and diverse businesses access to contract opportunities — supplier diversity.

Considering all the responsibilities and tasks involved in each of these jobs, and the level of importance each plays within the organization, performing both of them well is almost impossible. I have never seen a professional, no matter how amazing and empowered they are, effectively manage both of these functions simultaneously. This situation leaves the organization to suffer and the diversity leader frustrated and overwhelmed.

REMEMBER

If your organization is truly committed to each of these initiatives, impress upon it the significance of each role, how they're different, and why they should be managed separately in the best interest of long-term success.

Our Name Alone Will Deliver Program Results

Building relationships is the foundation to supplier diversity. And authenticity and transparency are what allow real relationship building to occur.

WARNING

Don't fall into the trap of relying solely on your organization's brand name or recognition to buoy your supplier diversity efforts. This move comes off like you're checking the boxes with no real commitment to supplier diversity or the people you're interfacing with. Entrepreneurs are people and can feel when the connections are genuine and the commitment to diversity is real. In this age of social media call-outs and cancel culture, having an attitude of "We're the big fish, and you should be honored to work with us" will spread across the Internet faster than you can blink (especially on a slow news day), and no one wants to be associated with damaging press. Such notoriety isn't likely to cause an organization to completely fall, but it may sting for a while.

Anybody Can Lead This Effort — Any Body

In the not-so-distant past, organizations that weren't necessarily committed to the full principles of supplier diversity viewed it as an add-on function or a volunteer effort, and anyone willing to take it on could step right up. After all, supplier diversity isn't tasked with building civilizations on another planet.

However, as supplier diversity has evolved, organizations have had to look at the intrinsic value it delivers. Delivering this value requires a combination of expertise, knowledge, interpersonal skills, and critical thinking. It's too important a function to be staffed randomly or unintentionally.

Conventional wisdom says you should hire for attitude and teach skill later. I agree in that supplier diversity can require a very specific temperament. Part 6 covers the education opportunities for professionals interested in building a career or expanding their knowledge in supplier diversity. This array of opportunities is vastly different from just a few years ago, when few, if any, programs were available for learning more about supplier diversity and sharpening your skill set.

We're Too Busy to Devote Energy to Supplier Diversity

I get it; everyone is hyper-busy! The relentless push to be better, stronger, and faster can leave employees over it, burned out, and unmotivated to commit to another thing. This effect is one reason a dedicated champion — someone who can do the heavy lifting to help internal departments better understand supplier diversity and how it applies to them respectively — is so important. This "dispensing in bite-sized bits rather than clobbering over the head" approach can help organizations avoid diversity fatigue and shift the thinking that supplier diversity is inherently burdensome to something that is a seamless and manageable part of their daily operations.

Supplier Diversity Will Lower Our Standards

Another big misconception is that you have to lower your standards and expectations in order to work with diverse suppliers. According to Hackett's 2017 Supplier Diversity Study, which surveyed leading companies with supplier diversity programs, nearly all the companies' diverse suppliers met or exceeded expectations, and the companies experienced no loss in efficiency. You can attribute this success to a variety of factors, including investments in small and diverse business development.

But just as organizations have asked more of their suppliers, internal departments have to raise the bar as well. Today's procurement departments rarely pay more than they have to for goods and services. However, many organizations have moved away from focusing solely on low price and are approaching procurement more strategically through strategic sourcing. This concept allows them to optimize their supply base by using a systematic and data-driven approach that focuses on the value proposition and quality of the delivery systems, not just price.

Index

external stakeholders, 17
  communication plan, 179
  local, 172
  SDM model, 37

F

facilities/construction department, 57–58
Fits-and-Starts Organizations, 109
Floyd, George, 46
foot-in-the-door (FITD) policy, 75, 150
force multipliers, 220
forecasting, 60–61
Forrester, 16
4 P's (people, policies, processes, and procedures), 74–79
  collision between policies and procedures, 78
  developing, 258
  key questions, 40
  management structure, 75
  people, 75
  policies, 75
  procedures, 78–79
  processes, 76–78
  SDM model, 40
  SDM process, 33, 35–37
Franklin, Aretha, 139
Franklin, Benjamin, 117

G

General Motors, 27
goals, 207–214
  action items, 122–123
  aligning supplier diversity program to strategic goals, 90–91, 115, 120, 208, 258. *see also* goals
  aligning with procurement strategies, 207–210
  capacity building, 151
  communication plan, 180–181
  competitor analysis, 212–213
  connecting program deliverables to, 258
  current utilization, 212
  disparity studies, 12, 210–212

KPIs aligned with, 14
  meeting goals vs. adding value, 213–214
  perception of market opportunities, 212
  SMART, 115–116
  utilization of, 12
Google Ngram, 14–15
government
  industry terminology, 235
  origins and history of supplier diversity, 22–24
  regulatory compliance, 19, 25, 27
  reporting problems, 223
graduate degrees, 246
Greater New England Minority Supplier Development Council, 214
group purchasing organizations (GPOs), 222–223
growth stage, 156, 158, 161–162

H

Hackett Group, The, 191
Hartsfield-Jackson International Airport, 26
Higher Ground, 190
Horsager, David, 138
hospitals, 222–223

I

IBM, 27
implicit biases, 10, 109–110, 139
industry standards, development of, 13
informing and preparing prospective vendors, 61, 63
in-reach programs, 104–105, 162
Institute for Supply Management (ISM), 240–244
internal (organizational) environment
  barriers to supplier diversity, 107–116
  benchmarks, 188
  building support for program, 97–106
  communication plan, 179
  goals and action items, 123
  key questions, 40
  KPIs, 188
  making the business case, 89–95

Title VII, 44

TopMBA, 103

total cost of ownership (TCO), 102

trainer coordinators, 234

transparency, 140–141

  cultivating, 140

  levels of, 141

  software for reporting, 191

trust

  KLT factor, 136

  pillars for building, 138–139

trust, respect, and transparency (TRT), 136–141

  respect, 139

  transparency, 140–141

  trust, 138–139

Trust Edge, The (Horsager), 138

Tuck Diversity Business Programs, 151

U

Udemy, 247

undergraduate degrees, 246

unique value proposition (UVP), 136

University of California at Santa Cruz, 46

upstream partners, 172

U.S. Census Bureau, 15–16, 29

U.S. Department of Commerce, 15, 24

U.S. Department of Labor, 23

UVP (unique value proposition), 136

V

value

  communicating value, 92–93

  defined, 90

  foundation for strategic goals, 91

  how supplier diversity adds value, 95

  opportunities for value creation, 91–92

  value add, 219

value creation opportunity model, 91–92

values-based consumers, 16

vendor capacity building evaluation template, 149

vendor onboarding/registration process (vendor portal), 61, 63, 82–83

  importance of paying attention to, 82–83

  often-missed points, 82

  startup stage, 160

vendor payment process, 83–84

vendor relationship management (VRM), 81–84

  connecting vendors to internal stakeholders, 83

  focus of, 81

  vendor onboarding process, 82–83

  vendor payment process, 83–84

veteran-owned businesses, 7, 16, 120, 262

W

Washington, Harold, 212

WBENC (Women's Business Enterprise National Council), 213, 216–217

'who-what-how' of organizational spend, 79–80

  how does organization buy, 80

  what does organization buy, 80

  who makes buying decisions, 79–80

WIIFT (what's in it for them), 106

win-win analysis, 133–135

women-owned businesses, 7, 120, 217, 262

  capacity building, 150–151

  disparity studies, 12, 76

  growth of, 16

Women's Business Enterprise National Council (WBENC), 213, 216–217

work culture, 9

workplace diversity, 9

Y

YouTube, 247

About the Author

Kathey Porter is an award-winning supplier diversity expert, nationally recognized small business strategist, author, lecturer, and entrepreneur. With a career spanning nearly two decades in marketing, small business development, supplier diversity, and entrepreneurship, Kathey is a sought-after subject matter expert, frequent keynote speaker, panelist, and workshop facilitator at conferences and events focusing on supplier diversity, small business development/entrepreneurship, women's entrepreneurship and empowerment, and diversity and inclusion.

Kathey is the founder and principal of Porter Brown Associates, a certified veteran-owned, woman-owned, DBE training and professional services consultancy that advises and works with corporations and public entities on how to build inclusive community business ecosystems through supplier diversity programs, inclusive diversity strategies, and targeted entrepreneurship training programs. Her company was recognized as a 2020 Small Business Subcontractor of the Year.

She is also founder and lead instructor for the Supplier Diversity Training Institute (sdti.co), a national training program for supplier diversity practitioners, procurement professionals, and organizational stakeholders looking to gain proficiency in supplier diversity and equitable inclusion.

Active in supplier development, Kathey is an executive coach/instructor for several national business accelerators, including *Inc.* magazine's Inc. 5000, the Small Business Administration's (SBA) Emerging Leaders Program, the National Minority Supplier Development Council (NMSDC), and the Black Women's Entrepreneurial Leadership (BWEL) program at Babson College.

In addition to *Supplier Diversity For Dummies,* Kathey is the author of *50 Billion Dollar Boss: African American Women Sharing Stories of Success in Entrepreneurship and Leadership*, which was nominated for an NAACP Image Award, and *Implementing Supplier Diversity: A Driver of Entrepreneurship* (both published by Palgrave Macmillan).

She was recognized as Supplier Diversity Advocate of the Year by the Florida State Minority Supplier Development Council (FSMSDC). She received her Certified Professional in Supplier Diversity (CPSD) credentials from the Institute of Supply Management (ISM). Her website is katheyporter.com.

Dedication

To my family — Hollis and Mason. #TeamPorterBrown

Author's Acknowledgments

I owe a huge debt of gratitude to the friends, colleagues, collaborators, and contributors who encouraged, supported, brainstormed, and pushed me through this project. You continue to inspire and motivate me every day. Happy to have you in my corner.

This book was written with the help and sacrifice of my family — my son, Mason, who can finally get a real meal (not just Sundays); my daughter, Hollis, for being patient when I couldn't answer calls; and my sisters for understanding canceled sisters' dinners and family vacations. Thank you to Markesia, Angela, Karima, Dr. Smith, and Juanita for just being there when I needed a chat, a break, or a pep talk. Also, thank you Dr. Fred for always being ready to dig in. WE DID IT!

I'd like to thank the Wiley editorial team — Tracy for supporting this project and believing I could do this and Chrissy and Kristie for keeping this project (and me) on track. Thanks to the entire *For Dummies* staff — graphic design, editing, proofreading, and indexing teams — for all your hard work in making this project turn out amazing. I am honored to be part of the *For Dummies* family!

Finally, thanks to the readers for buying and supporting this book.

Publisher's Acknowledgments

Senior Acquisitions Editor: Tracy Boggier

Project Manager and Development Editor:
Christina N. Guthrie

Managing Editor: Kristie Pyles

Copy Editor: Megan Knoll

Technical Editor:
Dr. Fred McKinney, BJM Solutions

Production Editor: Tamilmani Varadharaj

Cover Photos: © metamorworks/
Adobe Stock Photos

Dummies is the global leader in the reference category and one of the most trusted and highly regarded brands in the world. No longer just focused on books, customers now have access to the dummies content they need in the format they want. Together we'll craft a solution that engages your customers, stands out from the competition, and helps you meet your goals.

Advertising & Sponsorships

Connect with an engaged audience on a powerful multimedia site, and position your message alongside expert how-to content. Dummies.com is a one-stop shop for free, online information and know-how curated by a team of experts.

- Targeted ads
- Video
- Email Marketing
- Microsites
- Sweepstakes sponsorship

20 MILLION PAGE VIEWS EVERY SINGLE MONTH

15 MILLION UNIQUE VISITORS PER MONTH

43% OF ALL VISITORS ACCESS THE SITE VIA THEIR MOBILE DEVICES

700,000 NEWSLETTER SUBSCRIPTIONS TO THE INBOXES OF *300,000* UNIQUE INDIVIDUALS EVERY WEEK

# of dummies

Custom Publishing

Reach a global audience in any language by creating a solution that will differentiate you from competitors, amplify your message, and encourage customers to make a buying decision.

- Apps
- Books
- eBooks
- Video
- Audio
- Webinars

Brand Licensing & Content

Leverage the strength of the world's most popular reference brand to reach new audiences and channels of distribution.

For more information, visit dummies.com/biz

ENRICHMENT

Staying Sharp

9781119187790
USA $26.00
CAN $31.99
UK £19.99

Facebook
Carolyn Abram

9781119179030
USA $21.99
CAN $25.99
UK £16.99

Guitar
Mark Phillips
Jon Chappell

9781119293354
USA $24.99
CAN $29.99
UK £17.99

Investing
Eric Tyson, MBA

9781119293347
USA $22.99
CAN $27.99
UK £16.99

Beekeeping
Howland Blackiston

9781119310068
USA $22.99
CAN $27.99
UK £16.99

Digital Photography
Julie Adair King

9781119235606
USA $24.99
CAN $29.99
UK £17.99

Meditation
Stephan Bodian

9781119251163
USA $24.99
CAN $29.99
UK £17.99

Pregnancy
ALL-IN-ONE

9781119235491
USA $26.99
CAN $31.99
UK £19.99

Samsung Galaxy S7
Bill Hughes

9781119279952
USA $24.99
CAN $29.99
UK £17.99

iPhone
Edward C. Baig
Bob "Dr. Mac" LeVitus

9781119283133
USA $24.99
CAN $29.99
UK £17.99

Crocheting
Karen Manthey
Susan Brittain

9781119287117
USA $24.99
CAN $29.99
UK £16.99

Nutrition
Carol Ann Rinzler

9781119130246
USA $22.99
CAN $27.99
UK £16.99

PROFESSIONAL DEVELOPMENT

Windows 10
Andy Rathbone

9781119311041
USA $24.99
CAN $29.99
UK £17.99

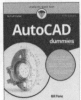

AutoCAD
Bill Fane

9781119255796
USA $39.99
CAN $47.99
UK £27.99

Excel 2016
Greg Harvey, PhD

9781119293439
USA $26.99
CAN $31.99
UK £19.99

QuickBooks 2017
Stephen L. Nelson, MBA, CPA, MBA in Taxation

9781119281467
USA $26.99
CAN $31.99
UK £19.99

macOS Sierra
Bob "Dr. Mac" LeVitus

9781119280651
USA $29.99
CAN $35.99
UK £21.99

LinkedIn
Joel Elad, MBAs

9781119251132
USA $24.99
CAN $29.99
UK £17.99

Windows 10
ALL-IN-ONE
Woody Leonhard

9781119310563
USA $34.00
CAN $41.99
UK £24.99

SharePoint 2016
Rosemarie Withee
Ken Withee

9781119181705
USA $29.99
CAN $35.99
UK £21.99

Fundamental Analysis
Matt Krantz

9781119263593
USA $29.99
CAN $31.99
UK £19.99

Networking
Doug Lowe

9781119257769
USA $29.99
CAN $35.99
UK £21.99

Office 2016
Wallace Wang

9781119293477
USA $26.99
CAN $31.99
UK £19.99

Office 365
Rosemarie Withee
Ken Withee
Jennifer Reed

9781119265313
USA $24.99
CAN $29.99
UK £17.99

Salesforce.com
Liz Kao
Jon Paz

9781119239314
USA $29.99
CAN $35.99
UK £21.99

Coding
Nikhil Abraham

9781119293323
USA $29.99
CAN $35.99
UK £21.99

dummies.com

dummies
A Wiley Brand